Unreal Engine 5
Best Practices

First Edition

The ultimate guide to advanced visual storytelling, design, lighting, and performance in UE5

Tyson Butler-Boschma

‹packt›

Unreal Engine 5 Best Practices
First Edition

Portfolio Director: Rohit Rajkumar
Relationship Lead: Tanisha Mehrotra
Project Manager: Sandip Tadge
Content Engineer: Anuradha Joglekar
Technical Editor: Tejas Vijay Mhasvekar
Copy Editor: Safis Editing
Indexer: Manju Arasan
Proofreader: Anuradha Joglekar
Production Designer: Aparna Bhagat
Growth Lead: Namita Velgekar
Marketing Owner: Nivedita Pandey

First published: December 2025

Production reference: 2090126

Published by Packt Publishing Ltd.
Grosvenor House
11 St Paul's Square
Birmingham
B3 1RB, UK.

ISBN 978-1-83620-565-4
www.packtpub.com

To my dear partner Ayla, my family, and my close friends, whose support, encouragement, and belief in me have fueled both my career and my passion for games. This book is as much yours as it is mine. Thank you for your endless love and support.

—Tyson Butler-Boschma

Foreword

Every industry has those rare individuals who don't just use tools, they find ways to build something with them, so unique, that others wonder: "How did they do that?"

Tyson is one of those creators.

I first met Tyson when he joined the Gameloft Brisbane studio, where I am happy to be the Studio Manager. From the very beginning, it was clear that Tyson was quickly going to bring our lighting, cinematics, cutscenes, and overall scene and immersive experiences to a whole new level. Tyson rapidly carved out a unique role within the studio. He brought with him a mix of deep technical mastery and great human qualities. His expertise in Unreal Engine, combined with his artistic sensibility, regularly left the entire team speechless. He delivered scenes that felt like magic: breathtaking environments, stunning lighting, powerful cutscenes, and Hollywood quality trailers that became "wow moments" we would remember and reference for months.

What makes Tyson truly unique is not only the quality of his output, but the way he creates it. He is always moving forward, learning, and creating opportunities for himself and others—even when none are obvious. He embodies collaboration, positivity, and fun. He lifts others up and makes people around him shine and grow.

With this book, I trust Tyson to make even more people shine, grow and take the path he once took. Tyson is sharing the knowledge and mindset that he has refined over years of practice. Not in a classroom, but on real productions, solving real challenges, and driving creative excellence forward. Within these pages, readers will find guidance on how to harness the most powerful features of Unreal Engine 5 to craft immersive experiences and striking visuals. Tyson introduces the tools, workflows, and ways of thinking that empower developers and artists to build worlds that feel alive, optimized, and full of wonder.

Tyson represents everything the video game industry needs more of. He is a new generation creative leader: visionary, highly skilled, deeply technical, and profoundly human. Anyone who gets the chance to learn from him, whether through a talk, a meeting, or through the pages of this book, is genuinely fortunate.

Manea Castet,

Head of Studio, Gameloft Brisbane

Contributors

About the author

Tyson Butler-Boschma is a multi-award-winning game developer, cinematic director, and lighting artist with over 13 years of industry experience. He is a Senior Lighting and Cinematic Artist at Gameloft Brisbane and the Founder and Creative Director of Toybox Games Studios, currently developing *Primordials Legends: Hollow Hero*.

Previously, Tyson was a Lead Lighter and Unreal Generalist on *Torque Drift 2*, *Battle Kitty (Netflix)*, and a **Fortnite** mini-series collaboration for **Epic Games** and **Universal Studios** called *We Will Be Monsters*. He has also created several award-winning projects, including the viral *Superman Flight Experience*, which amassed over 10 million views on YouTube alone, and over 100,000 players.

Tyson has an extensive educational background, having completed a "Masters in Animation, Games and Interactivity, a "Graduate Diploma in Creative Media," a "Bachelor of Interactive Entertainment," and a "Diploma in Information Technology."

In recognition of his talent and dedication, Tyson has earned numerous accolades throughout his career. He was named a *Develop Pacific 30 Under Thirty* in 2019 and won the *Unreal Engine Cinematic Summer* competition in 2019.

His projects have also been widely recognized on both national and international stages. *Primordials Legends: Hollow Hero* (2023) was the winner of the *PAX Australia People's Choice Award* and selected for the *PAX Australia Indie Showcase* and the *Future Games Show*. His earlier project, *Primordials: Fireborn* (2018–2019), was showcased at AVCON and became a finalist at the *Australian Production Design Guild Awards*.

In film and animation, Tyson's work on *Battle Kitty* (2022) was nominated at the *GLAAD Media Awards* and won Silver at the *AEAF Awards*, while *NBCUniversal: We Will Be Monsters* (2022) was a Spirit Medal Finalist at AEAF. Earlier in his career, his game *Heart of Zarar* (2013) won *Best Gameplay* and was a finalist for the *People's Choice Award*.

Across these achievements, Tyson's passion for games, storytelling, and visual craft is evident. His body of work reflects both creative excellence and a commitment to pushing the Australian games industry forward.

I would like to extend my deepest gratitude to the people who have stood beside me throughout the development of this book and my career. To my family, close friends, and the mentors who have guided me, I am truly grateful for your encouragement and belief in me.

A special thank you goes to my team at Toybox Games Studios, whose passion and dedication continue to inspire me every day, as well as the many incredible teammates and collaborators I've had the privilege to work with across various studios, but especially my current studio Gameloft. Your creativity and support have shaped not only this book, but also the way I approach my craft.

I would also like to thank Epic Games for their developer-first mindset and for building Unreal Engine, a world-class game development platform that has not only become the backbone of my career but also the foundation of the lessons and insights shared in these pages.

Finally, a heartfelt thanks to the team at Packt for their phenomenal support, patience, and guidance throughout this process. Your collaboration has been invaluable in turning this vision into a reality.

About the reviewer

Varun Kumar Gupta is a Technical Artist at Zitro, India, with a strong focus on procedural generation, rendering systems, and engine development. Holding a master's degree in computer science (augmented & virtual reality) from Trinity College, Dublin, he combines his deep understanding of mathematics, computer graphics, and real-time rendering to create scalable and efficient content generation tools.

Previously at Technicolor Games, Varun contributed to projects for Rockstar, EA, and Ubisoft. Developing procedural workflows, automation tools, and optimizing art pipelines. His current work involves Godot engine development, where he explores the intricacies of shader programming, GPU-based computation, and procedural workflows. He's passionate about pushing the boundaries of graphics programming and building intelligent systems that merge art with code.

He also served as a technical reviewer for *Unreal Engine 5 Character Creation, Animation, and Cinematics* (Packt Publishing, 2022) and continues to contribute to advancing real-time graphics and engine development.

I would like to thank my parents, my sister, my lovely girlfriend, and my friends for their unwavering support, encouragement, and invaluable feedback throughout my journey in developing games.

Table of Contents

Part III: Crafting Immersive Cinematic Storytelling   143

Chapter 7: Designing High-Quality Cinematic Sequences   145

Part IV: Optimizing Performance and Overcoming Complex Challenges 235

Chapter 10: Profiling and Performance Techniques 237

Preface

Welcome to *Unreal Engine 5 Best Practices*! Game development is an art, a craft, and—sometimes—an uphill battle! This book is here to help you face that challenge with clarity and confidence. **Unreal Engine 5 (UE5)** is more than just a tool; it's a revolutionary ecosystem that combines real-time rendering, next-gen lighting, advanced physics, cinematic storytelling, and world-class optimization workflows. Mastering all of this can feel overwhelming, but with the right approach, it becomes a playground for creativity.

This book is designed to be your guide through that playground. We'll explore not just *how* to use UE5's features, but *why* they matter, and how to turn them into design-driven workflows that elevate your projects. Think of it as a roadmap for bringing order to complexity, helping you create worlds that are not only technically sound but also artistically powerful.

Across these pages, we'll journey step by step: from the fundamentals of lighting and atmosphere, through advanced interactivity and physics systems, into the craft of cinematic storytelling, and finally, into the critical realities of optimization and troubleshooting. Each part builds on the last, creating a full pipeline of skills that will serve you no matter what kind of game or cinematic or interactive project you're building.

But this isn't just a book of technical checklists and settings to copy. It's much more about approaching Unreal Engine as a *creative medium*. You'll learn to think like both an artist and a problem-solver, using UE5 not just to build worlds but to communicate ideas, moods, and stories through design itself.

Whether you're an indie developer working solo, a student just starting your journey, or a member of a studio team tackling ambitious production goals, the workflows and principles here will give you the confidence to approach Unreal Engine with intent. By the time you finish, you'll understand that it's not just about knowing which buttons to press, but how to use UE5's tools to bring your vision to life in ways that feel efficient, scalable, and unforgettable.

Who this book is for

This book is written for game designers, developers, and artists who want to take their UE5 projects to the next level. Whether you're an environment artist looking to master lighting, a technical designer streamlining workflows, or a developer aiming to optimize performance, you'll find practical, actionable guidance here.

It's best suited for readers who already have some familiarity with Unreal Engine—intermediate users and experienced generalists will gain the most—but the lessons are presented in a way that allows motivated newcomers to follow along and grow into advanced concepts.

The material covers a broad spectrum of disciplines: optimization, animation, lighting, cinematic design, environment creation, and interactivity. If you're a technical artist seeking to refine pipelines, an indie developer pushing limited resources further, or an AAA veteran honing storytelling and visual fidelity, this book will help you sharpen your skills and work more effectively in UE5.

Above all, this book is for creators who see Unreal not just as a tool but as a creative medium. If you want to build worlds that run smoothly, look stunning, and tell powerful stories, then this is the book for you.

What this book covers

Chapter 1, Lighting with Lumen and Advanced Techniques, explores how to harness UE5's dynamic lighting to create both realistic and stylized environments. You'll learn how to set up Lumen for global illumination and reflections, and how to use lighting as a design tool to guide player focus and set the mood.

Chapter 2, Atmospheric Effects and Visual Storytelling, shows how fog, weather systems, and post-processing volumes can add depth and narrative power to your projects. This chapter covers practical setups alongside creative techniques for evoking emotion and reinforcing storytelling through atmosphere.

Chapter 3, Unreal's Advanced Modeling Tools, introduces in-engine workflows for blocking, sculpting, and refining geometry without needing to switch to external software. You'll discover how to prototype assets quickly, iterate efficiently, and leverage UE5's modeling suite for both simple and complex forms.

Chapter 4, Designing Engaging Game Environments, dives into layout, flow, and player-focused design principles. It emphasizes how environment design affects navigation, exploration, and gameplay engagement, equipping you with tools to design spaces that feel intuitive and compelling.

Chapter 5, Integrating Chaos Physics for Dynamic Gameplay Mechanics, demonstrates how to bring worlds to life with physics-driven interactivity. From destructible objects to real-time simulations, you'll see how Chaos can make environments feel dynamic, reactive, and fun to play in.

Chapter 6, Responsive and Adaptive Worlds, explores how to create systems that react dynamically to players and game states. You'll learn about procedural generation, adaptive events, and real-time environmental changes that make worlds feel alive and self-sustaining.

Chapter 7, Designing High-Quality Cinematic Sequences, teaches you how to use Sequencer to craft film-quality cutscenes, camera work, and visual storytelling moments. The focus is on building cinematic polish while keeping workflows efficient for iteration and collaboration.

Chapter 8, Environment as Narrative and Storytelling, highlights how spaces themselves can communicate story and mood. You'll see how props, lighting, and level design act as narrative devices, enabling players to experience the story through exploration rather than exposition.

Chapter 9, Adaptive Cutscenes and Interactive Paths, looks at branching, which refers to reactive narratives that keep players engaged. You'll explore how to design cutscenes that adapt to player decisions and how to blend cinematic storytelling seamlessly into gameplay.

Chapter 10, Profiling and Performance Techniques, covers how to measure and diagnose performance bottlenecks. You'll get hands-on with profiling tools, learning how to track down common issues and keep projects running smoothly during development.

Chapter 11, Advanced Optimization for Real-Time Rendering, digs into the best practices for balancing visual fidelity with efficiency. It explores rendering techniques, asset strategies, and engine settings that allow you to deliver beautiful results without sacrificing performance.

Chapter 12, Asset Management Best Practices, explains how to organize, track, and maintain clean, scalable projects. From naming conventions to version control and redirector cleanup, this chapter shows how proper asset management saves time and prevents headaches.

Chapter 13, Troubleshooting Common Development Challenges, gives you strategies to solve crashes, bugs, and roadblocks effectively. You'll learn systematic approaches for isolating problems, using UE5's built-in debugging tools, and developing habits that make troubleshooting less daunting.

To get the most out of this book

This book is based on Unreal Engine 5.4 and its associated toolset at the time of writing. Epic Games updates the engine frequently, and while the principles in this book will remain relevant, some features may evolve. Always refer to Epic's official documentation for the latest updates on cutting-edge features.

Copyright disclaimer

This book makes reference to and includes images of, third-party assets sourced from the Unreal Engine Marketplace, Quixel Megascans, Fab.com, and similar digital asset platforms. All such assets have been legally acquired and used in accordance with their respective license agreements, including the Unreal Engine Marketplace End User License Agreement and the Fab Standard License. These assets have been incorporated into original projects and demonstrations within Unreal Engine 5 solely for educational and illustrative purposes as part of this work.

All copyrights and intellectual property rights for these assets remain with their respective owners. The inclusion of these assets or images is not intended to imply ownership, endorsement, or sponsorship by the original creators or licensors.

Where applicable, credits have been provided alongside each image.

Download the color images

We also provide a PDF file that has color images of the screenshots/diagrams used in this book. You can download it here: `https://packt.link/gbp/9781836205654`.

This book contains long screenshots captured to provide you with an overview of the entire UE interface. As a result, the text on these images may appear small at 100% zoom. We recommend referring to the graphics bundle for the ease of understanding.

Conventions used

There are a number of text conventions used throughout this book.

`CodeInText`: Indicates code words in text, database table names, folder names, filenames, file extensions, pathnames, dummy URLs, user input, and Twitter/X handles. For example: "Use `r.Lumen.Reflections.Enable 0` or GI toggles to test trade-offs in bounce cost versus quality."

Bold: Indicates a new term, an important word, or words that you see on the screen. For instance, words in menus or dialog boxes appear in the text like this. For example: "Disable **Cast Shadows** on non-essential objects and lights (e.g., bottles, debris, decals, or candles)."

> Warnings or important notes appear like this.

> Tips and tricks appear like this.

Get in touch

Feedback from our readers is always welcome.

General feedback: If you have questions about any aspect of this book or have any general feedback, please email us at `customercare@packt.com` and mention the book's title in the subject of your message.

Errata: Although we have taken every care to ensure the accuracy of our content, mistakes do happen. If you have found a mistake in this book, we would be grateful if you reported this to us. Please visit `http://www.packt.com/submit-errata`, click **Submit Errata**, and fill in the form.

Piracy: If you come across any illegal copies of our works in any form on the internet, we would be grateful if you would provide us with the location address or website name. Please contact us at `copyright@packt.com` with a link to the material.

If you are interested in becoming an author: If there is a topic that you have expertise in and you are interested in either writing or contributing to a book, please visit `http://authors.packt.com/`.

Share your thoughts

Once you've read *Unreal Engine 5 Best Practices*, we'd love to hear your thoughts! Scan the QR code below to go straight to the Amazon review page for this book and share your feedback.

https://packt.link/r/1836205651

Your review is important to us and the tech community and will help us make sure we're delivering excellent quality content.

Free Benefits with Your Book

This book comes with free benefits to support your learning. Activate them now for instant access (see the *"How to Unlock"* section for instructions).

Here's a quick overview of what you can instantly unlock with your purchase:

PDF and ePub Copies

Next-Gen Web-Based Reader

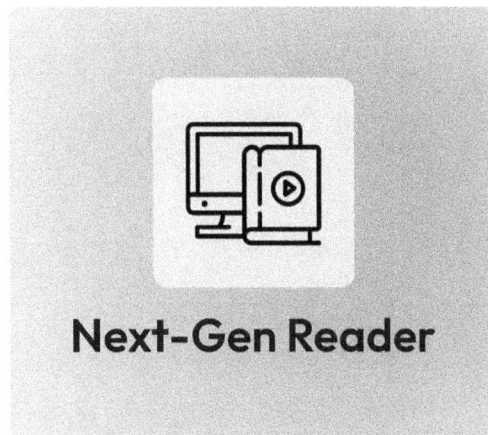

Free PDF and ePub versions

Next-Gen Reader

Access a DRM-free PDF copy of this book to read anywhere, on any device.

Use a DRM-free ePub version with your favorite e-reader.

Multi-device progress sync: Pick up where you left off, on any device.

Highlighting and notetaking: Capture ideas and turn reading into lasting knowledge.

Bookmarking: Save and revisit key sections whenever you need them.

Dark mode: Reduce eye strain by switching to dark or sepia themes.

How to Unlock

UNLOCK NOW

Scan the QR code (or go to packtpub.com/unlock). Search for this book by name, confirm the edition, and then follow the steps on the page.

Note: Keep your invoice handy. Purchases made directly from Packt don't require one.

Part 1

Mastering Lighting, Atmosphere, and Environment Design

In this first part of the book, we'll explore the foundational elements that bring a game world to life visually. From the technical power of Lumen to the artistry of atmospheric effects, you'll learn how to use light, fog, and advanced modeling tools not just as visual polish, but also as core design principles. By mastering these techniques, you'll be able to shape environments that are immersive, believable, and emotionally resonant.

This part of the book includes the following chapters:

- *Chapter 1, Lighting with Lumen and Advanced Techniques*
- *Chapter 2, Atmospheric Effects and Visual Storytelling*
- *Chapter 3, Unreal's Advanced Modeling Tools*

1

Lighting with Lumen and Advanced Techniques

Unreal Engine 5 offers unprecedented tools and workflows for crafting immersive games, stunning cinematic sequences, and detailed interactive environments. This book is your ultimate guide to UE5's advanced features and integrating them into your projects. From cutting-edge lighting techniques to optimization strategies, each chapter equips you with the practical knowledge and skills needed to elevate your creations to professional standards. Whether you're designing engaging gameplay environments, crafting interactive narratives, or achieving high visual fidelity without performance compromises, my hope is to ensure that you're ready to tackle the real-world challenges of game development, filmmaking, and virtual production to create unforgettable experiences.

Lighting is one of the most critical components in game development, cinematic storytelling, and virtual production, as it directly impacts atmosphere, realism, and player immersion. During my time as an artist, lighting has been single-handedly responsible for making or breaking a scene. I have seen poor assets elevated by good lighting, and excellent assets decimated by bad lighting. In this chapter, you'll dive into the power of **Lumen**, Unreal Engine 5's global illumination system, and explore advanced lighting techniques that elevate your scenes to the next level.

By the end of this chapter, you will have a strong grasp of Lumen's capabilities and practical insights into how to use it for dynamic, real-time lighting. You'll also gain valuable techniques for balancing visual fidelity with performance and combining Lumen with other advanced tools, such as volumetrics and emissive lighting, to create truly captivating environments.

Understanding and mastering these techniques will lay a strong foundation for the chapters to come, as lighting plays an integral role in environment design, cinematic storytelling, and overall project quality.

In this chapter, you will learn:

- How to set up and optimize Lumen in your Unreal Engine projects
- Techniques for achieving realistic indoor and outdoor lighting
- Advanced workflows for integrating volumetric effects, shadows, and emissive lighting
- Combining Lumen with advanced lighting techniques
- Tips for optimizing lighting to balance quality and performance
- Case studies: Lumen in action
- Troubleshooting Lumen issues

Free Benefits with Your Book

Your purchase includes a free PDF copy of this book along with other exclusive benefits. Check the *Free Benefits with Your Book* section in the Preface to unlock them instantly and maximize your learning experience.

Technical requirements

To follow along with this chapter, ensure that you have:

- Unreal Engine 5.4 or later installed on your system
- A PC capable of running Unreal Engine 5 with a recommended GPU supporting hardware ray tracing
- Basic knowledge of Unreal Engine's user interface and lighting tools
- Optional: A project with pre-built assets for testing and practice (or start with Unreal's sample projects)

> **Important note**
>
> This book uses several different Fab marketplace assets to show examples. While not required, it is recommended to have pre-built scenes of your choice to follow along or have one you have built yourself previously.

Overview of Lumen as a dynamic global illumination solution

Lumen is Unreal Engine 5's state-of-the-art solution for dynamic **global illumination (GI)**. Unlike traditional baked lighting techniques that require precalculations and often require significant time investments and computer power for baking, and lack adaptability, Lumen provides real-time feedback and dynamically calculates how light interacts with surfaces and environments. This makes it a revolutionary tool for artists and developers who need immediate visual accuracy without sacrificing creative flexibility.

Lumen achieves this realism by simulating the complex interplay of light rays as they bounce, scatter, and diffuse across surfaces. This technique brings lifelike realism to environments, where changes in lighting conditions, such as moving a light source or altering geometry, are instantly reflected throughout the scene.

Benefits of Lumen over baked lighting methods

Baked lighting has long been a staple in game development for its efficiency in static environments, and was one of my "go-to" solutions when developing games in the early 2010s, but it comes with significant limitations. Changes in lighting conditions require rebaking, which is time-consuming and often disrupts workflow. Additionally, baked lighting struggles with dynamic elements such as moving objects or changing light sources.

Lumen eliminates these bottlenecks by offering the following:

- **Time-saving workflow**: Artists can adjust lighting and see the results immediately, eliminating the need for lengthy baking processes.
- **Dynamic adaptability**: Lumen excels in projects that demand constant iteration, such as games with day-night cycles or real-time cinematics.
- **Improved realism**: Subtle effects such as light bleeding, color bouncing, and shadow softening are calculated in real time, enhancing visual fidelity.

Where Lumen excels

Lumen's real-time capabilities make it particularly effective in the following scenarios:

- **Indoor and outdoor environments**: Whether you're creating a dimly lit cave or a sunlit meadow, Lumen dynamically adapts to both enclosed spaces and open terrains.

- **Real-time interactivity**: It is perfect for gameplay where objects and light sources move frequently, such as opening a door to reveal a new light source or casting shadows from a swinging lantern.
- **Cinematic lighting**: For cutscenes or cinematic sequences, Lumen provides directors with the tools to manipulate light dynamically, ensuring that scenes look compelling from every angle.

While Lumen excels in many scenarios and is the focus area for lighting in this book, there are cases where traditional baked lighting or alternative methods still hold an advantage, and it's important to know why.

Where Lumen falls short

Here are just a few situations where Lumen doesn't excel compared to baked lighting:

- **Performance in low-end hardware:**
  - *Challenge*: Lumen's dynamic calculations require significant computational resources, which can impact performance on lower-end devices or older hardware.
  - *Advantage of baked lighting*: Precalculated lightmaps are far less resource-intensive, making them more suitable for games targeting mobile platforms or older PCs.

- **Extremely high-resolution details:**
  - *Challenge*: Lumen may struggle with fine details in GI, especially in highly detailed scenes with intricate geometry or dense materials
  - *Advantage of baked lighting*: Baked lightmaps can capture high-resolution lighting details with greater precision for these cases

- **Projects with memory constraints:**
  - *Challenge*: Lumen requires additional memory for handling dynamic lighting data, which can be problematic for projects with tight memory budgets
  - *Advantage of baked lighting*: Lightmaps are relatively lightweight, making them ideal for projects where memory optimization is a priority

- **VR and AR applications:**
  - *Challenge*: Virtual and augmented reality demand extremely high frame rates to ensure a smooth experience, and Lumen's real-time computations can cause performance dips

- *Advantage of baked lighting*: Prebaked lighting is more predictable and optimized for delivering consistent performance in VR and AR environments

Here, I have set up an example scene showing a static light setup versus the same scene rendered with Lumen, highlighting the differences in realism, adaptability, and shadow detail.

Figure 1.1 shows a side-by-side comparison of not using versus using Lumen GI:

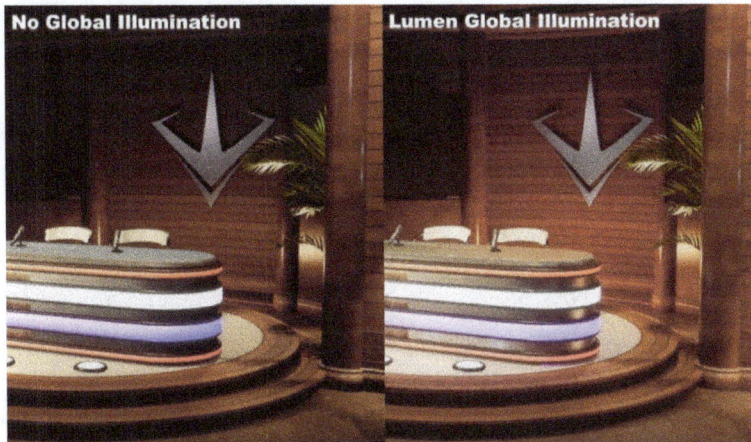

Figure 1.1: Showcasing static lighting versus dynamic lighting using Lumen

Figure 1.2 shows a visual breakdown of how Lumen is different with light bounces and reflections:

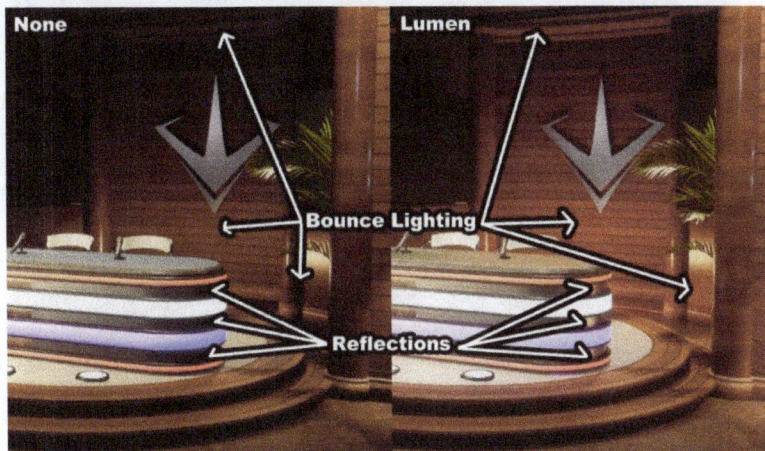

Figure 1.2: Showing how rays interact with surfaces in an environment

By understanding these limitations, we as artists can make informed choices about when to leverage Lumen's capabilities and when traditional lighting methods might be more suitable.

Now that we understand the transformative potential of Lumen as a dynamic GI solution, let's dive into the practical steps required to set it up in your Unreal Engine project.

Setting up Lumen in your project

To unlock Lumen's full potential, it's crucial to properly set up your project. This section provides a step-by-step guide to enabling Lumen, optimizing performance, and avoiding common pitfalls. Remember to check the *Technical requirements* section at the start of this chapter before you begin, and make sure you have the minimum specs required to run UE5 as shown here: https://dev.epicgames.com/documentation/en-us/unreal-engine/hardware-and-software-specifications-for-unreal-engine.

Enabling Lumen in Project Settings

Before you can start using Lumen's powerful dynamic lighting and reflections, you'll need to make sure it's turned on in your project. Don't worry—it only takes a minute. Here's how to enable Lumen in **Project Settings**.

1.　Open **Project Settings**:

　　a.　Navigate to the **Edit** menu and select **Project Settings...**.

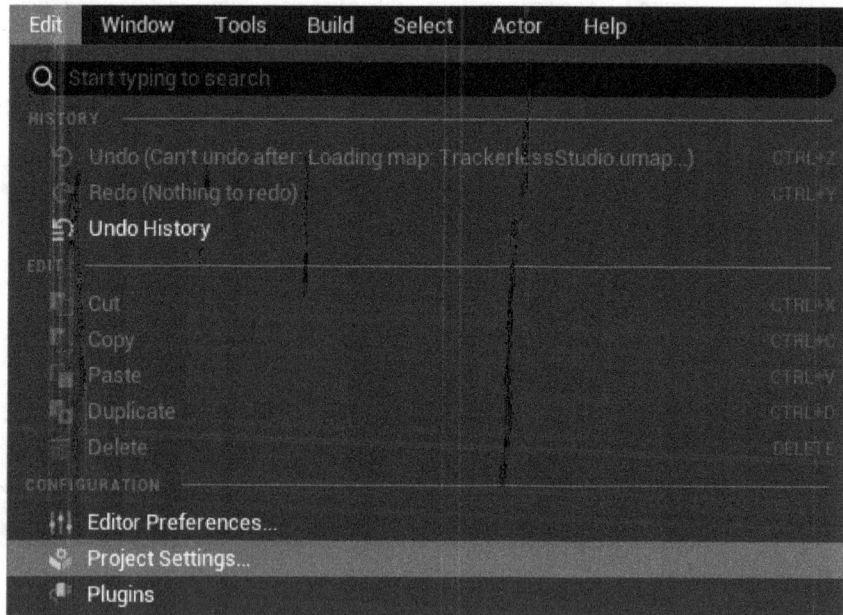

Figure 1.3: Project Settings 1 of 3

    b.   In the **Rendering** section, locate the **Dynamic Global Illumination Method** drop-down.

2.   Enable Lumen:

    a.   Set **Dynamic Global Illumination Method** to **Lumen**.

    b.   Ensure that **Reflection Method** is also set to **Lumen** to maximize its capabilities.

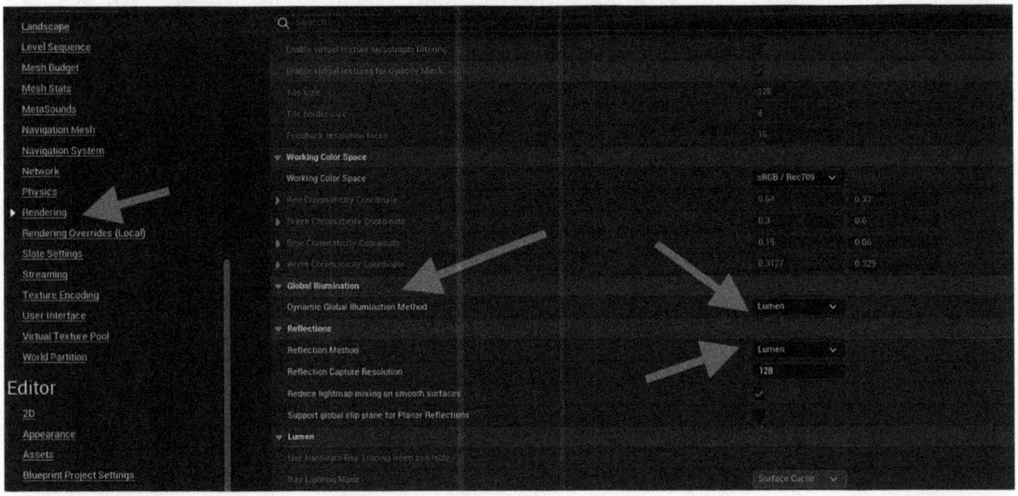

Figure 1.4: Project Settings 2 of 3

3.   Adjust **Hardware Ray Tracing**:

- If your system supports hardware ray tracing, enable it under the **Ray Tracing** settings for enhanced performance and visual fidelity.

- For systems without dedicated ray tracing hardware, Lumen will default to a software-based solution, which is less resource-intensive but may sacrifice some quality. Make sure to turn on **Generate Mesh Distance Fields**.

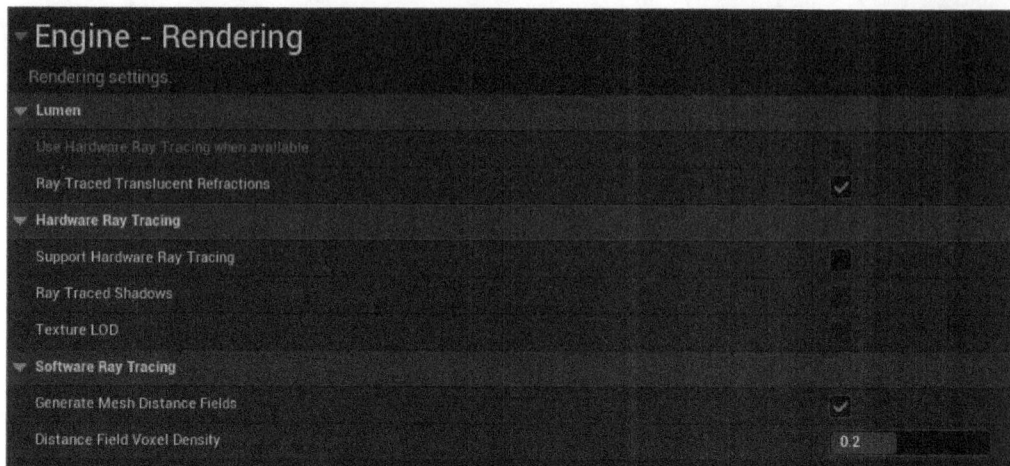

Figure 1.5: Project Settings 3 of 3

4.   Verify and save:

   a.   Restart your project to apply changes.

   b.   Test your scene to ensure that Lumen is functioning correctly.

Now that we have enabled Lumen in our project, we can discuss the technical specifications to achieve the best results.

Hardware requirements and performance considerations

While better hardware is obviously important, it's not essential. I, for example, still use a mid-tier 10-series graphics card for my testing, but here is what I recommend for your best experience:

- **GPU and hardware recommendations**:

  - A high-performance GPU with ray-tracing capabilities (e.g., NVIDIA RTX series or AMD RDNA 2) is recommended for optimal results.

  - Ensure that your system meets Unreal Engine 5's hardware baseline. See the minimum system specifications here: https://dev.epicgames.com/documentation/en-us/unreal-engine/hardware-and-software-specifications-for-unreal-engine.

- **Balancing quality and performance**:

  - In **PostProcessVolume**, adjust the **Global Illumination Quality** settings to balance performance with visual detail (see *Figure 1.6*).

- Use Unreal's built-in profiling tools to identify bottlenecks (e.g., the **GPU Visualizer**).

Optimizing settings for quality versus performance

Let's now adjust the following settings to match your project's needs:

- **Final Gather Quality**, **Lumen Scene Lighting Quality**, and **Lumen Scene Detail**: Higher values enhance indirect lighting but may impact frame rates.
- **Reflections Method**: For less demanding scenes, consider using Lumen's software mode.
- **Reflections Quality**: Fine-tune this in **PostProcessVolume** to improve reflection accuracy without unnecessary overhead.

These settings are shown in the following figure:

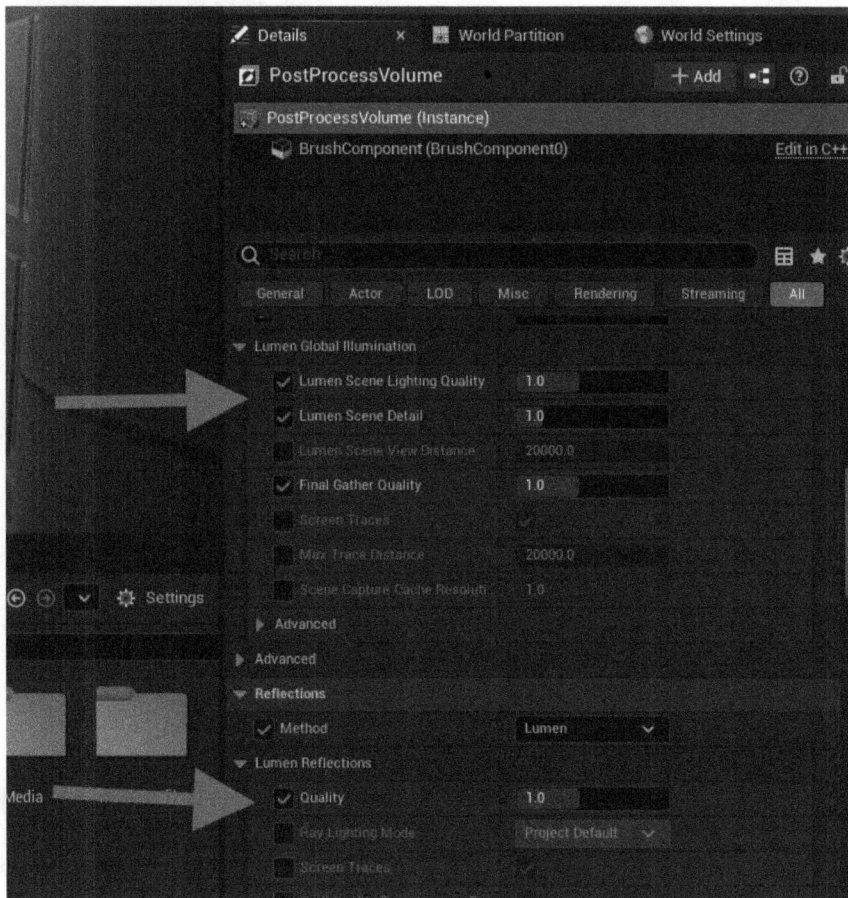

Figure 1.6: Lumen optimization settings within PostProcessVolume

With Lumen now integrated into your project, it's time to explore its application in indoor environments. The next section will focus on achieving realistic lighting setups for interiors, balancing natural and artificial light to enhance mood and immersion.

Mastering Lumen for indoor lighting

Lighting interiors effectively is a critical skill in Unreal Engine 5, as it requires balancing realism and visual appeal. Lumen is great for creating dynamic and immersive indoor environments by simulating natural and artificial light interactions in real time. This section will guide you through techniques to achieve lifelike interiors with Lumen while maintaining performance and artistic control.

Balancing natural and artificial light sources

Indoor spaces often rely on a blend of natural light, such as sunlight filtering through windows, and artificial sources such as lamps or overhead fixtures. Lumen enables the seamless blending of these light types (See the *Examples* subsection):

- **Natural light setup**: Use directional lights to simulate sunlight, positioning them to mimic real-world angles based on the time of day. Adjust the intensity and color temperature for a soft morning glow or a warmer evening ambiance. Ensure that windows and open spaces allow natural light to spill into the room, creating realistic patterns of light and shadow.

> **Tip**
>
> Combine Lumen with Unreal's Skylight for ambient outdoor light that enhances the realism of interior scenes.

- **Artificial light setup**: Add point or spotlights to represent artificial sources. Adjust their attenuation radius and intensity to ensure they complement, rather than overpower, natural light. Use color grading to match lightbulb hues, with cool tones for fluorescent lights and warm tones for incandescent bulbs.

> **Tip**
>
> Avoid over-lighting; let natural shadows and highlights create visual interest.

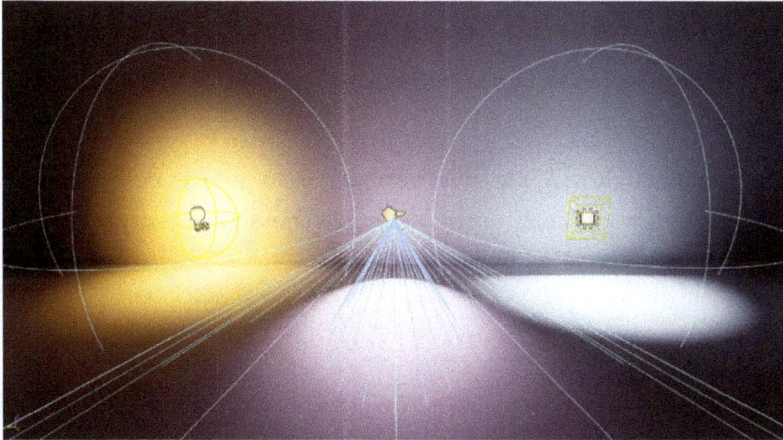

Figure 1.7: Color and temperature-balanced point, spot, and rectangle light

Achieving depth and contrast through indirect light bounces

Lumen's GI thrives in enclosed spaces where light bounces multiple times, illuminating otherwise dark areas. Mastering indirect light can elevate the depth and realism of your interiors:

- **Indirect lighting setup**: Ensure that primary light sources have enough intensity to cast multiple bounces. Adjust the indirect lighting intensity in the light's properties to fine-tune how far and bright the bounces travel.

> **Tip**
>
> In a room lit by a window, indirect light bounces can brighten corners and under-furniture areas, adding depth to the scene.

- **Contrast enhancement**: Use Lumen's GI to create contrast between light and shadow. Position objects strategically to block light and cast natural shadows, enhancing the sense of realism. Contrast helps draw the viewer's eye to focal points in your scene.

> **Tip**
>
> Experiment with soft and hard shadow settings to control the atmosphere, with soft shadows for cozy rooms and harder shadows for industrial environments.

Using emissive materials to enhance ambient lighting

Lumen allows emissive materials to act as light sources, opening up creative possibilities for ambient and accent lighting:

- **Creating ambient glow**: Apply emissive materials to surfaces such as computer screens, neon signs, or glowing panels. Set the material's emissive intensity to a realistic level and adjust its color for mood lighting.

> **Tip**
>
> In a cozy room, a glowing fireplace or lamp with an emissive material can add warmth and character.

- **Accentuating details**: Use emissive materials to highlight architectural features or props. For instance, a strip of LED lighting beneath shelving can add modern sophistication to an interior design.

> **Tip**
>
> Combine emissive materials with subtle bloom effects for a polished look.

> **Note**
>
> This emissive lighting feature is on by default! You may want to disable this feature and not have emissive materials affect GI. Disable it by clicking on the emissive asset and disabling **Affect Dynamic Indirect Lighting**.

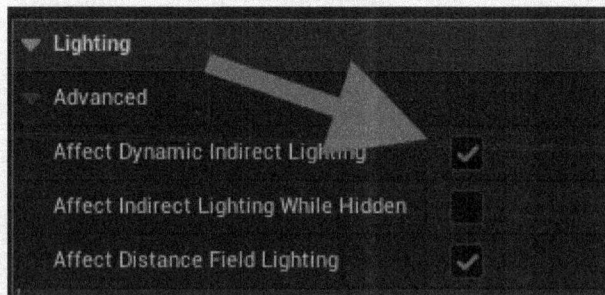

Figure 1.8: Disabling emissive GI, found in the details panel of an asset

Examples of interior scenes using Lumen

Here are a couple of quick examples of interiors using Lumen, as I have discussed. I have thrown these scenes together with existing Unreal assets:

- **Cozy room**: A warm and inviting living space for the holidays:

Figure 1.9: A warm and inviting living space, showcasing interior lighting using soft lighting (asset source: HQ Christmas Room by Darchall | fab.com)

Setup: Use directional light for sunlight, augmented by emissive materials on lights and a fireplace. Add point lights for localized lighting on the Christmas tree and candles with soft shadows to maintain a gentle atmosphere.

> **Tip**
>
> While realistic lighting is the goal, that does not mean it cannot be used in more stylized ways, like in this example. Realistic is the way light acts, more than something looking "real."

- **Industrial warehouse**: A more gritty, dramatic setting:

Figure 1.10: A more gritty, dramatic warehouse, showcasing interior lighting using soft lighting (asset source: Warehouse by Quixel | fab.com)

Setup: Use spotlights to simulate overhead fluorescent lights, casting strong shadows. Adjust the indirect bounce to brighten darker corners subtly.

Having mastered indoor lighting with Lumen, let's step outside. Outdoor environments pose unique challenges, from dynamic weather to expansive landscapes, and we'll explore how to harness Lumen's power to create breathtaking exteriors.

Advanced Lumen for outdoor environments

Designing breathtaking outdoor environments requires mastery of natural light and atmospheric effects. Lumen provides dynamic lighting capabilities that enable you to craft realistic, immersive outdoor scenes that respond to changing conditions. This section dives into advanced techniques for outdoor lighting using Lumen and its supporting features.

Harnessing directional light for natural sunlight and shadows

Directional light serves as the backbone of outdoor lighting in Unreal Engine. With Lumen, its interaction with the environment becomes dynamically adaptive, ensuring stunning visuals:

- **Simulating natural sunlight**: Adjust the intensity and color temperature of the directional light to represent different times of day. For example, use a warmer tone for sunrise or sunset and a cooler tone for midday.

Tips

Use the light's angle to define shadow lengths, which significantly influence the scene's mood and realism

Activates UE5's built-in **Sun Position Calculator** plugin to get a **Sun & Sky** asset that updates in real time based on directional light position

- **Dynamic shadows**: Dynamic shadows allow you to capture the natural movement of objects and characters in the environment. Adjust the shadow softness by expanding a light's radius to match the scale and intensity of the light source. Here is an example:

Figure 1.11: For a dense forest scene, let shadows from tree canopies create dappled light patterns on the ground (asset source: Mountain Grassland Landscape by FreshCan | fab.com)

Adjusting Skylight parameters for realistic ambient fill

Skylights complement directional light by simulating the ambient fill light created by the sky, providing subtle illumination to shaded areas:

- **Configuring Skylight settings**: Use a cubemap or the real-time captured sky to add depth and ambient color to your scene. Adjust the intensity to balance the overall brightness of the environment.

> **Tip**
>
> A slightly bluish tint in the skylight can best mimic natural outdoor light scattering.

- **Combining Skylight with Lumen GI: Skylight** works seamlessly with Lumen's GI to fill dark corners and soften harsh shadows. This is particularly effective in large, open environments. Here is an example:

Figure 1.12: In a rocky canyon scene, Skylight can brighten areas where direct sunlight doesn't reach, adding a realistic gradient of light and shadow (asset source: Nature Cave Cliff by shouhuzhedelang | fab.com)

Using fog and volumetric effects to amplify mood and depth

Atmospheric effects, such as fog and volumetrics, are essential for outdoor scenes that demand a sense of scale and mood:

- **Configuring fog parameters**: Use exponential height fog to simulate atmospheric scattering and distance haze. Adjust the density and falloff for desired effects—lighter fog for clarity or denser fog for mystery.

  For example, a foggy morning in a meadow can create a serene, immersive experience.

- **Volumetric effects**: Combine fog with volumetric lighting to enhance how light interacts with the atmosphere. This creates visible light shafts and subtle glow effects that add cinematic appeal.

> **Tip**
>
> For forest scenes, use volumetrics to simulate light rays filtering through the canopy.

We will delve deeper into this topic in the next chapter!

Practical use case for Lumen in outdoor environments

To really understand what Lumen brings to the table, it helps to see it in action. Here is just one example showing time-of-day changes:

- **Day/night cycles**: A seamless transition between day and night:

Figure 1.13: A showcase of different times of day possible in UE5

Setup: Animate the directional light's intensity and color temperature over time. Pair it with a dynamic skylight and subtle changes to fog density to reflect the time of day.

> **Tip**
>
> Check out **Ultra Dynamic Sky** on Fab for an excellent showcase regarding time of day, weather, and Lumen.

After covering indoor and outdoor lighting, the next step is to elevate your scenes by combining Lumen with advanced lighting techniques. The following section will show you how to layer traditional lighting methods with Lumen to achieve greater depth and realism.

Combining Lumen with advanced lighting techniques

Unreal Engine 5's Lumen delivers unparalleled realism and creative control by game engine standards, but combining it with traditional lighting techniques can elevate your scenes even further. This section focuses on layering additional lighting methods with Lumen to create more refined, cinematic, and visually striking environments.

Layering traditional lighting methods with Lumen

While Lumen handles GI dynamically, traditional lights such as spotlights, point lights, and area lights enable precise control over focal points and shadow diffusion:

- **Spotlights and point lights for focal highlights**: Use these lights to emphasize specific areas or objects in your scene, adding drama and guiding the viewer's attention.

  For example, in a gallery setting, a spotlight can highlight an artifact, while a point light adds a subtle glow to nearby objects for ambiance.

- **Area (Rect) lights for realistic shadow diffusion**: Area lights simulate broad light sources such as windows or fluorescent panels, creating soft, diffused shadows. They complement Lumen's GI to enhance realism in spaces such as offices or homes.

Tip

Position area lights near large emissive surfaces to mimic their glow naturally.

Figure 1.14: A showcase of different times of the day possible in UE5 (asset source: Virtual Studio by EpicGames | fab.com)

Leveraging light profiles (IES) for architectural realism

Here's a quick bit of context for the **Illuminating Engineering Society (IES)**:

- **Who they are**: They are a professional organization founded in 1906, dedicated to advancing the art, science, and practice of lighting.

- **What they do**: They set industry standards for lighting design, measurement, and application, covering everything from architecture to street lighting.

- **Why it matters in Unreal/3D**: The "IES light profiles" you use in engines such as Unreal are based on real-world photometric data published under their standards. These profiles simulate how specific light fixtures actually distribute light, bringing realism to virtual scenes.

In short, the IES defines how light should be measured and represented in the real world, and Unreal taps into that data so we can replicate real-world fixtures digitally.

So, how do we use IES profiles to simulate the behavior of real-world light fixtures, adding architectural accuracy to our scenes?

- **How to use IES profiles**: Import IES files into Unreal Engine to define the shape and distribution of light from a fixture. This is as simple as dragging and dropping a mask into your content browser, and these are perfect for environments where lighting realism is crucial, such as retail spaces, museums, or lobbies.

- **Integration with Lumen**: Lumen enhances the indirect illumination from IES-based lights, ensuring that their realistic patterns contribute to the scene's overall ambiance.

- **Further reading**: I highly recommend reading the full Unreal documentation on IES light profiles, which can be found here:

  ```
  https://dev.epicgames.com/documentation/en-us/unreal-engine/using-ies-
  light-profiles-in-unreal-engine.
  ```

Here is an example of how they can look and where to place them in a spotlight.

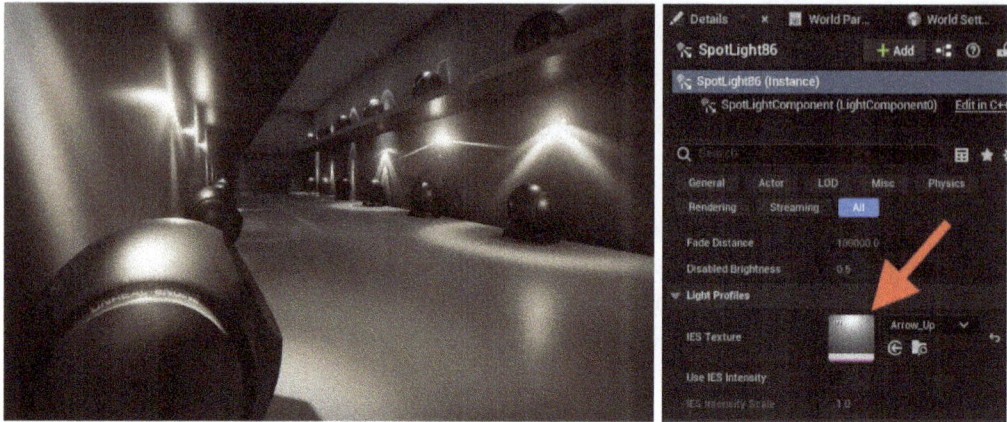

Figure 1.15: A room of detailed light patterns on the walls and floor using IES profiles

With light profiles covered, let's now take a look at how fog and light shafts can help create more cinematic and atmospheric scenes.

Using volumetric fog and light shafts for cinematic effects

Volumetric fog and light shafts amplify the atmospheric quality of a scene, creating depth and mood:

- **Volumetric fog**: Pair volumetric fog with Lumen to make light interact with the fog dynamically, adding depth to your environment. Adjust density and falloff for varying levels of visibility and ambiance.

  Here is an example:

*Figure 1.16: A distant mountain with deep cascading fog, dynamically lit by the sun
(asset source: EasyFog by William Faucher | fab.com)*

- **Light shafts:** Enable light shafts to create dramatic effects, particularly in scenes with strong directional lighting. These shafts are ideal for emphasizing natural light streaming through windows or foliage.

Here is an example:

Figure 1.17: Ruins with sunlight piercing through the ground above, highlighting dust particles in the air (asset source: Temples of Cambodia by Scans Factory | fab.com)

While Lumen offers incredible visual fidelity, it's important to maintain performance. In the next section, we'll explore optimization strategies to ensure your projects run smoothly, even on mid-tier hardware.

Optimizing Lumen for performance

Lumen's dynamic GI delivers impressive results, but balancing performance and quality is essential, especially for projects targeting a wide range of hardware. This section explores strategies to profile, tweak, and optimize Lumen's performance for smooth gameplay while maintaining visuals.

Profiling Lumen performance

Before optimizing, it's critical to identify bottlenecks in your project. Unreal Engine provides robust profiling tools to assess Lumen's impact on performance:

- **GPU profiling with the ProfileGPU command:** Use GPU profiling (**ProfileGPU** in console command) to view the time spent rendering each component, including Lumen's contributions. Look for areas where Lumen's cost spikes, such as scenes with complex geometry or numerous light interactions.

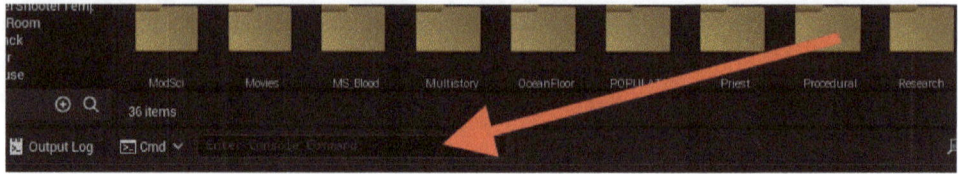

Figure 1.18: Console command location at the bottom of the Editor screen

> **Tip**
>
> The console command can be accessed within the editor by using the tilde (~) hot key.

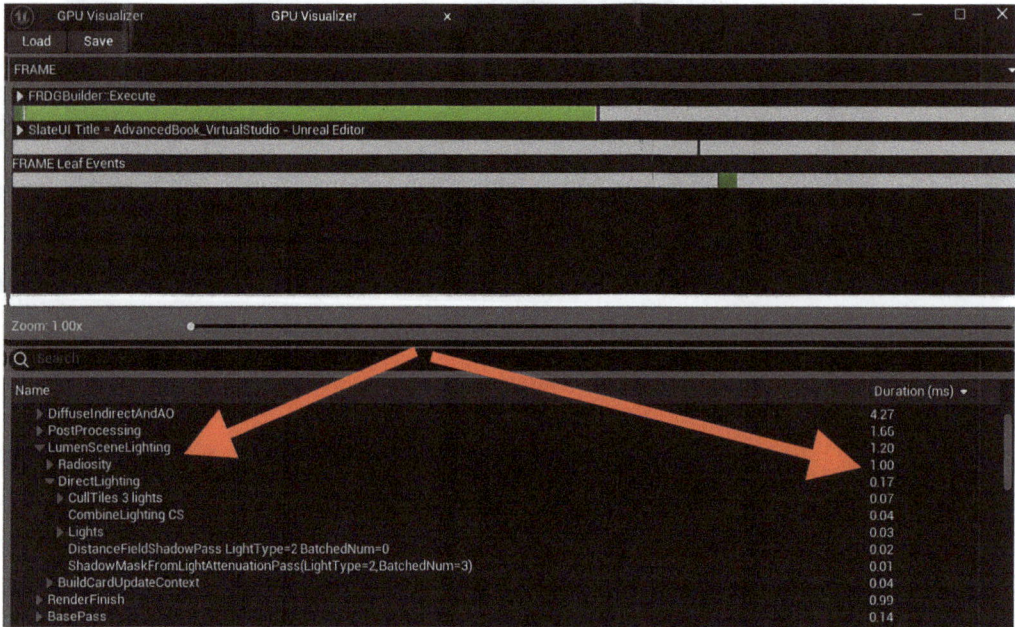

Figure 1.19: GPU profile window

- **Light complexity visualizer**: Unreal's built-in Visualizer allows you to analyze how Lumen calculates GI, screen traces, where lights are overlapping, and reflections. This tool is invaluable for diagnosing areas where performance can be improved.

> **Tip**
>
> Use the colored bar (see the red arrow in *Figure 1.19*) to see how good/bad your overlapping light complexity is.

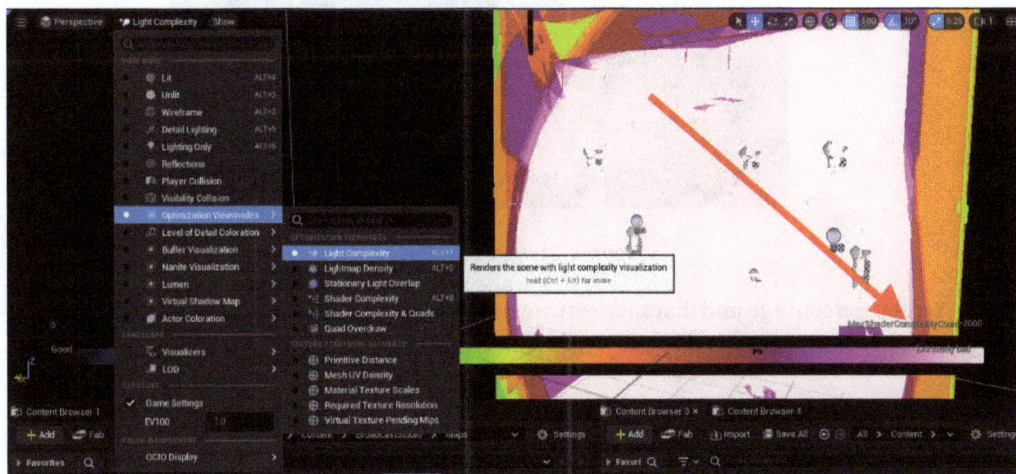

Figure 1.20: Light complexity visualizer with poor lighting overlap example

Once you've profiled how Lumen is performing in your scene, the next step is to fine-tune its settings to get the best results, especially on lower-end hardware.

Tweaking Lumen parameters to optimize for lower-tier hardware

For projects targeting mid-tier systems, adjusting Lumen settings can provide a significant performance boost without sacrificing too much visual fidelity:

- **Switching between screen traces and full GI**: Lumen supports screen-space traces for lower-cost indirect lighting, which can be activated in your levels post-process. Use this mode for less critical scenes where full GI is unnecessary.

- **Adjusting Lumen detail settings**: Reduce the Lumen quality setting within your post-process for less detailed lighting calculations. This is particularly effective in outdoor scenes where intricate lighting details may not be as noticeable.

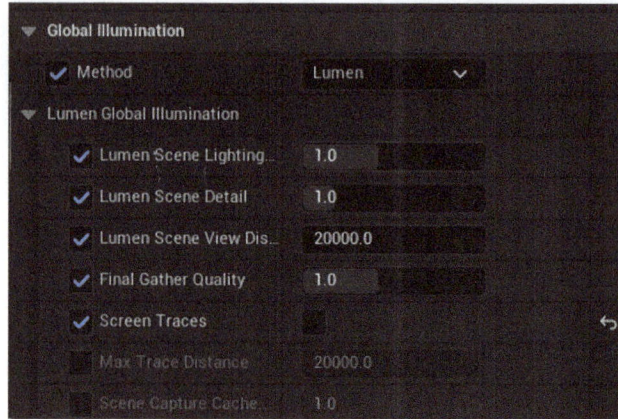

Figure 1.21: Post-process Lumen GI

- **Screen percentage and distance settings**: Modify **Screen Percentage** or set the light **Max Draw Distance** threshold to limit the complexity of far-off calculations.

> **Tip**
>
> **Draw Distance** is when the light turns off, whereas **Fade Distance** is how far it blends from 0 to your desired intensity, allowing for a smooth reveal of your lights instead of them just popping on. Distance is measured in centimeters (1,500 = 15m distance).

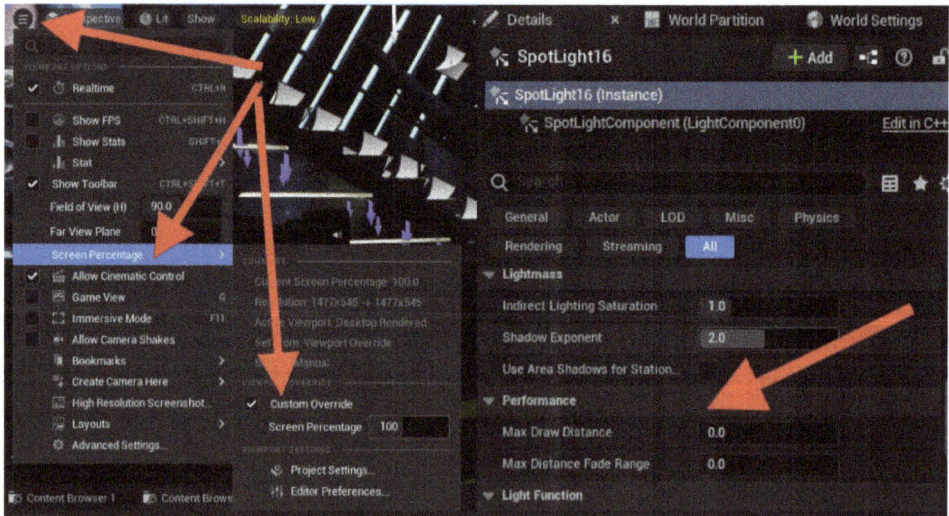

Figure 1.22: Where to find Screen Percentage and Performance

With optimization strategies in hand, it's time to see Lumen in action. Through real-world examples, we'll showcase how these techniques come together to create immersive environments.

Case studies: Lumen in action

To fully appreciate the versatility of Lumen, we'll explore two simple real-world applications: a moody dungeon scene and a vibrant outdoor market.

Case study 1: Creating a moody dungeon scene

Atmospheric interiors such as dungeons are perfect settings to showcase Lumen's GI and shadowing:

1. Setting up flickering torches with emissive light:

    a. Place torches strategically along the walls, using emissive materials for realistic flame glows.

    b. Add dynamic point lights near each torch to simulate the flickering effect. Adjust the light intensity and color slightly over time for authenticity.

    c. Enable Lumen's GI to capture subtle light bounces off stone walls.

    Here is an example:

Figure 1.23: No lights vs. point lights added to dungeon scene (asset source: Multistory Dungeons by Mana Station | fab.com)

2. Adding volumetric fog for eerie depth:

    a. Introduce a directional light and volumetric fog to create atmospheric layers within the dungeon. Here is an example:

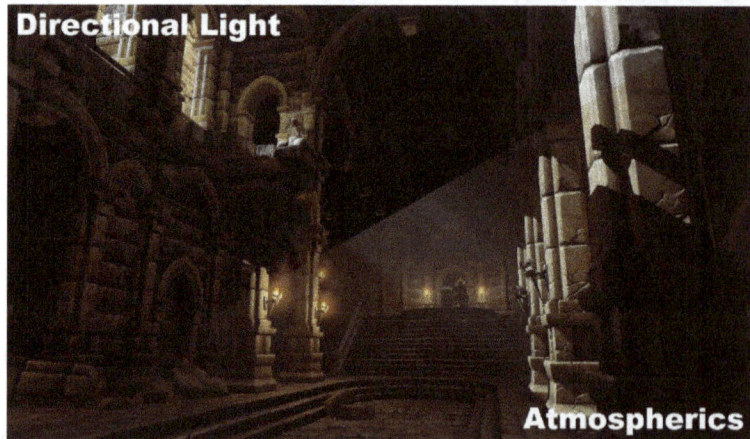

Figure 1.24: Directional light vs. atmospherics added to dungeon scene

    b. Place fog volumes near light sources such as torches for enhanced interaction between light and mist. Here is an example:

Figure 1.25: Visual guide to light placements in dungeon scene

    c. Adjust the density and scattering properties to balance visibility with mood.

From the eerie depths of a dungeon to the vibrant energy of an outdoor market, we'll now explore how Lumen enhances dynamic lighting in bustling, colorful environments.

Case study 2: A vibrant outdoor market

Lumen excels in vibrant outdoor scenes, such as a bustling market at sunset. Here's how to light such a dynamic, colorful environment effectively:

1.   Using directional lights for realistic sunlight:

   a.   Position a directional light to mimic the setting sun, with warm tones and soft shadows.

   b.   Adjust the light's intensity and angle to create dramatic, long shadows cast by market stalls and decorations.

Here is an example:

Figure 1.26: Visual guide to light placements in market scene (asset source: Bazaar by Quixel | fab.com)

2.   Adding dynamic lighting for highlights:

   a.   Place dynamic point/rect lights to add contrast, shadow, and vibrancy to the market.

   b.   Use lights where necessary to "fake" light transfusion through materials, such as the cloth above the markets. This can imply the cloth is not entirely opaque and makes the scene feel more realistic.

Here is an example:

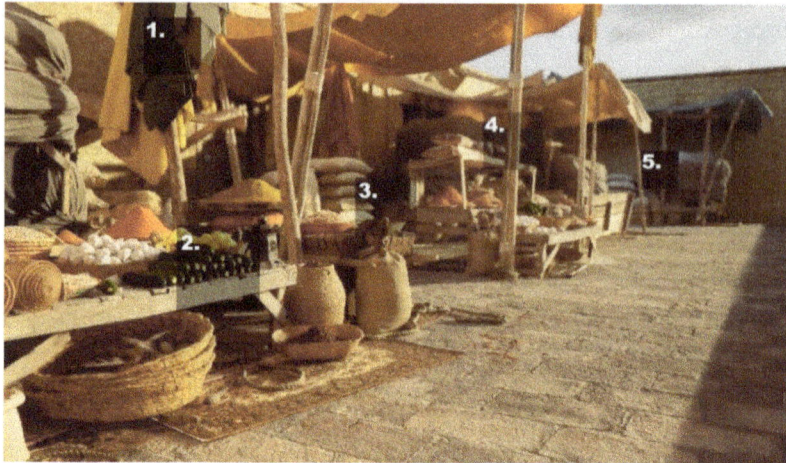

Figure 1.27: Look at the numbers for examples of color before rect lights were added to the market scene for added depth and shadow

Finally, even the most advanced tools have their challenges. In this concluding section, we'll address common issues with Lumen, offering troubleshooting tips and solutions to keep your projects on track.

Troubleshooting Lumen issues

While Lumen is a powerful lighting solution, it is not without its challenges. Developers may encounter visual artifacts or performance limitations, particularly in complex scenes. In this section, we'll identify some common issues and provide actionable solutions to help you maintain high-quality visuals and optimize your workflow.

Common issues with Lumen

Here are a few common issues with Lumen, along with their causes and solutions to overcome them:

- **Artifacts in light, reflections, and shadows:**

  - *Issue*: Reflections and GI may appear noisy or distorted, especially on glossy or reflective surfaces, while shadows might flicker or lack definition.

  - *Cause*: These issues often stem from insufficient screen-space data or incorrect light settings.

- *Solutions*:

  - Adjust **Reflection Method** under the Lumen settings to prioritize **Hardware Ray Tracing** (if supported by your system) for higher-quality reflections.

  - Increase **Final Gather Quality** in the GI settings to reduce noise in reflections and improve shadow definition.

  - For specific objects, enable **Two-Sided Shadow Casting** in the material or mesh properties to ensure accurate shadow rendering.

- **Performance drops in complex scenes**:

  - *Issue*: Large or detailed environments can cause frame rate drops when using Lumen, particularly with high-quality settings.

  - *Cause*: High triangle counts, excessive dynamic lights, or poorly optimized Lumen parameters can overwhelm hardware.

  - *Solutions*:

    - Optimize the scene by using Nanite for high-poly models, reducing draw calls, and minimizing redundant dynamic lights.

    - Lower **Max Trace Distance** in the Lumen settings to reduce the computation load for global illumination and reflections.

    - For less critical areas, use a combination of non-shadow and shadow-casting lights to balance quality and performance.

Best practices for resolving challenges

Here are some of my recommended best practices for resolving common challenges when using Lumen:

- **Use debugging tools**: Utilize Unreal Engine's **Visualize Lumen** view mode to identify problem areas in lighting, such as insufficient GI or overdraw in reflections.

- **Profile early and often**: Use the **GPU Profiler** and **Stat GPU** commands to pinpoint which aspects of Lumen are causing the most performance impact.

- **Fallback strategies**: For hardware that struggles with Lumen, implement fallback solutions such as lower-quality **Screen Traces** or non-shadow casting while maintaining dynamic Lumen lighting for key areas.

- **Stay updated**: Ensure that you're using the latest version of Unreal Engine, as Lumen improvements are frequently rolled out in updates.

By addressing these challenges head-on and implementing the solutions provided, you'll not only improve the visual fidelity of your projects but also ensure a smoother development process. With proper troubleshooting and optimization, Lumen becomes a reliable tool for delivering stunning real-time lighting.

Summary

In this chapter, we delved into the power of Unreal Engine 5's Lumen system and explored advanced lighting techniques to enhance your projects. By now, you should have a deeper understanding of how to effectively utilize Lumen in various scenarios, optimize its performance, and troubleshoot common issues.

Here's a list of the key takeaways:

- **Streamlining workflow efficiency**: Lumen eliminates time-consuming light baking, enabling rapid iteration and seamless integration into interactive and cinematic projects

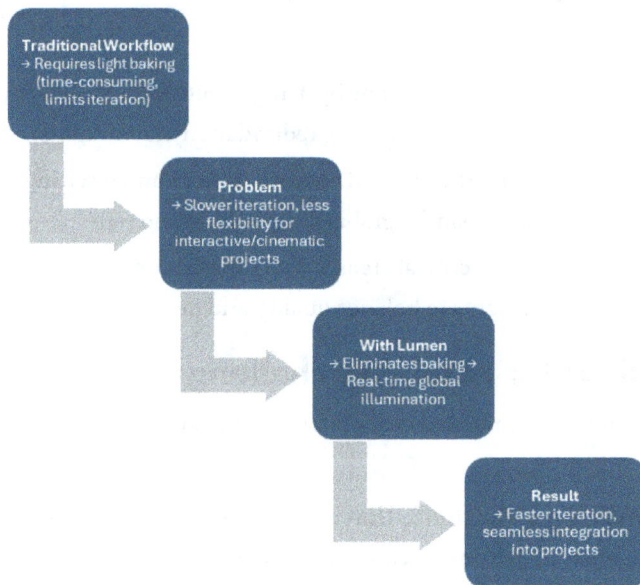

Figure 1.28: Traditional light baking versus Lumen-enabled workflows

- **Realistic lighting across scenarios**: Techniques for balancing natural and artificial light sources indoors and achieving stunning realism in outdoor environments through directional lights, volumetric fog, and dynamic weather systems.

- **Advanced techniques for lighting enhancement**: Combining Lumen with traditional lighting methods and volumetric effects allows for heightened realism and creative control

- **Performance optimization**: Practical strategies for balancing visual fidelity with performance, ensuring smooth results even on mid-tier hardware.

- **Practical application**: Case studies illustrated how to use Lumen in diverse settings, such as a moody dungeon or a vibrant outdoor market, demonstrating its versatility and impact.

Mastering Lumen is just the beginning. Experimentation, study, and refinement will unlock even more creative possibilities in your projects. Use the techniques and tools covered in this chapter as a foundation to push the boundaries of what you can achieve with Unreal Engine 5 and explore the *Further reading* section for an even greater understanding of lighting.

In the next chapter, we'll delve into how to use tools such as volumetric fog, particle systems, and post-processing to create compelling environments that enhance narrative and mood. These techniques will further build on the lighting principles covered in this chapter, ensuring that your projects captivate and inspire.

Further reading

- *Lighting, Exposure, and Contrast*: Explore advanced techniques for achieving realistic exposure and contrast in your lighting setups. Read more here: `https://www.artstation.com/blogs/shinsoj/p0Vv/lighting-exposure-and-contrast`

- *Daylight*: Dive into the science and principles of daylight to better understand its impact on lighting design. Read more here: `https://www.velux.com/what-we-do/research-and-knowledge/deic-basic-book/daylight/daylight-calculations-and-measurements`

Subscribe to Game Dev Assembly!

We are excited to introduce **Game Dev Assembly**, our brand-new newsletter dedicated to everything game development. Whether you're coding, designing, animating, or managing a studio, we've got insights, trends, and expert advice to help you create, innovate, and thrive. Sign up now and get exciting benefits.

```
https://packt.link/gamedev-newsletter
```

Get This Book's PDF Version and Exclusive Extras

Scan the QR code (or go to packtpub.com/unlock). Search for this book by name, confirm the edition, and then follow the steps on the page.

Note: Keep your invoice handy. Purchases made directly from Packt don't require one.

UNLOCK NOW

2

Atmospheric Effects and Visual Storytelling

Atmosphere is a cornerstone of immersive game environments and cinematic storytelling, shaping the mood, tone, and emotional impact of your scenes. In all my years developing virtual worlds, the word "atmosphere" is something that comes up more than all others, implying mood, or a feeling we want to invoke, but how do we achieve that in a literal sense? In this chapter, we'll explore UE5's advanced tools for creating atmospheric effects and learn how to use them to reinforce your narrative and captivate your audience.

By the end of this chapter, you will understand how to craft visually compelling environments that can resonate with players and viewers alike. You'll gain practical insights into using **volumetric fog**, **particle systems**, and **post-processing** effects to create depth and mood while integrating weather effects for a truly holistic visual storytelling experience.

Mastering these atmospheric techniques will not only enhance the visual quality of your projects but also establish a cohesive narrative foundation for the chapters ahead, as atmosphere plays a pivotal role in environment design and emotional engagement.

In this chapter, you will learn:

- The role of atmosphere in visual storytelling
- How to use volumetric fog and light shafts to create depth and mood
- Approaches to integrating weather effects to enhance narrative impact
- Methods for using color grading and post-processing to set the scene's tone
- Combining visual cues to build a seamless storytelling experience

Technical requirements

To follow along with this chapter, ensure you have:

- Unreal Engine 5.4 or later

- A system with real-time ray tracing support (optional but recommended)

- A basic understanding of the interface, Niagara particles, lighting, and Blueprints in Unreal Engine

- Optional: A project with pre-built assets for testing and practice (or start with Unreal's sample projects)

The role of atmosphere in visual storytelling

Atmosphere goes beyond mere aesthetics—it is a core element of storytelling that communicates mood, reinforces themes, and immerses players in your world. When used effectively, atmospheric effects can do the following:

- **Evoke emotions**: A dimly lit cavern shrouded in fog can spark feelings of unease, while a bustling marketplace bathed in warm light can evoke comfort and liveliness.

- **Guide player focus**: Subtle shafts of light highlighting an ancient doorway or particles swirling around a magical artifact can direct attention to key narrative elements.

- **Enhance world-building**: Weather effects such as thunderstorms, hazy deserts, or snow-covered peaks deepen the believability of your setting.

For instance, a shadowy forest enveloped in thick fog immediately conveys mystery and danger, setting the tone for exploration or conflict. Conversely, a tranquil meadow illuminated by golden sunlight evokes a sense of peace and optimism.

Atmosphere is not just a backdrop—it shapes how players perceive and engage with your narrative, often without conscious realization.

Here, I have set up an example scene showing a setup with no **atmospherics** (left side of *Figure 2.1*) versus the same scene rendered with **Volumetric Height Fog** (right side of *Figure 2.1*), highlighting the differences in mood, look, and presentation.

Figure 2.1 shows a side-by-side comparison of not using atmospherics versus using atmospherics:

Figure 2.1: Showcasing no atmospherics versus atmospherics in the same scene (asset source: Viking Village Environment by Leartes Studios | FAB.com)

Balancing realism and artistic intent

While realism often anchors players in a believable world, it's not always the ultimate goal. Stylized or exaggerated atmospheric effects can heighten storytelling and create memorable visuals. Unreal Engine provides the flexibility to strike the perfect balance between realism and creative expression.

- **When to emphasize realism**: A grounded setting like a modern cityscape or military simulation benefits from realistic atmospheric conditions, accurate weather, lighting, and material interactions.

- **When to prioritize artistry**: In fantasy or sci-fi worlds, you can use bold, stylized effects such as glowing fog, saturated skies, or surreal particle swirls to enhance the otherworldly vibe.

Practical tips for balancing artistic choice and realism

Here are some practical tips to consider when treading the line between artistic choice and realism:

- Use **post-processing tools** to tweak **contrast**, **saturation**, and **color grading**, amplifying the mood you want to convey.

- Layer effects like fog, ambient lighting, and particles to create depth and complexity in your scene.

- Experiment with Unreal's atmospheric tools, such as **Sky Atmosphere** and **Volumetric Fog**, to achieve a cohesive look that aligns with your artistic vision.

Balancing realism and artistic intent allows you to tell your story in a way that feels both authentic and impactful, aligning with your project's tone and genre.

Figure 2.2 shows a side-by-side example of atmospheric stylization, such as a hyper-realistic urban park versus a stylized natural setting, demonstrating how different approaches can achieve distinct narrative goals:

Figure 2.2: Side-by-side of a realistic versus stylized atmosphere (asset sources: left -City Park Environment by SilverTim | FAB.com; right -Stylized Environment by Polyart Studio | Dreamscape)

Now that we've established how atmosphere serves as a powerful narrative tool, let's dive into specific techniques. We'll start by exploring volumetric fog and light shafts, two key elements for crafting depth and mood in your scenes that will follow on nicely from what we explored in *Chapter 1*—specifically, the dungeon scene, which already uses a few of the techniques we are about to discuss.

Creating atmosphere with volumetric fog and light shafts

Volumetric fog is a powerful tool for crafting depth and mood in your environments, offering an immediate sense of atmosphere. From eerie, dense fog in a haunted forest to soft, ethereal mist drifting over a serene lake, this feature lets you fine-tune the emotional tone of your scene.

The following subsections will guide you on how best to approach atmosphere with regard to fog and lighting setup.

Volumetric Fog

Volumetric Fog is an optional extension of the **Exponential Height Fog** component that makes fog feel three-dimensional and dynamic. Instead of being a flat layer, it calculates how light interacts with tiny particles in the air throughout the camera's view. This means fog can vary in density, react to multiple light sources, and create dramatic effects like God-rays or shafts of light cutting through mist.

I recommend reading the UE documentation below for more information:

https://dev.epicgames.com/documentation/en-us/unreal-engine/volumetric-fog-in-unreal-engine.

To implement volumetric fog in Unreal Engine, follow these steps:

1. Add an **Exponential Height Fog** actor to your scene.
2. In the actor's settings, enable **Volumetric Fog**.
3. Adjust key parameters to achieve the desired effect:

    - **Fog Density**: Controls how thick or opaque the fog appears. Use higher values for dense fog and lower values for subtle mist.
    - **Scattering Distribution**: Determines how light interacts with the fog, ranging from forward scattering (bright edges) to isotropic scattering (even light diffusion).

- **Albedo:** Sets the fog's base color, which can dramatically influence the mood, white for purity, green for toxicity, and so on.

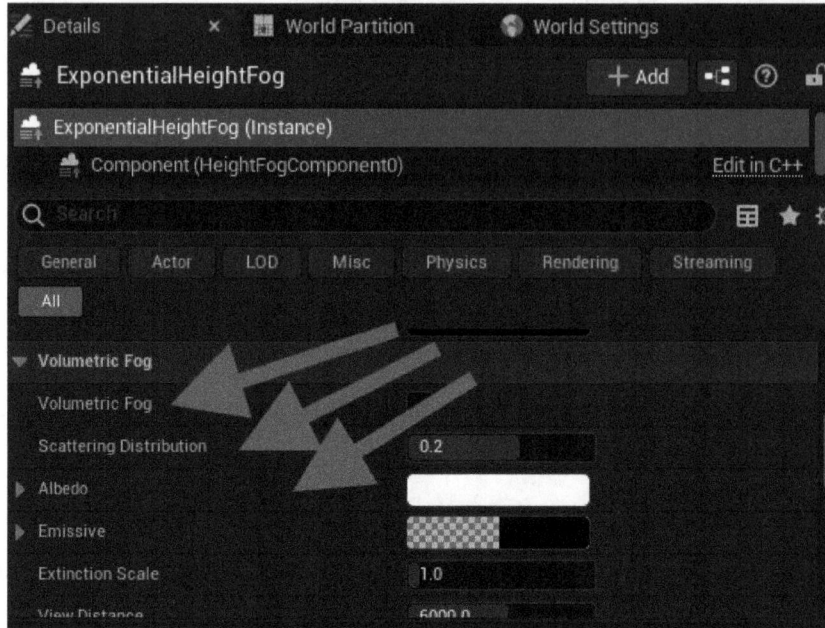

Figure 2.3: What a few parameters look like within Exponential Height Fog

> **Note**
>
> The **Albedo** setting will be influenced by the light in your scene when using **Volumetric Fog**; blue may not look "blue" if your light is red, and so on.

Layering fog

Creating realistic fog involves more than a single, uniform layer. Manipulate the fog's multiple height falloff settings to introduce variations in height and density.

Example: In a forest scene, apply denser fog close to the ground for mystery and thinner fog at higher altitudes for depth.

Practical use cases for atmospheric fog and lighting

Here are some common practical use cases for atmospheric fog and lighting.

- **Dense fog for horror or mystery**: Combine heavy fog with dim lighting to obscure visibility, evoking suspense or dread.

- **Thin mist for dreamy or ethereal scenes**: Use low-density fog with soft lighting to create a tranquil or otherworldly ambiance.

> **Tip**
>
> Subtle adjustments can make a big difference. Overusing fog can obscure detail, so find a balance that complements your scene.

Figure 2.4 demonstrates the start of fog in a forest scene, showing the evolution from a clear environment to one with a fog layer.

Figure 2.4: Basic atmosphere sky with no other elements (left) and adding sky polish and volumetric clouds (right)

Figure 2.5 continues from *Figure 2.4*, showing the progressive layers of fog in a forest scene, showing an eventual scene rich with atmospheric depth.

Figure 2.5: Adding Volumetric Height Fog to the left side of the image and then adding denser fog to change the mood even further on the right

Enhancing light shafts for cinematic effects

Light shafts simulate the scattering of light through particles in the air, creating striking beams of light that add cinematic drama and realism to a scene. There are two kinds of light shafts you can create, and they work great together as well.

Volumetric light shafts

We have already explored volumetric fog, and that automatically creates light shafts when doing the following:

- Adjusting **Volumetric Scattering Intensity** of a light source to control how much the fog interacts with it. A higher intensity makes the light more visible in fog, while a lower intensity reduces its effect.

- Enabling **Volumetric Shadow** for dynamic volumetric light shafts.

Directional light shafts

To enable and adjust light shafts, start with these steps:

1. Add a **Directional Light** to your scene and go to its properties.

2. Enable **Light Shaft Bloom** and **Light Shaft Occlusion** to simulate light scattering and shadowed areas.

3. Adjust the following parameters for customization:

    *   **Bloom Scale**: Controls the intensity of the light beams. Higher values create more pronounced shafts.

    *   **Occlusion Mask Darkness**: Determines how much shadow is cast by objects blocking the light. Increase this value for stronger contrasts.

    *   **Bloom Tint**: Allows you to tint the light shafts to match your scene's color palette (e.g., golden hues for a sunset).

Tips for effective use

Here are a few things to consider to effectively use light shafts to their maximum potential:

*   **Strategic placement**: Place light sources near openings like windows, tree canopies, or cracks in walls to create natural light shafts.

*   **Pairing with fog:** Combine light shafts with volumetric fog to amplify their impact. Fog particles interact with light beams, enhancing their visibility and creating a layered effect.

*   **Use in storytelling:** Position light shafts to draw attention to key elements, such as a sacred altar illuminated by beams of light through a cathedral's stained glass.

Light shafts work best in areas where there is a clear interaction between light and shadow. Avoid using them excessively, as they can overwhelm the scene and lose their cinematic value.

In *Figure 2.6*, I am showing how light shafts can dramatically improve a scene, especially when combined with other atmospherics. The top image is an adequately lit scene, but I think we can agree, the scene below is greatly enhanced in its mood and feel when atmosphere and light shafts are added.

Figure 2.6: The difference between a lit scene with and without atmospheric light shafts (asset source: Multistory Dungeons by Mana Station | Fab.com)

Volumetric fog and light shafts are indispensable for creating atmospheric scenes that captivate players and enhance storytelling. Together, they bring depth, emotion, and cinematic quality to your virtual worlds.

With a solid understanding of how volumetric effects shape depth and lighting, let's move on to weather-based particle systems. While particle systems like falling leaves or dust motes can provide the finer details of atmosphere, for the context of this book, we will focus on larger-scale weather effects that can transform entire environments. Let's explore how to simulate rain, snow, and other dynamic weather conditions to amplify our project's immersion and storytelling.

Simulating weather effects for dynamic worlds

Dynamic weather systems can transform static environments into living, breathing worlds. By simulating rain, snow, or other weather phenomena, you can add an immersive layer to your project, making players feel truly embedded in the environment. Unreal Engine 5's particle systems, volumetric fog, and Blueprints provide all the tools needed to create stunning weather effects that can elevate your storytelling.

However, building a whole weather system could be a book in itself, so for this section, we will instead focus on some actionable techniques and theories to make your weather systems more advanced.

Rain, snow, and beyond

In this section, we will investigate some tips and theory on how to set up weather effects, rather than the full breakdown of exactly how this system would be built. Creating weather effects involves combining particle systems with fog and lighting for a cohesive and realistic appearance. We will discuss creating rain and snow effects and go beyond with a dynamic layering effect.

Rain effects

Rain effects are a great way to add atmosphere, tension, or realism to a scene, whether you're setting the tone for a cinematic moment or enhancing environmental storytelling. There are several ways to create rain, each with its own pros and cons depending on your performance needs and artistic goals, but let's take a look at how you might get started.

- **Rain particles:**

    1. Use **Niagara** to create elongated particles for raindrops.
    2. Add subtle velocity variations for a natural appearance.
    3. Make sure your rain material is set to **Lit** so that it can be affected by the light around particle raindrops. Here is a great tutorial to follow on the subject of rain: https://dev.epicgames.com/community/learning/tutorials/5nKZ/unreal-engine-5-rain-and-thunder-tutorial

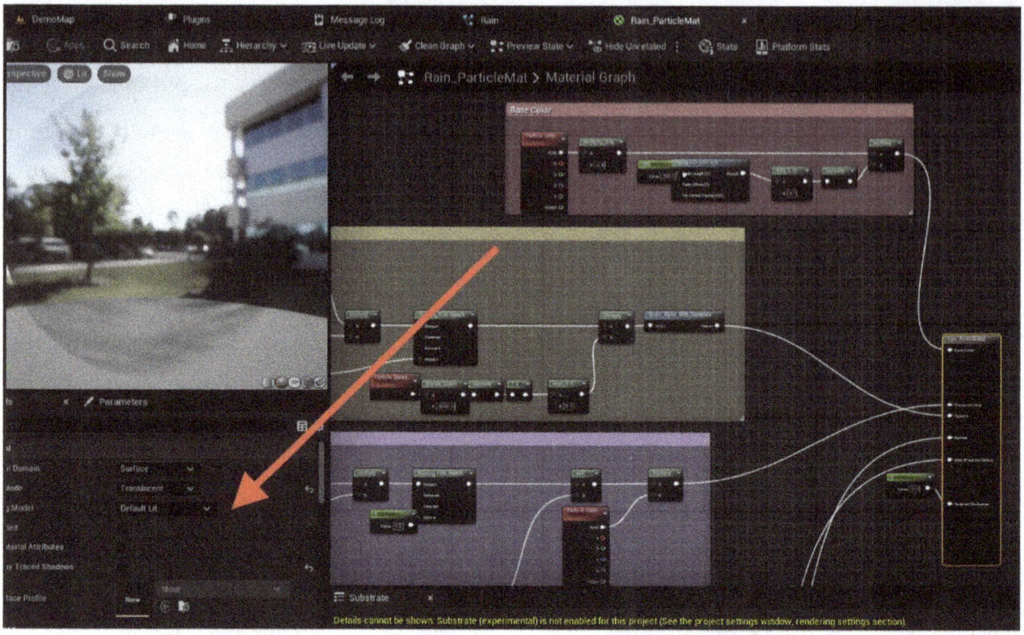

Figure 2.7: Where to make sure your Rain material is set to Lit

- **Rain mist:**

  1. Pair with **Exponential Height Fog** to simulate mist near the ground or surfaces.

  2. Adjust scattering and density to create the illusion of rain diffusing in the air.

  3. You can also place large translucent planes in the distance with a looping rain texture or particle effect applied. This technique fakes the look of rainfall far away without rendering thousands of individual particles, helping performance while still adding to the layered, realistic depth of a rainstorm.

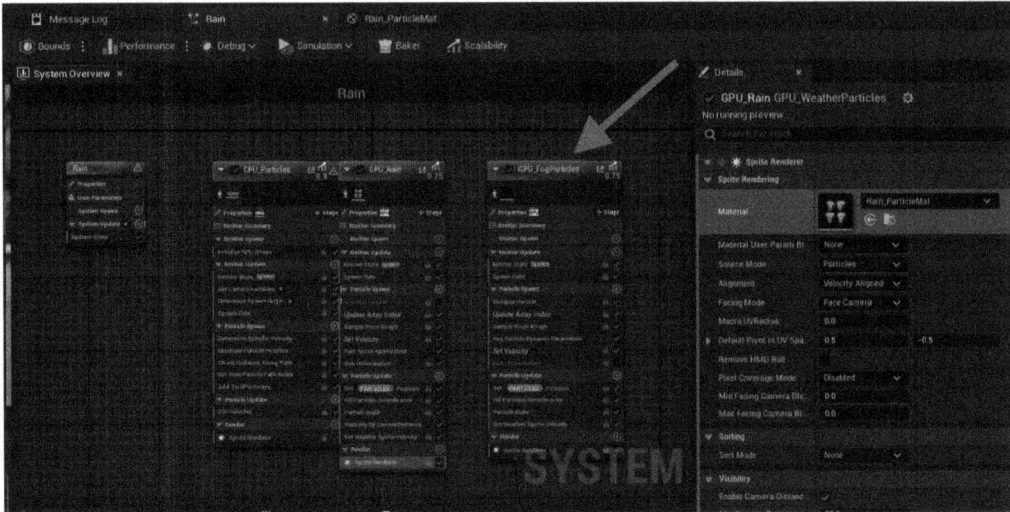

Figure 2.8: Showing how we can have multiple systems (like rain mist/fog) within one Niagara system

- **Puddles and reflections:**

  Use wetness for materials on surfaces to reflect the environment dynamically. This is easily controlled by affecting a material's **roughness**.

Snow effects

Like rain, snow effects can instantly transform a scene, adding mood, seasonality, or a sense of isolation and calm. In Unreal, snow can be approached in different ways, ranging from GPU particles to material-based accumulation, depending on your desired look and performance budget.

> **Tip**
>
> Instead of simulating every snowflake, you can use materials to make snow appear to build up naturally on surfaces. This is what I mean by "material-based accumulation." This usually means blending a snow material on top of existing assets using height or slope-based masks, so snow gathers on flat, upward-facing areas while leaving vertical or sheltered areas clear. You can also add displacement or parallax effects for extra depth, but even simple blend shaders go a long way in selling the illusion of snow piling up over time.

Here's how to start thinking about building snowy environments that feel immersive and dynamic.

- **Snow particles:**

  - Create particles with slow, floating velocities to mimic drifting snowflakes.

  - Add randomized rotations and variations in size for realism.

- **Snowy haze:**

  Use fog with cool tones and low density to simulate the visual softness of snowy weather.

- **Accumulation:**

  Implement **dynamic materials** that adjust to display snow buildup on objects and terrain.

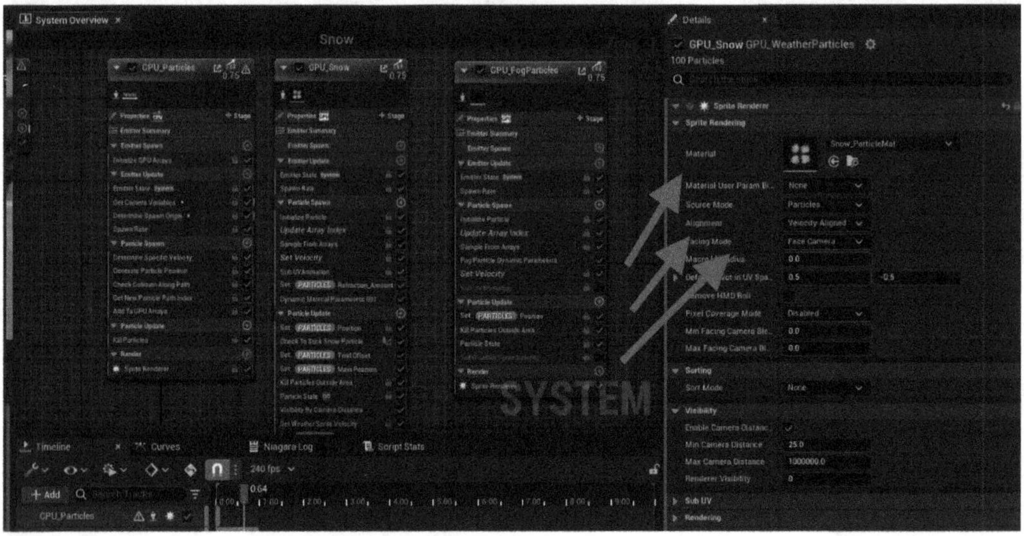

Figure 2.9: Settings to consider within Niagara when building a snow particle

> **Tip**
>
> While I have focused on snow here, this advice works just as well with any other weather-based particle system, especially things like dust or sandstorms; you're basically just changing the color and speed.

Dynamic layering or effects

Dynamic layering is the layering of effects to greater realise a look of an effect beyond its core idea. For example, rain is the overall effect, but ripples are a dynamic layer that can add to it. Here are a few examples:

- **Puddle and ripples:** Use animated decals or shaders to depict raindrops hitting puddles. These effects can add texture and movement to surfaces.

- **Snow trails:** Implement deformation or vertex paint systems to show footprints in snow, adding interactivity and storytelling potential.

- **Lightning and shadows:** For storms, use directional lights to simulate lightning flashes. Pair these with sudden changes in shadows for a dramatic, natural effect.

Figure 2.10 is a showcase of how weather can drastically affect the atmosphere of the same scene. Here, we have 5 examples (from left to right). We have: 1 – Dry, 2 – Fog, 3 – Wet, 4 – Sandstorm, and finally, 5 – Snow. The same scene, but different weather:

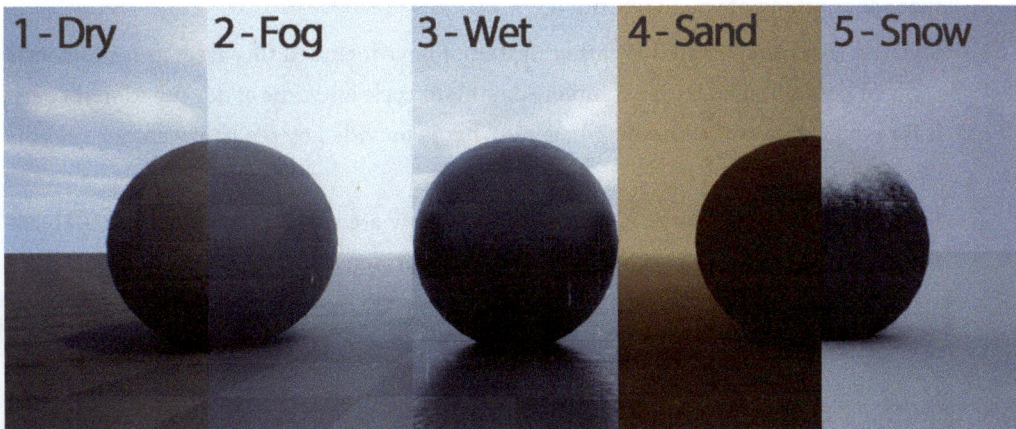

Figure 2.10: A showcase of different weather effects on the same scene

Pre-built systems

We have gone over the very basics of what weather can do for your projects, but building these systems from scratch is well beyond the scope of this book.

So, let's instead look at some incredible systems available for you to use on the Fab Marketplace, and then we can use the theory we have just discussed to enhance our worlds and storytelling with the use of these pre-built systems.

- **Ultra Dynamic Sky**: Ultra Dynamic Sky (UDS) is a versatile sky and weather system built for realism and ease of use. Designed to be more realistic and versatile than many existing packages, it offers extensive customization options through an intuitive, performance-focused interface. UDS also includes a full weather system out of the box, supporting everything from rain and snow to sandstorms. Out of all the weather-based systems available on the Unreal Marketplace (Fab), this is the one I've relied on most throughout my professional career.

- **Weather System – Free**: I have included "Weather System – Free" simply because it is a phenomenal system for being a free asset that anyone reading this book can get right now at no cost and test the principles we have discussed as part of this chapter. While I don't think it's quite as powerful as its paid counterpart, UDS, it is still an incredible system that asks nothing of you in return.

- **Stylized Dynamic Sky and Weather System**: I have included this asset as it provides a stylized sky combined with a complete day-night cycle and time of day functionality—it is for you if you want something beyond what is provided by realistic weather systems like UDS.

- **EasyRain and EasySnow**: EasyRain and EasySnow are separate systems, but both are made by William Faucher and work together in harmony.

Figure 2.11: The Fab store page for EasySnow by William Faucher

EasyRain is a streamlined Blueprint and Niagara-based system designed to help us artists quickly implement realistic rain effects. Whether you're aiming for a gentle drizzle or a heavy summer downpour, it offers flexible controls to dial in the perfect atmosphere with minimal setup. **EasySnow**, on the other hand, delivers a high-fidelity snowfall system. It gives you full control over the mood and density of your winter scenes in seconds. I use both these systems regularly for game development, both professional and indie, and my personal film projects.

> **Disclaimer**
>
> I am in no way affiliated with these products and have no monetary or personal stake in them or their success. These are purely my personal opinions/recommendations for tools that I use on a daily basis in my professional career.

Weather effects, when executed effectively, enhance the believability of your world and deepen player immersion. By mastering the tools provided by UE5 and systems provided by the Fab community, you can craft dynamic, visually engaging weather systems that adapt to your storytelling needs.

While weather effects add motion and texture to your worlds, post-processing is where you can truly refine your visual tone. Let's take a closer look at how color grading, exposure adjustments, and other post-processing techniques can elevate your scene's mood and cohesion.

Using post-processing for visual impact

Post-processing is a powerful tool in Unreal Engine 5 for refining the mood and atmosphere of your scenes. By adjusting **color grading**, **exposure**, and other settings, you can guide the player's emotional response and enhance the narrative of your environment. Properly utilizing post-process volumes can make the difference between a flat, uninspiring scene and one that captivates your audience. Post-processing is my personal favorite tool in Unreal as an artist, as it is so versatile in controlling the look and feel of a scene.

Let's see how you can advance your visual impact through color grading and exposure within your Post Process Volume.

Color grading for atmosphere and emotion

Color grading is one of the most effective ways to set the tone of your scene. By manipulating **colors**, **contrast**, and **saturation**, you can align the visual presentation with your narrative.

Adjusting color grading

Adjust these values to achieve a bunch of different results, from warm nostalgia to cold mystery.

- **Warm tones for comfort and nostalgia**: Use a combination of yellow, orange, and red hues to evoke warmth, safety, or happiness. This works well for sunsets, cozy interiors, or nostalgic flashbacks.

    - Increase **Temperature** and **Tint** in the color grading panel to shift toward warm tones.

    - Slightly enhance **Saturation** to make the colors more vivid.

- **Cool tones for mystery and tension**: For icy landscapes, night scenes, or suspenseful moments, emphasize blues, purples, and greens.

    - Decrease **Temperature** and adjust **Contrast** to create a stark, moody effect.

    - Add subtle desaturation for a more subdued, somber tone.

- **High-contrast settings for drama**: Increasing contrast between highlights and shadows can draw attention to specific areas or create a more cinematic feel.

    - Use the **Global Contrast** slider for overall adjustment or fine-tune highlights, mid-tones, and shadows individually.

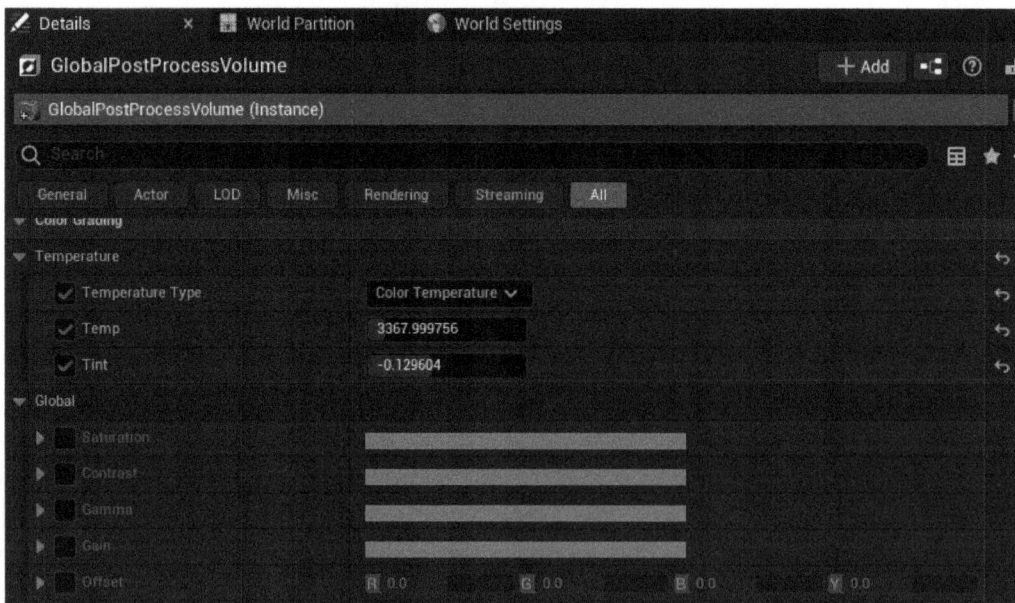

Figure 2.12: Temperature controls in a Post Process Volume

Creating narrative intent

Pairing color grading with an environment's theme helps reinforce the emotional tone and narrative intent of a scene. For example, a desaturated, cool-toned palette can evoke feelings of isolation or mystery, while warm, saturated tones might suggest comfort, safety, or nostalgia. By aligning the color grade with the story's emotional beats, you create a subconscious connection for the player that strengthens immersion and narrative clarity.

Here are some other examples:

- **Post-apocalyptic**: Desaturated colors with high contrast
- **Dreamscapes**: Overexposed whites and pastel tones for a surreal look
- **Action sequences**: Vibrant, high-saturation palettes with sharp contrasts

Figure 2.13 shows a scene that I have dramatically affected using different color-grading techniques that we have just discussed, showing how different the same scene can look when using (from left to right) neutral, cold, and warm color grading, respectively.

Figure 2.13: The visual differences temperature and color grading can achieve on the same scene (asset source: The Bazaar by Meshingun Studio | FAB.com)

Exposure adjustments for realism and impact

Exposure settings allow you to mimic the natural way human eyes adjust to light, adding another layer of immersion to your scenes.

Auto exposure for dynamic adaptation

Auto exposure in Unreal Engine 5 automatically adjusts brightness based on the lighting conditions within the camera's view. This mimics real-world eye adaptation and is particularly useful in environments with varying light levels, such as the following:

- **Dark interiors leading to bright exteriors**: The player's view will brighten as they step outside, simulating human eye adjustment.
- **Dimly lit areas**: Auto exposure can help retain visibility without sacrificing atmosphere.

To enable and tweak auto exposure:

1. Open the **Post Process Volume** settings in your scene.
2. Locate the **Exposure** section.
3. Adjust **Min Brightness** and **Max Brightness** to define the range for adaptation.
4. Set the **Speed Up** and **Speed Down** values to control how quickly the exposure adapts to changes in light.

Manual exposure for artistic control

While auto exposure is dynamic, manual settings are ideal for static scenes where you want full control over brightness and contrast.

1. Adjust **Exposure Compensation** to balance your scene's overall brightness.
2. Use **Histogram Mode** in the Viewport to analyze the exposure levels and ensure no areas are over- or underexposed.

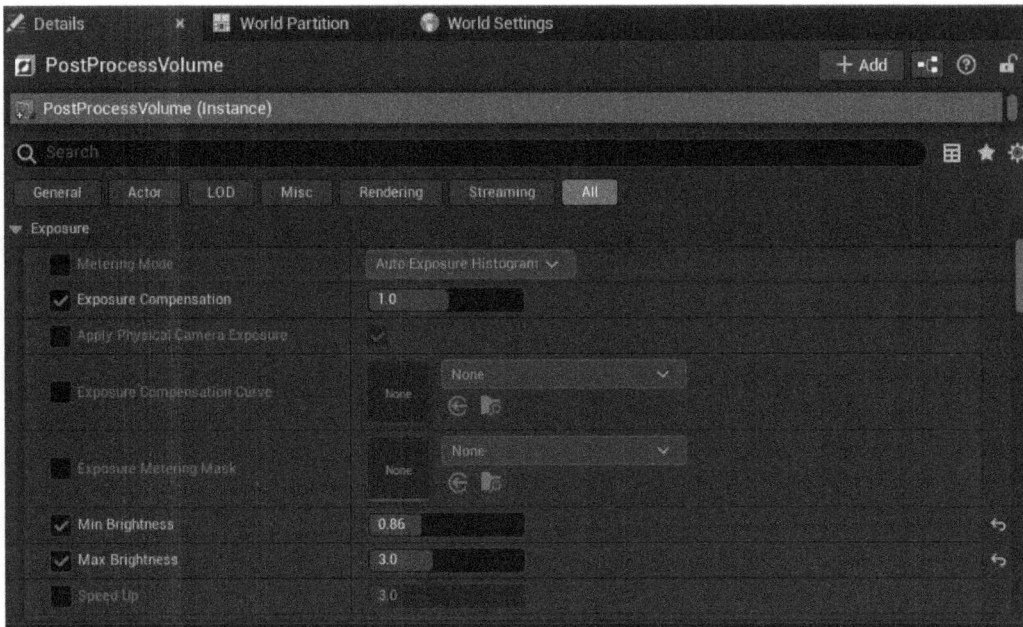

Figure 2.14: Exposure controls in a Post Process Volume

Practical workflow — setting correct Exposure values

Here's a practical workflow for setting up a scene to use the correct **Exposure** values.

1. Begin with neutral settings to establish your scene's baseline lighting.
2. Activate the Post Process Volume and gradually layer in adjustments, starting with color grading, then exposure, and finally contrast and vignette effects.
3. Regularly compare the raw version of your scene to the post-processed version to ensure the enhancements align with your intended mood and narrative.

Post-processing is not just about making your scene look polished; it's about storytelling through visual refinement. By mastering color grading and exposure adjustments, you can convey emotion, enhance immersion, and guide the player's journey in a way that feels both natural and compelling.

With all these tools at your disposal, it's time to focus on tying them together for narrative impact. In the following section, we'll explore how atmosphere can subtly guide player focus and build tension to complement your storytelling.

Combining atmosphere with narrative elements

Atmosphere isn't just about creating visually stunning environments—it's also a powerful tool for guiding players and reinforcing narrative elements. By strategically integrating atmospheric effects with storytelling techniques, you can craft immersive experiences that captivate players and keep them engaged. Let's have a look at some theory and principles for guiding the player and building your narrative moments.

Guiding player focus with atmospheric effects

Players naturally gravitate toward areas of visual contrast or dynamic movement within a scene. By using atmospheric effects to subtly guide their focus, you can ensure they interact with critical elements of the environment or narrative.

Lighting as a guide

Lighting is one of the most effective tools for directing attention within a scene.

- **Highlighting key areas:** Use contrasting light and shadow to draw the player's eye. Here are some examples:

    - Brightly lit doorways against a dimly lit corridor

    - A spotlight effect on an important object or character

- **Directional lighting**: Place light beams or shafts to guide players along a path. Here are some examples:

    - In a dense forest, beams of sunlight breaking through the canopy can subtly point toward an exit

    - In indoor environments, lights spilling through windows or cracks can signal the next room to explore

- **Dynamic lighting for interaction**: Employ flickering lights, glowing objects, or changes in color temperature to draw attention to interactive elements. For example, a flickering torch near a hidden lever encourages exploration.

Environmental cues

Atmospheric effects can work in tandem with the environment to provide players with visual or contextual cues.

- **Fog and density variations**: Use fog density to differentiate safe areas from dangerous ones. Here are some examples:
  - A clear path leading through thick mist can reassure players they're heading in the right direction
  - Denser fog paired with faint red hues can indicate danger or a high-stakes encounter

- **Particle trails for subtle guidance**: Add subtle particle effects like glowing embers or drifting leaves to suggest movement or direct attention. Here are some examples:
  - A trail of sparkling particles leading to a magical artifact
  - Wind-blown leaves subtly moving toward a hidden path

Building tension through atmosphere

Dynamic atmospheric changes are a powerful way to evoke emotions and heighten tension in gameplay.

Dynamic weather events

Sudden shifts in weather can set the tone for pivotal moments in your game.

- **Approaching storms**: Gradually darkening skies, stronger wind effects, and distant thunderclaps can signal an impending threat, such as a boss battle or narrative climax.
- **Rain and lightning for drama**: Heavy rain combined with occasional lightning flashes can amplify tension in chase scenes or survival sequences.
- **Transitioning calm to chaos**: Begin with a serene setting—gentle fog or soft lighting—and disrupt it with sudden, dramatic changes like gusting winds or swirling mists to signal danger.

Fog density changes for suspense

Fog is not only a mood-setter but also a tool for suspense and unpredictability. Use thickening fog to obscure the player's view during moments of uncertainty or tension. Here are some examples:

- A player exploring an abandoned village is gradually enveloped in dense fog, hiding potential threats.

- As fog dissipates, distant enemies or story-critical elements are revealed, creating a dramatic effect.

Atmospheric visual syncing

While focusing on visuals, timing atmospheric changes with subtle environmental effects can enhance immersion. Here are some examples:

- A distant, glowing storm draws closer as lightning briefly illuminates the horizon
- Fog disperses to reveal a foreboding silhouette in the distance

Practical workflow – combining atmosphere with narrative elements

Here is a simple workflow to follow in order to start combining atmosphere with your chosen narrative elements.

1. Begin by identifying key narrative beats or moments in your game.
2. Map out how atmospheric elements like lighting, fog, and weather transitions can complement these beats.
3. Test player behavior during key scenes to ensure the atmospheric cues effectively guide their focus without feeling forced.

Atmospheric effects, when combined with thoughtful narrative design, are a powerful tool for shaping player experience. Whether guiding their focus, building tension, or reinforcing key story moments, these techniques allow you to craft immersive, emotionally impactful worlds that leave a lasting impression.

We've covered a wide range of atmospheric tools, theories, and techniques in this chapter. Before we move on, let's summarize the key takeaways and consider how these elements can enhance your future projects.

Summary

Mastering atmospheric effects in Unreal Engine 5 allows you to elevate your environments into dynamic, immersive storytelling platforms. By integrating techniques such as volumetric fog, light shafts, particle systems, and post-processing, you can craft visually stunning scenes that resonate emotionally with players and reinforce your narrative goals.

In this chapter, you've explored a comprehensive range of atmospheric tools and techniques:

- **Volumetric fog and light shafts**: You learned how to use volumetric fog to create depth and mood, and light shafts to enhance cinematic quality. These tools bring realism and artistic flair to your scenes, allowing you to evoke specific emotions and focus attention on key elements.

- **Particle systems and weather effects**: You delved into dynamic weather systems, exploring how rain, snow, and transitions between weather states can add life and unpredictability to your worlds, and where you can access these systems to easily bring them into your projects.

- **Post-processing for visual impact**: Post-process volumes were highlighted as a tool for refining the visual tone of your scenes. You discovered how to use color grading and exposure adjustments to set the mood and direct the player's perception effectively.

- **Narrative integration with atmosphere**: Finally, you explored how atmospheric elements can guide player focus, build tension, and reinforce key narrative beats. By harmonizing visuals with storytelling, you can create a cohesive and immersive experience.

Through practical workflows, theory, and illustrative examples, you've gained the knowledge to confidently apply these techniques in your own projects.

In the next chapter, we'll shift focus from atmosphere to form as we dive into Unreal's advanced modeling tools. You'll learn how to block out assets and refine geometry directly in the editor without ever leaving the engine.

Further reading

To deepen your understanding of atmospheric effects and their storytelling potential, explore the following resources:

- *Unreal Engine documentation*: The official Unreal Engine documentation provides a thorough overview of all its atmospheric tools, including setup guides and best practices. Read more here: https://dev.epicgames.com/documentation/en-us/unreal-engine/unreal-engine-5-5-documentation

- *The Role of Light in Visual Storytelling*: This article delves into the impact of lighting and atmospheric cues on audience perception, offering valuable theoretical context to complement your technical skills. Read more here: https://agifineart.com/advice/light-in-visual-storytelling/

Subscribe to Game Dev Assembly!

We are excited to introduce **Game Dev Assembly**, our brand-new newsletter dedicated to everything game development. Whether you're coding, designing, animating, or managing a studio, we've got insights, trends, and expert advice to help you create, innovate, and thrive. Sign up now and get exciting benefits.

`https://packt.link/gamedev-newsletter`

Join our community on Discord

Join our community's Discord space for discussions with the authors and other readers:

`https://packt.link/unrealengine`

3

Unreal's Advanced Modeling Tools

As we have covered in previous chapters, UE5 is widely recognized for its cutting-edge real-time rendering capabilities, but it has also evolved into a powerful creation suite with **built-in modeling tools** that can rival traditional **3D software**. With these tools, you can **model**, **edit**, and **refine** assets directly within the engine, eliminating the need for constant back-and-forth between external applications. Whether you're setting up Level design shapes, **prototyping Levels**, or fine-tuning details on in-game objects, **Unreal's modeling suite** can provide you with a solid and efficient workflow.

In this chapter, we'll dive deep into the advanced modeling features UE5 has to offer. You'll learn how to create and modify assets using tools such as **Modeling Mode**, explore procedural workflows for rapid prototyping, and refine models using **Boolean operations**, **sculpting tools**, and **UV mapping**. These techniques will help you initially design and then craft complex environments while keeping performance and iteration speed in mind.

In this chapter, you will learn:

- Why we might use modeling tools within a game engine
- How to utilize Unreal's Modeling Mode to create and edit meshes
- How to use tools/functions similar to those in third-party software for non-destructive modeling
- Where to leverage procedural modeling techniques for efficient asset creation
- Techniques for optimizing assets using UV mapping and mesh simplification

Mastering these tools will not only enhance your workflow but also empower you to create high-quality environments and assets entirely within Unreal Engine, making your development process more efficient than ever.

Technical requirements

To follow along with this chapter, ensure you have:

- Unreal Engine 5.4 or later
- A system with real-time ray tracing support (optional but recommended)
- A basic understanding of the Unreal Engine interface, modeling principles, and textures in Unreal Engine
- Optional: A project with pre-built assets for testing and practice (or start with Unreal's sample projects)

The evolution of Unreal's modeling tools

For many years, game developers primarily relied on external 3D modeling software such as **Blender, Maya**, and **3ds Max** to create assets, which were then imported into Unreal Engine for scene assembly and rendering. This workflow, while effective, and to be fair is still used by myself and my colleagues in a professional context, can often introduce inefficiencies, requiring frequent back-and-forth adjustments, file exports, and compatibility checks between software.

Recognizing the need for a more integrated approach, Epic Games has continuously expanded Unreal Engine's built-in modeling capabilities. Today, Unreal's **Modeling Mode** provides a robust suite of tools that allow artists and designers to create, edit, and refine 3D assets directly within the engine. This means that many essential modeling tasks, such as mesh editing, UV unwrapping, and procedural modeling, can now be performed without ever leaving Unreal.

The integration of these tools has been particularly transformative for Level design and rapid prototyping, which is the context in which I use these tools the most. Instead of spending hours refining assets in external software before seeing them in-engine, artists can now model and iterate in real time, making immediate adjustments based on lighting, gameplay, and scale. This native modeling workflow can not only accelerate development but also foster a more intuitive creative process, allowing designers or artists like us to experiment and refine ideas with unprecedented speed.

By leveraging Unreal's evolving modeling suite, developers can do the following:

- **Quickly block out environments** for Level design using primitive shapes and editable meshes.
- **Use non-destructive Boolean operations** to merge, subtract, and refine shapes seamlessly.
- **Sculpt and refine assets** directly within the engine, reducing dependency on external sculpting software.
- **Utilize procedural modeling techniques** to create parametric assets that can be easily adjusted on the fly.

As Unreal Engine continues to develop, these modeling tools are becoming an essential part of the asset creation pipeline. In the following sections, we'll explore these tools in a bit more depth and demonstrate how they can streamline your workflow, enhance efficiency, and unlock new creative possibilities for your projects.

Setting up and accessing modeling tools

Before diving in, we need to ensure that the necessary tools are enabled and ready to use. Unlike traditional modeling software, where all features are immediately accessible, Unreal Engine keeps certain toolsets modular to optimize performance and streamline the interface.

Enabling the Modeling Mode plugin

Unreal's modeling tools are contained within a dedicated Modeling Mode, which is available as a **plugin**. By default, this plugin may not be active, so you'll need to enable it:

1. Launch UE5 and open an existing project or create a new one.
2. Open the **Plugins** window by navigating to **Edit | Plugins** in the top menu bar.
3. In the search bar, type Modeling to quickly locate the **Modeling Tools Editor Mode** plugin.
4. Enable the plugin by checking the box next to its name.
5. Click **Restart Now** when prompted, allowing Unreal to reload with the modeling tools activated.

Once the plugin is enabled, you will gain access to a full suite of modeling features directly within Unreal Engine.

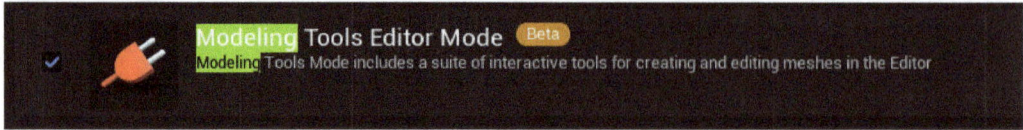

Figure 3.1: Showcasing static lighting versus dynamic lighting using Lumen

Important note

At the time of writing, this is still considered a feature in "beta" and as such is still experimental. While I haven't personally found this to be an issue, it is important to remember that it means that the tool could change or could disappear altogether if Epic decides to discontinue support.

Accessing Modeling Mode

With the plugin now active, you can enter Modeling Mode to begin creating and editing 3D assets. To do this, do the following:

1. Locate the mode selector in the top-left corner of the Unreal Engine interface (by default, it displays **Select Mode**; see *Figure 3.2*).

2. Click the dropdown and choose **Modeling Mode** from the list.

Tip

Alternatively, you can press the *Shift + 5* hotkey to open Modeling Mode.

This will replace the standard toolbar with an expanded modeling panel, giving you access to a variety of tools such as mesh editing, Booleans, deformations, UV editing, and sculpting.

Figure 3.2 shows two images of where in the editor to find Modeling Mode (left) and what the options look like within that mode (right and bottom):

Figure 3.2: Modeling options (top left) and Modeling Mode location in UE (top right). The bottom shows the location of the zoomed option above

Understanding the modeling tool categories

Once in Modeling Mode, you'll see several key categories of tools, each serving a different purpose:

- **Create**: Generate primitive shapes such as cubes, cylinders, spheres, and planes. Edit geometry with extrusions, subdivisions, and edge/vertex manipulation.

- **XForm**: Modify pivots and transforms of imported or created assets. Adjust position, rotation, and scale with precision.

- **Model** and **Mesh**: Merge, subtract, and intersect meshes for complex shape creation.

- **Deform**: Apply sculpting and smoothing operations to refine your meshes.
- **UVs**: Unwrap and modify UV layouts directly in Unreal.
- **Texture**: Paint vertex colors and apply simple textures for material previews.

With these tools at your disposal, you can perform a range of essential modeling tasks directly inside Unreal Engine, reducing reliance on external software and streamlining the asset creation process. While we can't go through all of them in this chapter, we will focus on the tools I think will provide you the most mileage and usefulness in your projects based on my own experience.

In the next section, we'll explore creating and manipulating geometry in Unreal Engine, starting with primitive shapes and moving toward more advanced modeling techniques.

Primitive modeling and basic geometry

Modeling in UE5, much like in Maya or Blender, begins with **primitive shapes**, which serve as the foundation for more complex structures. These basic geometric forms, such as **cubes**, **spheres**, and **cylinders**, allow artists and designers to rapidly prototype environments, refine spatial layouts, and even create finished assets directly within the engine.

Let's explore how primitives can be used for effective Level blockouts and rapid layout prototyping.

Using primitives for Level blockouts

One of the most effective ways to start designing an environment is by **blocking out** the Level using primitive geometry. This technique is widely used in Level design, architectural visualization, and game development to establish the layout before committing to high-detail assets.

These are the benefits of blocking out Levels with primitives:

- **Rapid iteration**: Quickly test Level flow, spacing, and player navigation.
- **Early gameplay testing**: Use rough geometry to evaluate mechanics before finalizing assets.
- **Scalability**: Adjust proportions easily before adding details.

Here are the steps to block out a Level with primitives:

1. Enter Modeling Mode by selecting it from the **Mode** menu in the top-left corner of the Unreal editor.

2. In the **Create** panel, choose from the available primitive shapes:

    - **Cube**: Ideal for walls, floors, and basic architectural forms.
    - **Sphere**: Useful for rounded objects, decorations, or placeholders.

- **Cylinder**: Works well for columns, barrels, and pipes.
- **Plane**: Useful for ground surfaces, ceilings, or water bodies.

3. Place and arrange your chosen primitives in the scene by clicking and dragging them into the viewport.

4. Modify the **Scale**, **Position**, and **Rotation** values to fit the desired layout.

Once the basic structure is in place, you can gradually replace primitives with detailed assets or refine them using the modeling tools.

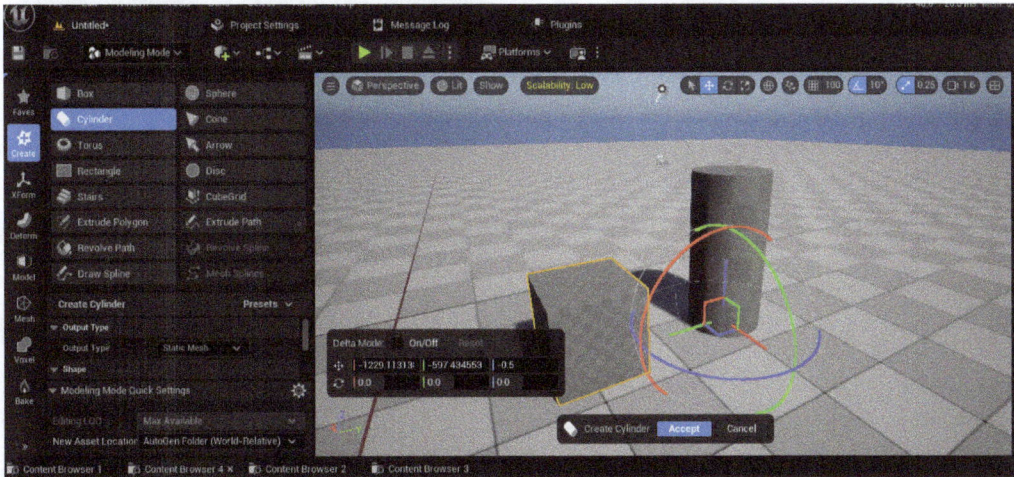

Figure 3.3: An example of a few of the basic shapes available

Adjusting shape properties: Real-time geometry editing

Beyond simple placement, Unreal's modeling tools allow for real-time editing of primitive shapes, giving designers more flexibility in shaping their environments without switching to external software.

Here are the key geometry adjustments:

- **Vertex editing**: Move individual points to reshape objects dynamically.
- **Edge and face manipulation**: Adjust edges and surfaces to refine models.
- **Extrusion**: Extend geometry outward to create new forms.
- **Subdivision and smoothing**: Increase mesh complexity for rounded or organic shapes.

Here are the steps to modify primitives in Unreal Engine:

1. Select a primitive in the viewport and enter **Modeling Mode**.

2. Choose the **PolyEdit** toolset to enable vertex, edge, and face selection.

3. Use **Move**, **Rotate**, and **Scale** tools to reshape the object.

4. Apply Boolean operations to merge or subtract shapes for more intricate designs.

5. Refine the model using deformation tools such as smoothing and beveling.

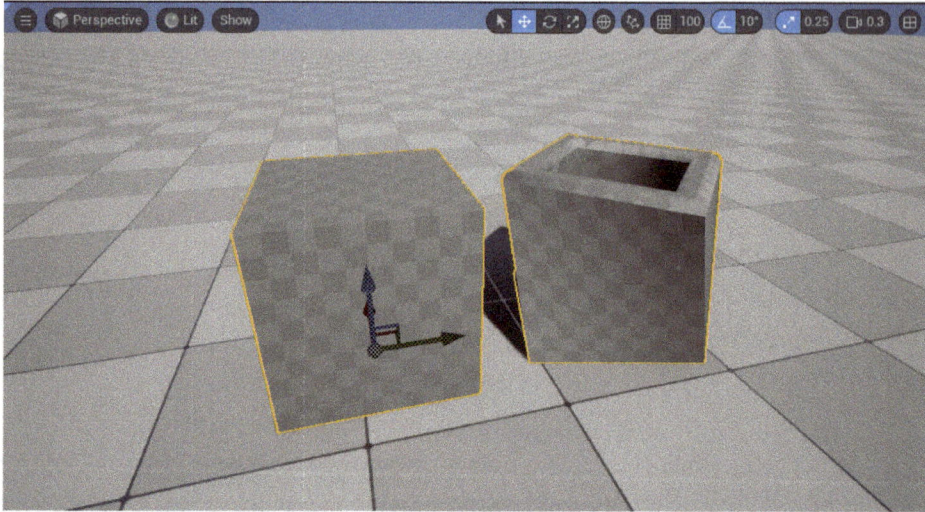

Figure 3.4: A side-by-side comparison between a cube, and the same cube modified using things such as PolyEdit and Boolean operations

From blockout to final asset

Primitives aren't just for placeholders—they can be refined into final models using editing tools. The following are examples:

*   A simple cube can be transformed into a detailed building with extrusions and bevels.

*   A cylinder can evolve into a sculpted column by adjusting segments and adding edge loops.

*   A sphere can be reshaped into organic terrain (rocks) using deformation tools.

When understanding primitive modeling and real-time geometry adjustments, we can create flexible, modular environments that adapt to our project's needs, all without leaving the engine.

Now that we've established the fundamentals of primitive modeling, it's time to take your creations further. In the next section, we'll explore Boolean operations and mesh editing, unlocking the ability to craft custom shapes and intricate designs directly inside Unreal.

Boolean operations for complex shapes

Boolean operations are a powerful modeling technique that allows for dynamic merging, subtraction, and intersection of meshes. These tools enable artists and designers to quickly create complex structures, intricate details, and custom geometry without needing to manually model every element. Whether you're designing a futuristic sci-fi corridor, sculpting destructible objects, or refining architectural elements, Boolean operations provide an efficient way for us to manipulate shapes directly within UE5.

Understanding Boolean operations

In Unreal's Modeling Mode, Boolean operations work by combining two or more meshes based on their overlapping geometry. There are three primary Boolean functions:

- **Union**: Merges two or more meshes into a single object while maintaining a clean topology.
- **Subtraction**: Removes the volume of one mesh from another, ideal for cutting windows, doors, or negative space.
- **Intersection**: Extracts only the overlapping area between two meshes, useful for creating detailed cutout shapes.

Applying Boolean operations

With Booleans explained, here are the steps for activating Boolean mode:

1. Activating the **Boolean** mode: Here are the steps for activating **Boolean** mode:

    a. Select the meshes you want to modify.

    b. Navigate to **Modeling Mode | Model | Boolean** in the toolbar.

    c. Choose the desired Boolean operation (**Union, Subtraction,** or **Intersection**).

    d. Adjust parameters such as **Retain Original Meshes**, allowing you to keep the original meshes if desired to refine the result.

2. Using **Union** for mesh merging: The **Union** operation is useful for combining objects into a seamless whole. For example, if you're constructing a modular building, you can merge walls, floors, and ceiling components into a single optimized mesh. Here are the steps for using the **Union** operation:

    a. Select two meshes and apply **Union** to fuse them.

    b. Enable **Merge Materials** to preserve texturing.

    c. Use the **Weld Edges** option to ensure proper geometry connectivity.

> **Tip**
>
> Think of assets in their basic forms. Much like how you might start drawing with circles to make a character, a chair is just a bunch of basic primitive shapes to make legs, seats, and so on.
>
> Then you can merge individual furniture components (legs, tabletop, and supports) into a single cohesive asset!

3. Creating negative space with **Subtraction**: The **Subtraction** operation is commonly used for cutting openings, such as windows, doorways, or intricate mechanical details. Here are the steps for using the **Subtraction** operation:

    a. Position a cutting mesh (e.g., a cube) inside the base object.

    b. Apply the **Subtraction** Boolean to carve out the negative shape.

    c. Adjust the **Offset** parameter to fine-tune the cut depth.

> **Use case**
>
> Carving out pipes, vents, or embedded sci-fi paneling into walls.

4. Extracting detail with **Intersection**: The **Intersection** operation retains only the overlapping portion of two meshes, which is ideal for crafting unique modular pieces. Here are the steps for extracting details with **Intersection**:

    a. Align two meshes with overlapping geometry.

    b. Apply the **Intersection** Boolean to isolate the shared area.

    c. Use **Remesh** to ensure clean topology after extraction.

Optimizing Boolean workflow

While Boolean operations are highly efficient, they can sometimes create messy or dense geometry. To ensure smooth results, do the following:

*   **Use Remesh and Simplify**: After a Boolean operation, clean up topology using **Remesh** to generate even polygons.

*   **Adjust normal smoothing**: If shading artifacts appear, tweak the **Smooth Normals** setting or use auto UVs to reapply texture coordinates.

- **Convert to Nanite meshes**: Unreal's Nanite system handles high-detail Boolean objects efficiently, eliminating polycount concerns.

Figure 3.5 shows two images where we see the start and end of three objects creating one complex mesh using Boolean operations:

Figure 3.5: Side-by-side comparison of models before and after Boolean operations.

Figure 3.6 shows two images of what these three objects look like while editing (notice the transparent torus being used to remove the mesh):

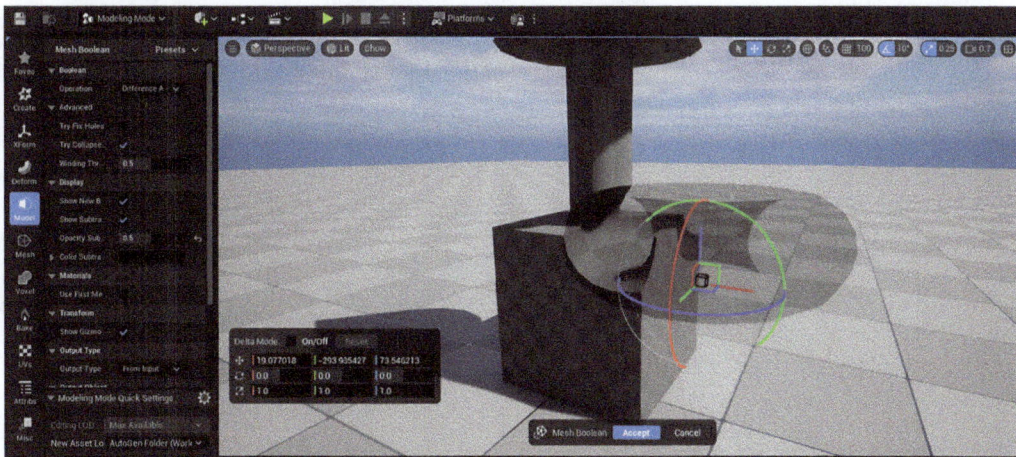

Figure 3.6: Showcasing Union, Subtraction, and Intersection in action

With Boolean operations, you can rapidly create intricate models and refine your designs without needing external 3D software. Whether you're crafting environmental assets, hard-surface props, or architectural elements, Boolean modeling in UE5 streamlines the creative process while maintaining flexibility.

Now that we've explored how Boolean operations can help you create complex shapes by merging or cutting geometry, let's move on to **sculpting and mesh editing**. This next step is similar in many ways to Boolean operations but there are extra tools that allow for more options and even finer control over your models, enabling you to craft organic shapes and refine details with brush-based tools.

Sculpting and mesh editing with DynaSculpt

Unreal's **Dynamic Sculpt (DynaSculpt)** tool provides another powerful way to refine and shape 3D models directly within the engine. Whether you are creating intricate terrain details, fine-tuning character assets, or modifying environmental props, Unreal's sculpting tools offer the flexibility needed to enhance organic and hard-surface models.

Mesh sculpting: Refining organic forms

DynaSculpt, which you can find in the **Deform** tab of the modeling tools window, provides a brush-based interface for shaping geometry, making it possible to create smooth, organic surfaces or add fine surface details. These tools are ideal for terrain editing, rock formations, and other natural assets.

Here are the key sculpting techniques:

- **Smooth and inflate**: Use the **Smooth** brush to refine surfaces and remove jagged edges, while the **Inflate** tool can push out areas of the mesh, adding volume.
- **Pinch and flatten**: The **Pinch** tool creates sharper creases, which is useful for carving fine details, while the **Flatten** tool helps even out surfaces for structured forms.

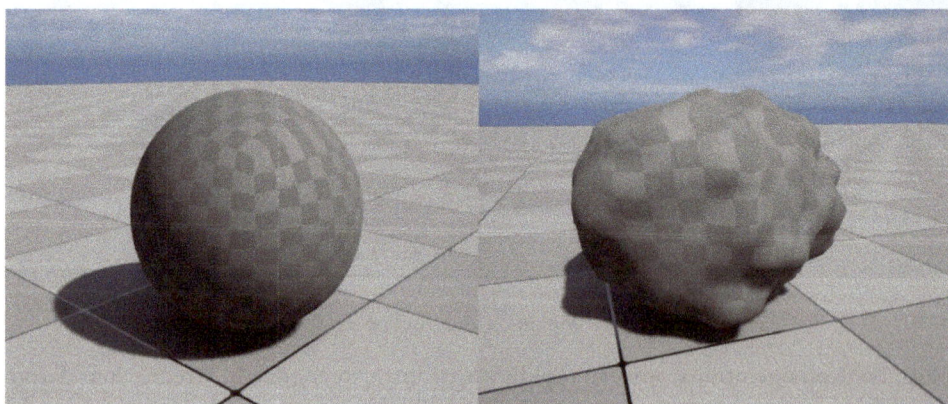

Figure 3.7: Before and after sculpting a rock from a basic sphere, demonstrating different brush effects

> **Important note**
>
> This is not a lesson on how to sculpt 3D models since that is far beyond the scope of this chapter and is its own discipline for a reason. Instead, I am showing you how to access and approach these tools within the context of Unreal Engine. Combine what we discuss here with the resources in the *Further reading* section to gain a complete sculpting experience.

Retopology tools: Optimizing mesh topology

Once a model has been sculpted, it is essential to optimize its topology to ensure smooth deformations, efficient UV mapping, and game-ready performance. Unreal Engine provides built-in retopology tools to automatically or manually refine mesh topology.

Here are the retopology techniques:

- **Decimation and polygon reduction**: Use the **Remesh** and **Simplify** tools to reduce unnecessary polygons while maintaining detail. This is crucial for performance optimization, especially for mobile and VR applications.

- **Adaptive mesh reduction**: The **Remesh** feature dynamically adjusts polygon density based on surface complexity, keeping high detail where needed and reducing complexity in flatter areas.

Practical applications of sculpting and retopology in game development

Knowing what retopology tools are is one thing, but how and why are they used? Here are some examples:

- **Environmental sculpting**: Artists can sculpt cliffs, caves, and organic ground formations directly in Unreal, refining details without needing external tools.

- **Character and creature prototyping**: Quickly sculpt basic character forms, then refine topology before finalizing in external software.

- **Prop creation**: Modify assets within the engine, making last-minute changes without going back to a 3D modeling suite.

The ability to sculpt, refine, and optimize directly within the engine can significantly enhance flexibility and iteration speed in asset production.

Once your models are sculpted and refined, it's time to focus on **UV mapping and texturing**. Proper UV mapping ensures that textures are applied correctly, giving your models the visual detail and realism they need to stand out in your scenes.

UV mapping and texturing

Efficient and accurate UV mapping and texturing are crucial for achieving high-quality visuals in game development. UE5 offers some pretty robust tools to generate, edit, and optimize UV maps directly within the engine. Whether you are applying realistic materials to props or fine-tuning textures for complex environments, being aware of Unreal's UV tools can significantly enhance your workflow.

Auto-generated UVs: Rapid UV mapping in Unreal

Unreal Engine provides an **auto UV** feature that automatically generates UV coordinates for meshes. This is particularly useful for prototyping or when working with procedural textures, as it eliminates the need for manual unwrapping.

Here are the key benefits of auto-generated UVs:

- **Speed and efficiency**: Instantly creates UV maps for assets, reducing manual work.
- **Great for prototyping**: Quickly apply materials to placeholder assets before finalizing UVs.
- **Useful for dynamic objects**: Ideal for objects that won't have complex texture details, such as background props or procedurally generated assets.

Here are the steps for using auto UVs in UE5:

1. Select a static mesh in the **Modeling Mode** panel.
2. Navigate to the **UV Tools** section and enable **Auto UV**.
3. Adjust settings such as **Angle Threshold** for better accuracy.
4. Apply and inspect the generated UVs in the **UV Editor**.

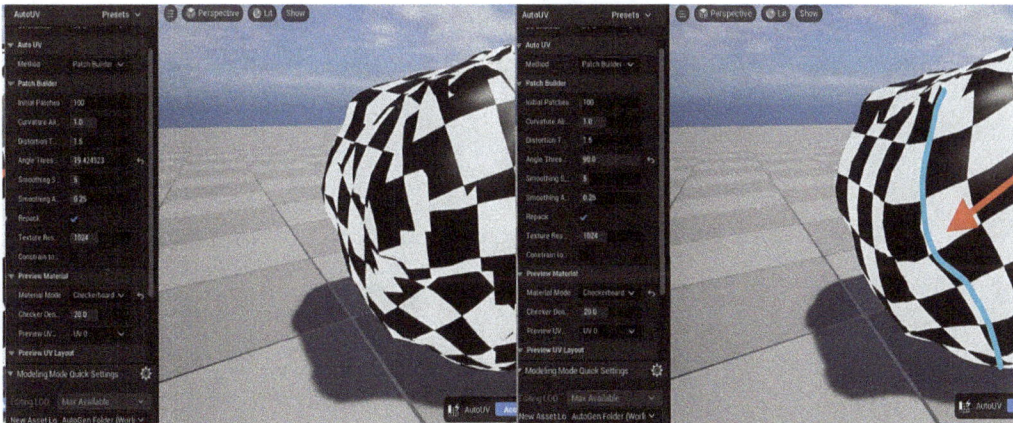

Figure 3.8: A side-by-side comparison of a model before and after applying auto UVs, demonstrating how textures align differently when changing the angle threshold

Unwrapping techniques: Manual UV adjustments for precision

While auto-generated UVs are useful, more complex models often require manual UV unwrapping for precise texture alignment. UE5 includes a *UV Editor* that allows artists to unwrap, adjust, and optimize UV layouts without external software.

Here are the key unwrapping techniques:

- **Planar mapping**: Best for flat surfaces such as walls or floors, applying UVs from a single direction.
- **Cylindrical and spherical mapping**: Ideal for rounded objects such as pipes, barrels, or characters.
- **Seam placement and island packing**: Manually defining UV seams ensures that textures wrap naturally without visible stretching.

Here are the steps for manual UV unwrapping in Unreal:

1. Enter **Modeling Mode** and select your mesh.
2. Open the UV Editor and choose **Project UVs**.
3. Use **Planar**, **Box**, or **Custom Projections** to map UVs based on the object's shape.
4. Adjust seams, flatten the UV islands, and pack them efficiently to minimize wasted texture space.

5. Apply a checkerboard material to preview distortion and refine if needed.

Figure 3.9: A UV layout comparison showing a poorly projected UV map with Planar versus an optimized version cleaner version with Box

Best practices for UV mapping and texturing

Here are some best practices to consider for UV mapping and texturing now that we have a solid base:

- **Avoid overlapping UVs (unless using tileable textures)**: Overlapping UV shells can cause visual artifacts unless intentional for repeating patterns.

- **Maintain even texel density**: Ensure UV islands are scaled appropriately to prevent texture distortion.

- **Use a checkerboard preview material**: This helps identify UV stretching or misalignment before applying final textures.

By familiarising yourself with UV mapping in UE5, you can ensure that textures are applied seamlessly across models, enhancing the overall realism and quality of your scenes, or at the very least, easily edit assets you have created in other software to speed up the iterative process when required.

With your models now textured and ready, let's wrap up with a summary of key techniques and best practices we have learned that will help you streamline your modeling pipeline and workflow.

Summary

UE5's modeling tools have evolved into a **powerful, in-engine alternative** to traditional 3D asset creation workflows. No longer just a game engine, Unreal now offers a fully integrated modeling suite, enabling us as artists and designers to prototype, refine, and finalize assets without needing external software. By leveraging these tools, we can significantly accelerate iteration times and improve creative flexibility, all while working in a workflow that minimizes destructive edits, allowing us to duplicate, adjust, and refine models in real time without leaving Unreal.

While Unreal still has a long way to go to compete with some third-party DCCs, it's well on its way to being a fully integrated modeling suite with each new update.

Throughout this chapter, we explored how Unreal's modeling tools can be applied across different aspects of asset creation:

- **Primitive modeling and Boolean operations**: Building foundational structures and refining shapes dynamically.
- **Sculpting and mesh editing**: Creating organic, high-detail models directly within the engine.
- **UV mapping and texturing**: Ensuring precise texture application through auto-generated UVs and manual adjustments.

By mastering these tools, we can streamline our asset creation pipeline, maintain an efficient modeling workflow, and deliver high-quality visuals without sacrificing performance. Whether you're crafting immersive game environments, prototyping new Levels, or fine-tuning details for cinematic sequences, these modeling tools provide the speed and flexibility needed to bring our creative visions to life.

As you continue your journey, consider experimenting with different workflows, combining procedural techniques with hand-crafted details, and integrating Unreal's modeling tools alongside external software to build a pipeline that best suits your project needs.

Looking ahead, we'll dive into interactive and dynamic design techniques and theories, as well as exploring how Unreal's Blueprint system and advanced interactivity tools can bring your environment to life.

> **Important note**
>
> Asset creation is a massive and diverse discipline that can easily fill the pages of several books, and we have barely scratched the surface in this chapter. I hope that what you have read in this chapter provides you with some solid tips and tricks on how to approach asset creation in Unreal itself, but I also recommend going through the resources in the *Further reading* section to really expand on this complex and immense art form.

Further reading

This list of further readings is from other authors under the Packt Publishing label that I recommend for getting a solid basis and understanding of 3D workflows and design. While not specifically Unreal Engine related, the lessons taught in these books directly overlap with what we have discussed in this chapter and any potential future modeling work you may undertake in the future, whether in UE5 or otherwise.

- *Blender 3D Incredible Models*: A comprehensive guide to hard-surface modeling, procedural texturing, and rendering. Read more here: `https://amzn.asia/d/7qHZ60G`

- *3D Environment Design with Blender*: Enhance your modeling, texturing, and lighting skills to create realistic 3D scenes. Read more here: `https://amzn.asia/d/d4LKdFa`

- *Sculpting the Blender Way*: Explore Blender's 3D sculpting workflows and latest features, including face sets, mesh filters, and the Cloth brush. Read more here: `https://amzn.asia/d/4bPHyBM`

Subscribe to Game Dev Assembly!

We are excited to introduce **Game Dev Assembly**, our brand-new newsletter dedicated to everything game development. Whether you're coding, designing, animating, or managing a studio, we've got insights, trends, and expert advice to help you create, innovate, and thrive. Sign up now and get exciting benefits.

`https://packt.link/gamedev-newsletter`

Get This Book's PDF Version and Exclusive Extras

UNLOCK NOW

Scan the QR code (or go to packtpub.com/unlock). Search for this book by name, confirm the edition, and then follow the steps on the page.

Note: Keep your invoice handy. Purchases made directly from Packt don't require one.

Part 2

Advanced Interactivity and Game Design

In this part, we'll move beyond static worlds and dive into interactivity. This part focuses on how to design environments that respond to player actions, integrate physics-based mechanics, and feel truly alive. By combining thoughtful game design with tools such as Chaos Physics and adaptive systems, you'll create spaces that don't just look good—they react, challenge, and evolve with the player.

This part of the book includes the following chapters:

- *Chapter 4, Designing Engaging Game Environments*
- *Chapter 5, Integrating Chaos Physics for Dynamic Gameplay Mechanics*
- *Chapter 6, Responsive and Adaptive Worlds*

4

Designing Engaging Game Environments

Creating an engaging game environment goes beyond simply placing assets in a scene—*it's about crafting a world that tells a story, guides the player, and supports the overall gameplay experience.* Whether designing open-world landscapes, confined interior spaces, or dynamic battle arenas, the way an environment is structured directly influences player immersion, navigation, and emotional engagement.

The principles of **Level design** transcend any one engine, which is why this chapter will be far heavier on *theory* than raw technique or implementation, but UE5 does offer a comprehensive suite of tools to help bring our game worlds to life. With the right knowledge, you can build breathtaking, responsive environments that enhance gameplay and storytelling. However, mastering environment design requires more than just a knowledge of the tools or chosen engine; it also requires a delicate blend of *artistic sensibility* and *technical know-how*.

In this chapter, we will break down the core principles and workflows necessary for creating compelling game spaces. We'll cover foundational design concepts, advanced techniques for visual storytelling, and the use of UE5's latest tools to elevate your Levels.

In this chapter, you will learn:

- **The foundations of game environment design**: Exploring the fundamental core of what environment design is, why it matters, and how to get started.
- **The principles of effective environment design**: Understanding how composition, scale, and player psychology impact the feel of a game world.

- **Using Unreal's procedural tools for environment creation**: Leveraging basic procedural generation techniques and Blueprint to create natural landscapes and complex urban layouts efficiently.

- **Lighting and atmosphere for emotional impact**: Taking what we learned from *Chapter 1* and applying it here, by using Lumen and other lighting tools to craft mood, direct player attention, and enhance realism.

- **Case studies: Real-world examples of strong environment design**: Analyzing successful implementations of environment design techniques in existing projects.

- **Troubleshooting common environment design issues**: Discussing a few key design issues that are prevalent, especially in environments built by less experienced designers, and how to avoid them.

By the end of this chapter, you'll have the knowledge and techniques to design rich, immersive environments that not only look great but also serve your gameplay and narrative needs.

Technical requirements

To follow along with this chapter, ensure you have:

- Unreal Engine 5.4 or later

- A system with real-time ray tracing support (optional but recommended)

- A basic understanding of the Unreal Engine interface, design principles, and grayboxing in Unreal Engine

- An understanding of lighting and atmosphere in Unreal (see *Chapters 1* and *2*)

- Optional: A project with pre-built assets for testing and practice (or start with Unreal's sample projects)

The foundations of game environment design

Before diving into UE5, it's essential that we understand some fundamental principles of game environment design. These core concepts serve as the foundation for crafting interactive, visually appealing, and functionally sound spaces that engage players. Strong environment design is not just about making a game world look good—it's about shaping the player's experience, guiding their movement, and reinforcing the game's narrative and mechanics.

This chapter is a stepping stone into the next two chapters of this book, where we will dive deeper into the topics we cover here. But for now, let's explore some of these more fundamental principles!

> **Fun fact!**
>
> Before I became a cinematic and lighting artist, I studied game design at both the bachelor's and master's levels. While it is not a major part of my day-to-day job now, it played a significant role in shaping my career path.
>
> In my experience, lighting as an art form overlaps more with the principles of design than any other aspect, and I still help my fellow design colleagues guide a player with lighting and environments today, which is why I wanted to include this chapter in this book.

Visual composition: Creating cohesive and readable environments

Composition is a fundamental aspect of environment design that influences how players perceive and navigate a space. Proper use of composition ensures that a Level remains aesthetically pleasing, functional, and easy to interpret. Key compositional techniques include the following:

- **Framing and focal points**: Directing player attention by placing key landmarks, objectives, or interactable objects in prominent positions within the scene. The *rule of thirds* and *leading lines* can be used to guide the player's eye naturally.

- **Depth and layering**: Creating a sense of scale and distance by using foreground, midground, and background elements effectively. This technique enhances spatial readability and helps establish atmosphere.

- **Contrast and hierarchy**: Differentiating important areas from background elements using light, color, or unique architectural features. This makes objectives and pathways stand out while maintaining overall harmony in the environment.

To read more on composition, the rule of thirds, and leading lines, refer to the *Further reading* section.

Figure 4.1 shows a render I captured within Epic's *Dark Ruins* MegaScans pack, illustrating all the key points we have discussed in this section.

Figure 4.1: An example of an environment applying composition principles, demonstrating the impact of proper framing, focal points, and depth (asset source: Dark Ruins by Quixel | FAB.com)

The red arrows highlight the leading lines in the geometry, guiding the eye upward toward the focal point marked by the green circle. The doorway is further emphasized through strong contrast, with its dark, mysterious silhouette standing out against the lighter rock surroundings. Additionally, the foreground elements (Blue lines) before the cliffs create a sense of depth and layering, resulting in a scene that clearly and intuitively directs the player toward their destination.

Guiding the player: Environmental cues and intuitive navigation

A well-designed game environment naturally leads the player without the need for excessive UI elements or explicit instructions. This can be achieved through the following:

- **Lighting as a guide**: Brightly lit areas, spotlights, or subtle glow effects can draw attention to objectives, exits, or interactable elements.

- **Color theory and contrast**: Warm colors (reds, oranges, and yellows) tend to grab attention, while cooler colors (blues and greens) create calming or background elements. High contrast between key locations and surrounding areas helps reinforce navigation.

- **Architectural flow and Level layout**: Pathways should be structured in a way that naturally leads players forward. Curved roads, open doorways, and sightlines to distant landmarks encourage progression.

- **Environmental storytelling elements**: Use props, textures, and environmental details to hint at objectives or past events within the world. A broken bridge, a trail of footprints, or flickering lights can subtly suggest the next step to the player.

By mastering these techniques, you can create Levels that feel intuitive and immersive without excessive hand-holding.

> **Tip**
>
> In games, *hand-holding* refers to guiding players with explicit instructions, tutorials, or overly direct cues. While helpful for new/casual players, excessive hand-holding can reduce exploration, undermine player agency, and diminish the sense of discovery.
>
> For example, forcing the camera to focus on an object with a constantly "pinging" objective would be considered hand-holding.

Balancing aesthetics and gameplay

One of the biggest challenges in environment design is finding the right balance between visual appeal and functional gameplay. While stunning environments can elevate a game's atmosphere, overly complex or cluttered designs may interfere with gameplay clarity. Key considerations include the following:

- **Maintaining readability**: Avoid excessive visual noise or overcomplicated details that may distract or confuse the player. Essential gameplay elements should always be distinguishable.

- **Minimizing visual clutter**: While realism and detail are important, too many assets or overly dense foliage can obscure visibility and impact performance. Strategic asset placement ensures both beauty and usability.

- **Performance optimization**: Highly detailed environments must be optimized for real-time performance. Using **Level-of-Detail (LOD)** models, culling techniques, and efficient material setups prevent frame rate drops while maintaining visual fidelity.

- **Ensuring playability**: Testing Levels from a player's perspective ensures that the environment remains engaging and free from unintentional bottlenecks or confusing layouts. Playtesting can reveal issues that might not be obvious during development.

A well-balanced environment maintains a seamless blend of aesthetics and function, ensuring that players remain immersed while still being able to navigate and interact with the game world effectively.

> **Tip**
>
> Gameplay is king! There are plenty of beautiful games out there that are terrible to play, and vice versa. Yet history shows that the "fun" games with strong gameplay and design always end up being more successful. With that in mind, while you should always strive for a beautiful game, it should always be in service to the game design itself.
>
> Don't forget the importance of fun while in pursuit of visual beauty; they both matter!

By applying these fundamental principles, we can craft environments that are not only visually stunning but also enhance player engagement, storytelling, and gameplay flow.

Now that we've covered the core principles of game environment design, it's time to explore how these elements can be used to tell a story. Strong environmental storytelling begins with a strong layout. Once the spatial structure and gameplay flow are in place, the environment becomes a canvas for narrative intent. Whether it's subtle environmental clues or overt visual storytelling, these narrative layers build upon the foundation of functional design—ensuring that each space is not only practical to navigate but meaningful to experience. With that in mind, let's now explore how we can use different tools and techniques to craft environments that communicate a story through set, mood, and detail.

Environmental storytelling through design

A well-crafted game environment can tell a story without a single line of dialogue. Through the thoughtful arrangement of props, the use of environmental cues, and strategic lighting, designers can weave narratives that deepen a player's connection to the game world, elevating the existing Level design foundation. UE5 offers us powerful tools to achieve this level of storytelling, allowing us to create spaces that speak volumes through our design.

Props and set dressing

Props and **set dressing** play a crucial role in communicating the story of a place. The strategic placement of objects can offer players insights into the world, its history, and its characters.

Set dressing is the process of placing props, decorations, and environmental details in a scene to enhance realism, storytelling, and visual appeal. It's a term we adopt from the film industry where artists "literally" dress the set of a scene with real props.

Here's what we should consider when set dressing:

- **Choosing the right props**: Select assets that align with your game's setting and narrative. For example, a broken-down wagon in a medieval village suggests abandonment or a past conflict.

> **Tip**
>
> I utilize the massive **Quixel Megascans** library to match my desired visual style quickly and efficiently. You can too!

- **Telling stories with placement**: Arrange props to imply past events. A knocked-over chair and a spilled drink can suggest a hasty departure, while a campsite with still-burning embers hints at recent activity.

  Use clusters of objects to create "story vignettes" that players might discover while exploring.

- **Adding layers of detail**: Incorporate small, subtle details that reward observant players. Graffiti on a wall, a journal left open on a table, or a half-eaten meal can all add narrative depth.

  Blend props with environmental effects. For instance, use decals to add dirt, blood, or water stains around objects to reinforce their story.

> **Tip**
>
> Balance storytelling props with gameplay clarity. Avoid cluttering important paths or creating visual noise that might distract from gameplay objectives.

Figure 4.2 features two images demonstrating how thoughtful set dressing can significantly enhance a scene.

Figure 4.2: A scene before and after set dressing, showing how the addition of carefully chosen props can transform a generic space into a story-rich environment (asset source: Dark Ruins by Quixel | FAB.com)

On the left, a rocky coastline stands strong and, to be fair, is visually appealing on its own. On the right, the same landscape is transformed with additional set dressing, adding a layer of storytelling that the first image lacks. With just a few extra assets, the scene shifts from a generic cliffside to ancient ruins long forgotten, with a fresh rowboat in the foreground. This subtle addition sparks curiosity—what is this place, what happened here, who recently arrived, and why? All of this is conveyed without a single word.

Environmental clues

Environmental clues are subtle hints embedded in the environment that guide players to draw conclusions about the world and its lore. These clues can be as simple as a cracked wall or as elaborate as a staged scene that reveals a story moment:

- **Using visual cues:** Broken structures, such as collapsed bridges or crumbling walls, can indicate the age of a location or past battles.

  Abandoned objects, such as suitcases or toys, can evoke emotions and spark curiosity about what happened to their owners.

- **Leveraging Unreal Engine tools**: Use decals to add non-intrusive storytelling elements, such as footprints, blood splatters, or graffiti.

  Utilize particle systems (Niagara) for dynamic storytelling elements—such as floating embers, dust motes, or dripping water—that add life to the environment.

- **Encouraging player interpretation**: Not every clue needs to be obvious. Sometimes, less is more. Leave space for players to interpret the story in their own way.

  Place clues along optional paths or hidden areas, rewarding exploration with narrative depth.

> **Tip**
>
> Combine clues to create layered storytelling. For example, a boarded-up door, a rusted medical kit, and a flickering light can imply a quarantine or past tragedy.

Figure 4.3 builds directly on the ideas from *Figure 4.2*, once again showcasing how a scene can tell an entire story without a single word.

Figure 4.3: A small scene showing how subtle environmental clues—such as a dead warrior surrounded by gold—can evoke a backstory without explicit explanation

The top image features a dark, mysterious rocky cave. The bottom image transforms the same space with the subtle addition of a long-dead warrior surrounded by treasure. This simple change enhances the scene in multiple ways—it draws the player in with the promise of loot, builds tension within the environment, and sparks curiosity. How did the warrior die? Was it greed or bad luck, or is the treasure cursed? These details add depth to the world, making it more immersive and engaging for the player.

Lighting for mood

As we discussed in *Chapter 1*, **lighting** is one of the most powerful tools for setting the mood and reinforcing the story of a game environment. It can turn a cheerful village into a sinister, haunted location with just a few adjustments:

- **Setting the tone with color**: Use warm, soft lighting to create a sense of safety and nostalgia, while cooler, harsher tones can evoke unease or danger.

  Implement color grading in Unreal's **Post Process Volume** to apply overarching color tones to entire environments.

- **Directing attention**: Highlight key storytelling elements with focused lighting. For example, use a shaft of light to draw attention to a crucial prop or clue.

  Implement light and shadow to control player movement, guiding them through a Level naturally.

- **Enhancing narrative moments**: Use dynamic lighting changes to indicate shifts in the story. A sudden loss of light can signal danger, while sunlight breaking through clouds might symbolize hope.

  Utilize Unreal's lighting tools such as **volumetric fog**, **light shafts**, and **dynamic light sources** to add atmosphere and emotion to scenes.

> **Tip**
>
> Avoid over-lighting environments. Shadows and darkness can be just as powerful in storytelling, creating mystery and tension.

Figure 4.4 shows how lighting alone can affect a scene.

Figure 4.4: A comparison of the same scene with different lighting setups—one bright and welcoming, the other dark and foreboding—to illustrate how lighting influences mood (asset source: Scifi Kitbash Level Builder by Denys Rutkovskyi | FAB.com)

In this scene, I started with a well-lit space station that looks functional and inviting, and with just a few light and atmosphere adjustments, I changed it into a darker, more "horror-esque" scene. You'll notice how we can keep a design idea intact... I left the yellow door in the distance unchanged; here is a clear signifier of where I might want my player to go and it works in both examples.

Practical example: Storytelling in a deserted cabin

Let's imagine designing a deserted cabin in a survival horror game by following these steps:

1. Start with set dressing—place worn-out furniture, scattered papers, and a rusted lantern.
2. Add environmental clues, such as a shattered window, claw marks on the wall, and a child's drawing left on the floor.
3. Use lighting to enhance the mood. Cast harsh, angular shadows using a single flickering light source to evoke unease.
4. Introduce audio elements such as creaking wood and distant whispers to reinforce the narrative atmosphere.

I expect that you can already visualise what this scene might look like in your mind, with props, clues, and lighting all combining to create a powerful sense of place and story.

Environmental storytelling transforms a game's world from a static backdrop into an active participant in the narrative. Through the placement of props, embedding subtle clues, and using lighting to evoke emotion, you can create immersive experiences that resonate with your players on a deeper level.

While environmental storytelling helps establish mood and narrative, efficiency in Level creation is just as important. One of the best ways to streamline development and maintain consistency is by using modular assets or pieces that can be reused and rearranged to quickly build complex environments.

Creating modular and reusable assets

Creating large and intricate game environments can be a time-consuming process. However, adopting a **modular** approach can significantly boost efficiency while maintaining high-quality visuals and gameplay design. UE5 makes it pretty easy for developers to build modular kits and implement blueprints. These techniques not only accelerate development but also contribute to a cohesive and polished end product.

Modular kit design

A modular kit is a collection of reusable assets—such as walls, floors, doorways, and props—that can be combined in different ways to build diverse environments. By designing modular assets with uniform dimensions and seamless edges, you can construct environments quickly while ensuring they remain visually consistent:

- **Planning your kit**: Before creating assets, analyze the type of environments you need. A sci-fi corridor kit, for example, might include wall panels, floor tiles, ceiling pieces, and modular door frames.

  Break down your designs into repeatable sections. Design assets with a grid-based approach (e.g., 1x1 m or 2x2 m) to ensure compatibility.

- **Building modular assets**: Create assets with standardized pivot points and consistent scale. This allows assets to snap together easily when assembling environments in UE5.

  Use Unreal's built-in modeling tools or external software such as Blender or 3ds Max to design modular pieces.

- **Assembling environments**: Import your modular assets into Unreal Engine and use the grid snapping feature to place them accurately.

Experiment with different arrangements of the same kit to create varied yet cohesive environments.

> **Tip**
>
> Maintain a balance between modularity and uniqueness. Introduce a few "hero" assets—unique models or features—to break up the repetition of modular elements.

Figure 4.5 shows a blueprint assembled with multiple assets to make one reusable modular asset.

Figure 4.5: An example of a modular BP kit with labeled components

This is a great way to create a feast across a whole dining hall by only making the assembly once.

Using Blueprint for dynamic environments

UE5's **Blueprint** system allows designers to add interactivity and dynamic elements to their environments without needing deep programming knowledge. Combining blueprints with modular assets can elevate the player's experience by introducing responsive game worlds:

- **Interactive elements**: Use Blueprints to create dynamic objects such as doors, elevators, moving platforms, or destructible walls.

  Implement triggers and events, allowing objects to respond to player actions (e.g., doors opening when a player approaches or platforms moving when a button is pressed).

- **Basic procedural generation**: Blueprints can be used to randomize certain aspects of environments. For instance, you could create a blueprint that spawns different props each time a Level loads, adding variety to modular setups.

- **Enhancing modular workflows**: Combine modular assets with blueprints to create modular prefabs—pre-assembled chunks of environments that can be placed quickly.

  For example, build a blueprint for a modular hallway that spawns randomized decorations each time it's placed.

> **Tip**
>
> Avoid overcomplicating blueprints. Modular assets combined with simple, reusable blueprints can achieve impressive results without introducing unnecessary complexity.

Modular workflows are a cornerstone of efficient Level design. By adopting modular kit creation and leveraging blueprints for interactivity, developers can produce high-quality environments with speed and consistency.

Building modular assets allows for flexible and efficient Level design, but to truly make a game world feel alive, interactivity is key. From physics-based objects to dynamic elements that respond to the player, adding interactive features enhances both immersion and gameplay.

Enhancing gameplay with interactive environments

While stunning visuals can draw players in, as I have mentioned previously, true engagement comes from interaction. A well-designed game environment isn't just a backdrop—it is a living, responsive world that reacts to the player's actions. UE5 provides some pretty powerful tools to bring this interactivity to life, from physics-based objects to destructible environments and dynamic elements. In this section, we will explore some basics of how to use and set up these tools, in preparation for the next chapter, which will dive deeper into what we will discuss here.

Physics-based objects

Physics-based objects use UE5's **Chaos Physics** system to simulate realistic movement, collisions, and interactions. These elements make environments feel tangible and alive, allowing players to push, pull, or manipulate objects naturally:

- **Setting up physics on objects**: To make an asset physics-based, enable **Simulate Physics** in the object's **Static Mesh Component** within Unreal Engine.

  Adjust properties such as the **mass**, **friction**, and **damping** to match the desired behavior. For example, a metal crate should be heavier and less bouncy than a rubber ball.

- **Adding physics constraints**: Constraints limit how an object can move. For example, a door might only rotate on its hinges, or a pendulum might swing in a fixed arc.

  Use **Physics Constraint Components** to set up these restrictions and create more controlled interactions.

- **Incorporating gameplay mechanics**: Combine physics-based objects with blueprints to trigger events. For example, a pressure plate activated by placing a heavy object on it could open a door or reveal a hidden path.

Create puzzles that rely on realistic physics interactions, such as rolling boulders or stackable objects.

> **Tip**
>
> Avoid overusing physics-based objects in complex environments, as too many dynamic elements can impact performance or cause unforeseen glitches. Use them strategically to enhance interactivity where it matters most.

Figure 4.6 shows where to tick the check box in its "details panel" to allow an asset to be affected by physics.

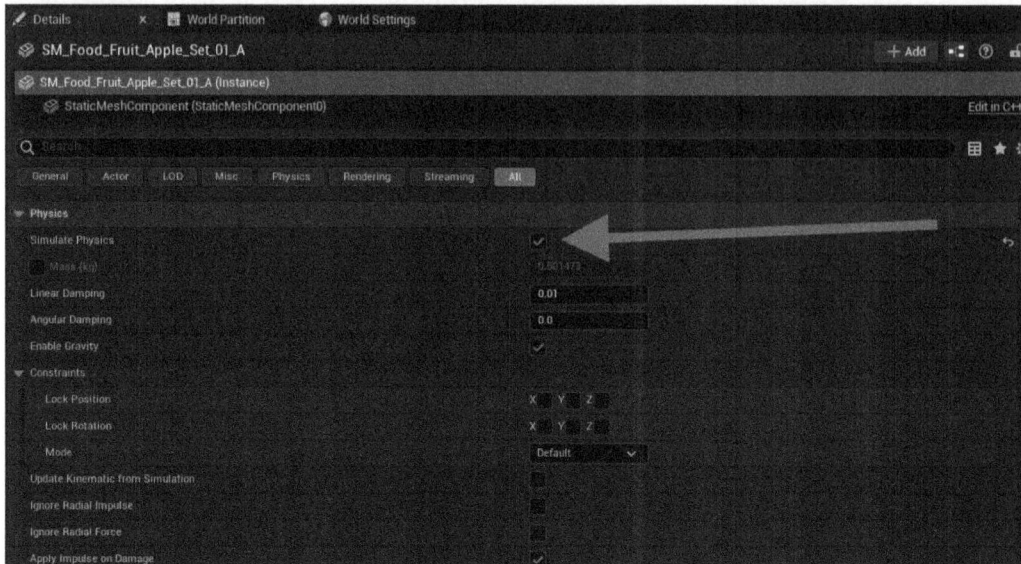

Figure 4.6: A diagram showing the setup of a physics-based object in UE5, highlighting the
key settings for simulation and constraints

Destructible environments

Destructible environments allow players to alter the game world dynamically, whether through combat, exploration, or scripted events. Implementing breakable walls, shatterable objects, or deformable terrain adds a layer of realism and excitement, enhancing both gameplay and narrative. This is a very surface-level view, and we will explore it further in the next chapter, but for now, let's look at some basics!

- **Creating destructible meshes**: Use UE5's **Chaos Destruction** tools to convert static meshes into destructible assets.

  Set **fracture types**, such as **clustered**, **uniform**, or **radial**, depending on the desired effect.

- **Implementing destruction in gameplay**: Use blueprints to trigger destruction events. For example, when a player throws an explosive, a wall could fracture realistically.

  Tie destructible objects to gameplay mechanics. Perhaps breaking a floor reveals a hidden passage, or shattering a barrier unlocks a new area.

- **Performance considerations**: Limit the number of active destructible objects in the scene to maintain performance.

Interactive environments are key to crafting memorable game experiences. By utilizing Chaos Physics, destructible systems, and dynamic elements, you can create worlds that not only look stunning but also respond meaningfully to player actions. When done right, these interactions transform static spaces into **living worlds**, driving player engagement and storytelling to new heights.

We've explored a range of techniques for building efficient, fun game environments, but how do these principles apply in real-world projects? In this section, we'll examine case studies that showcase effective environment design across different genres.

Case studies: Effective game environment design

Examining real-world examples of environment design can provide us with valuable insights into the practical application of the tools and techniques we have discussed. So, in this section, we'll explore two distinct case studies: a **futuristic sci-fi research facility** and a **dense medieval village**. Each scenario demonstrates different approaches to modular design, atmosphere creation, and interactivity, offering a well-rounded perspective on building engaging game environments.

Case study 1: Designing a sci-fi research facility

Designing a sci-fi research facility involves blending clean, futuristic aesthetics with a sense of mystery and unease. This environment design leverages **modular assets**, **real-time reflections**, and **atmospheric lighting** to create a polished vibe.

Using modular assets for a futuristic setting

Modular design is essential for constructing the sleek, repetitive architecture often seen in sci-fi environments:

- **Kit design**: Create a modular kit including walls, floors, ceilings, doorways, and trim pieces that snap together seamlessly. This approach enables rapid Level construction while maintaining consistency in design.
- **Efficient iteration**: By using modular assets, we can quickly test different layouts and iterate on the Level design without needing to remodel assets.
- **Customization**: Introduce **material instances** to adjust surface properties (e.g., metallic sheen or emissive glow) and add variety without creating new assets.

Real-time reflections for a high-tech aesthetic

To emphasize the facility's advanced technology, integrate **real-time reflections** using **Lumen**:

- **Reflective surfaces**: Apply **highly reflective materials** to floors, screens, and glass partitions. The dynamic reflections help convey a sense of cleanliness and precision.

- **Light interaction**: Utilize **light panels** with emissive materials to create glowing elements that enhance the sci-fi atmosphere.

- **Optimizing reflections**: For performance, strategically place **reflection captures** and consider using **Screen Space Reflections (SSRs)** in less critical areas.

Crafting an eerie atmosphere with lighting

A sci-fi research facility often walks the line between high-tech marvel and eerie isolation. Use lighting and sound to build tension:

- **Lighting techniques**: Create contrasting lighting with cool blues and sterile whites, then introduce pockets of shadow to evoke mystery.

- **Dynamic lighting**: Add flickering lights or emergency lighting sequences triggered by gameplay events.

Figure 4.7 shows the result of a moody lighting setup for a sci-fi facility based on the case study we have just discussed:

Figure 4.7: Case study 1: Example render of a sci-fi facility (asset source: Scifi Modular by Jonathon Fredrick | FAB.com)

Case study 2: Building a dense medieval banquet

Designing a medieval banquet requires a different approach—focusing on organic layouts, lived-in textures, and bustling interactivity. This project highlights **procedural tools** and **atmosphere** to create an immersive historical setting.

Using procedural tools for building and prop placement

In a medieval setting, a dense, natural layout enhances realism and player immersion:

- **Procedural generation**: Use **pre-built blueprints** of food and drink props to rapidly build your scene.

- **Randomization**: Introduce slight rotation and scaling variations to break the grid-like pattern of procedural placement of food.

- **Custom rulesets**: Set up placement rules to ensure objects such as plants, food, and chair items appear in logical, story-driven locations.

Crafting an energetic atmosphere with lighting

A medieval banquet often gives off warmth and a sense of celebration. Create contrasting lighting with **warm temperatures** and **soft shadows**.

Dynamic interactivity

Many medieval games (*TES: Skyrim*, for example) let players have fun by turning on physics for all the food on the tables so they can kick and throw assets around:

- **Physics for fun**: Turn on **Simulate Physics** on objects in Unreal, to let players make a mess of the environment. Optional player-triggered chaos using physics adds levity and immersion.

Figure 4.8 shows the result of a warm, inviting lighting setup based on the case study we have just discussed:

Figure 4.8: Case study 2: Example render of a medieval banquet (asset source: Medieval Banquet by Quixel | FAB.com)

Key takeaways from the case studies

While each environment had unique challenges and requirements, both benefited from the following:

- **Modular design:** Streamlining the construction process and enabling rapid iteration
- **Lighting and atmosphere:** Tailoring visual and auditory elements to reinforce the narrative
- **Interactivity:** Engaging players with dynamic and responsive elements

These case studies demonstrate how versatile UE5 is in creating environments that not only look stunning but also enhance gameplay and storytelling. By adopting these techniques, you can apply similar strategies to your own projects, regardless of setting or genre.

With these studies concluded, and with a new suite of tools and techniques at your disposal, let's finish up this chapter by looking at how to troubleshoot some common environment design pitfalls that may diminish your environments.

Troubleshooting common environment design issues

Designing engaging game environments is a complex process, and even experienced developers encounter challenges. Whether dealing with things such as flat layouts, or maybe cluttered spaces, recognizing and addressing these problems early can save time and enhance the final product. This section covers just a few common pitfalls I see in environment design and offers some practical solutions using Unreal's tools and workflows.

Flat and uninteresting layouts

Flat environments can lead to dull and uninspiring gameplay experiences. Without variation in elevation or visual interest, players may find the world unmemorable or difficult to navigate.

Here are the key solutions:

- Add elevation changes:

    - Introduce **hills, ramps, platforms**, or **multi-story structures** to create verticality.
    - Utilize Unreal's **Landscape** tools to sculpt terrain with naturalistic height variations.
    - Apply **modular assets** such as staircases, ladders, and bridges to promote exploration.

- Create focal points:

    - Use **landmarks** (e.g., a towering statue or a glowing portal) to draw player attention.
    - Implement **leading lines** through the environment using pathways, light, or asset placement to guide movement.

- Encourage exploration:

    - Design *hidden* paths, elevated viewpoints, or underground areas to reward curiosity.
    - Place collectibles or environmental storytelling elements in less obvious locations to entice players to explore.

> **Tip**
>
> Use cameras to preview the player's perspective and identify areas that feel flat or visually monotonous before even starting gameplay testing—trust your instincts and eyes!

Overly cluttered or sparse areas

Balancing detail density is crucial. Overly cluttered areas can overwhelm players and obscure important gameplay elements, while sparse environments may feel unfinished or lifeless.

Here are the key solutions:

- Assess density with player view in mind:

    - Regularly *playtest environments* in third-person or first-person views to gauge clutter levels.

    - Use Unreal's editor view modes, such as **Wireframe** or **Lighting Only**, to spot unnecessary objects or empty spaces.

- Balance visual detail:

    - Introduce **decorative assets** such as **foliage, props**, or **small debris** to fill empty areas naturally.

    - In cluttered spaces, group items logically and remove non-essential assets to improve readability.

- Guide the player through design choices:

    - Use **lighting**, **color contrasts**, or **movement** (e.g., waving flags or flowing water) to direct attention.

    - Implement **visual-driven highlights** on interactive objects to ensure they stand out in dense environments.

By proactively identifying and resolving these simple common environment design issues, you can create more immersive and visually appealing game worlds.

With a solid understanding of environment design principles, storytelling techniques, modular workflows, and interactive elements, you now have the tools to create engaging, immersive worlds. Before we move on to some more practical lessons in the following chapters, such as how to use Unreal's physics engine, **Chaos**, let's recap the key takeaways from this chapter.

Summary

Designing game environments is more than just assembling assets—it's about crafting immersive worlds that enhance gameplay, storytelling, and the player experience.

Throughout this chapter, we've explored a few essential components of environment design, from the fundamental principles of composition and player guidance to advanced techniques such as procedural generation. By combining these strategies, you can create Levels that feel alive, responsive, and narratively rich.

Throughout this chapter, we explored the following principles and workflows behind designing engaging game environments in UE5:

- **The foundations of game environment design**: Leveraging composition, lighting, and player guidance to create immersive spaces.
- **Environmental storytelling through design**: Enhancing world-building with props, lighting, and environmental clues.
- **Modular workflows for efficient Level design**: Utilizing reusable assets, blueprints, and material variations for streamlined development.
- **Interactive and dynamic elements**: Adding physics-based objects and reactive game elements.
- **Case studies: Effective game environment design**: Examining real-world applications of these techniques in sci-fi and medieval settings.
- **Troubleshooting common environment design issues**: Addressing flat layouts and asset placement best practices.

Mastering environment design is an iterative process that blends creativity with technical problem-solving. By refining your workflows and thoughtfully placing assets, we can craft environments that captivate players and elevate the overall gaming experience.

With the knowledge and techniques covered in this chapter, you're well equipped to design Levels that are not only visually stunning but also enhance gameplay and storytelling. As you continue to refine your skills, remember that the most engaging game worlds are those that seamlessly blend artistry with interactivity—where every element has a purpose, and every detail contributes to the player's journey.

> **Important note**
>
> Like "modeling" in the previous chapter, "design" is a massive and diverse discipline that can easily fill the pages of several books, and something I studied at the tertiary level for half a decade. I hope that what you have read in this chapter provides you with some solid tips and tricks on how to approach Level creation in Unreal itself, but I also recommend going through the resources in the *Further reading* section to really expand on this complex and nuanced discipline.

Further reading

This list of further readings is from other authors under the Packt Publishing label, and a few of my personal favourites that I recommend for getting a solid basis and understanding of game design as an art and discipline. While not specifically Unreal Engine related, the lessons taught in these books directly overlap with what we have discussed in this chapter and any potential future game design and world-building work you may undertake in the future, whether in UE5 or otherwise.

- *Practical Game Design*: A modern and comprehensive guide to video game design. Read more here: `https://amzn.asia/d/3mHnaPy`

- *Rules of Play: Game Design Fundamentals*: This is a golden oldie but still one of my personal favorites in my hardcover collection to refer to. Read more here: `https://amzn.asia/d/6tFIKNG`

- *Making Video Games: The art of creating digital worlds*. Read more here: `https://amzn.asia/d/gQlNaRn`

Subscribe to Game Dev Assembly!

We are excited to introduce **Game Dev Assembly**, our brand-new newsletter dedicated to everything game development. Whether you're coding, designing, animating, or managing a studio, we've got insights, trends, and expert advice to help you create, innovate, and thrive. Sign up now and get exciting benefits.

```
https://packt.link/gamedev-newsletter
```

Join our community on Discord

Join our community's Discord space for discussions with the authors and other readers:

```
https://packt.link/unrealengine
```

5

Integrating Chaos Physics for Dynamic Gameplay Mechanics

Physics-driven interactions are often a core component of immersive gameplay, shaping *how players interact with the game world* in a tangible and engaging way. UE5's **Chaos Physics** system offers a powerful and efficient framework for simulating realistic movement, destruction, and environmental interactions. Whether it be *dynamic destruction*, *real-time cloth simulation*, or *physics-based character interactions*, Chaos Physics allows us to create highly responsive game worlds.

In this chapter, we will explore the key features of Chaos Physics and how to effectively integrate it into your UE5 projects. You'll learn how to harness the power of **Chaos rigid bodies**, implement destructible environments, and utilize advanced physics simulations such as soft body dynamics.

In this chapter, you will learn:

- The fundamentals of Chaos Physics and its advantages over legacy physics systems
- Implementing Chaos rigid bodies for dynamic object interactions
- Setting up destructible environments using the Chaos Destruction system
- Implementing cloth physics for realistic movement

By the end of this chapter, you will have a solid understanding of how to integrate Chaos Physics into your projects, allowing you to create more interactive and visually compelling game environments.

Technical requirements

To follow along with this chapter, ensure you have:

- Unreal Engine 5.4 or later
- A system with real-time ray tracing support (optional but recommended)
- A solid understanding of the Unreal Engine interface
- Some understanding of physics terminology
- Optional: A project with pre-built assets for testing and practice (or start with Unreal's sample projects).

What is Chaos Physics?

Chaos Physics is Unreal's advanced **physics simulation system**, designed to provide more accurate, scalable, and performance-friendly physics interactions than the legacy **PhysX system**. Chaos is built to handle large-scale destruction, real-time rigid body interactions, soft body dynamics, and complex vehicle physics, making it a crucial tool for us developers looking to create immersive and interactive game worlds.

Before Chaos, Unreal relied on NVIDIA's PhysX for physics simulations, which, while effective, had limitations in areas such as large-scale destruction, real-time performance, and cloth simulation. Chaos Physics overcomes these constraints by offering more precise collision detection, real-time fracturing, and an improved solver that efficiently handles complex interactions between objects. This allows developers, for the most part, to integrate physics-driven mechanics that feel more natural and reactive without causing performance bottlenecks.

> **Fun fact!**
>
> I started my game development journey experimenting with PhysX in **Unreal Development Kit (UDK)** and UE4 as part of my master's degree, where I made a game that has the player shooting colored bouncy balls to paint a room. This was fun, and I have fond memories of it, but what we can achieve with Chaos now would have taken that game to the next level!

Specifically, let us take a look at some key benefits of Chaos Physics:

- **More accurate and efficient physics calculations**: Chaos Physics introduces a robust solver system that improves the accuracy of physics interactions while optimizing performance. It means we can simulate highly dynamic environments with multiple interacting objects without excessive computational overhead.

- **Real-time destruction and fracture simulations**: One of the standout features of Chaos is its ability to simulate real-time destruction. The **Chaos Destruction system** enables objects such as walls, bridges, or entire buildings to break apart dynamically based on impact forces, explosion physics, or scripted events. Unlike traditional pre-baked destruction sequences, Chaos allows for **procedural fracturing**, ensuring unique destruction outcomes every time. This makes gameplay feel more reactive and unpredictable, increasing immersion.

- **Cloth and soft-body physics for realistic movement**: Chaos extends beyond rigid body physics to include soft-body and cloth simulations, enabling realistic interactions with fabric, ropes, and deformable objects. The system supports dynamic cloth physics that react to wind, movement, and collisions, allowing for more believable clothing, flags, or organic materials.

Chaos Physics represents a major leap forward in physics simulation for UE5, providing us with the tools to create highly interactive and visually compelling game worlds. By leveraging its robust feature set, we can create physics-driven gameplay mechanics that enhance realism, immersion, and player engagement.

Now that we have an understanding of the fundamentals of Chaos Physics, let's explore its most commonly used feature—rigid body dynamics. Whether it's objects reacting to forces, player interactions, or environmental influences, rigid body physics serves as the foundation for realistic movement and interactions in UE5.

Rigid body dynamics and object interactions

Rigid body physics form the backbone of most physics-driven interactions in UE5. Whether it's objects tumbling down a hill, crates responding to player collisions, or debris scattering from an explosion, Chaos rigid bodies ensure these interactions feel natural. Chaos provides fine-tuned control over physical properties such as mass, friction, and restitution. Unlike **kinematic** or **static** objects, rigid bodies can move and rotate in response to applied forces, gravity, and collisions. This enables a wide range of physics-driven mechanics, from simple object movement to complex, interconnected systems such as destructible props, swinging platforms, or even physics-based puzzles.

> **Important note**
>
> In Unreal, *kinematic* refers to objects that are moved manually (via code, Blueprints, or animations) rather than being affected by physics forces such as gravity or collisions. Kinematic objects can influence other physics-driven objects but are not themselves affected by external physics forces.

Implementing Chaos rigid bodies is relatively straightforward. By enabling physics simulation on a mesh, you can make objects respond to gravity, collisions, and external forces. The following is a step-by-step guide to setting up and refining rigid body interactions.

Converting an object into a rigid body

To turn any Static Mesh into a physics-driven object, take the following steps:

1. Select the Static Mesh:

    a. Click **Static Mesh** in Blueprints or place the mesh into the scene.

    b. In the **Details** panel, locate the **Physics** section.

    c. Enable **Simulate Physics** to allow the object to move freely.

2. Adjust the physical properties of the Static Mesh:

    a. **Mass:** Defines the object's weight. Unreal can auto-calculate mass based on volume and density, but you can override it for more precise control.

    b. **Linear and Angular Damping**: Controls how quickly movement and rotation slow down over time. Increasing damping makes objects feel heavier and more resistant to motion.

    c. **Enable Gravity**: Controls whether the object should or should not be controlled by Unreal's built-in gravity values, and can be affected by manipulating the previous values.

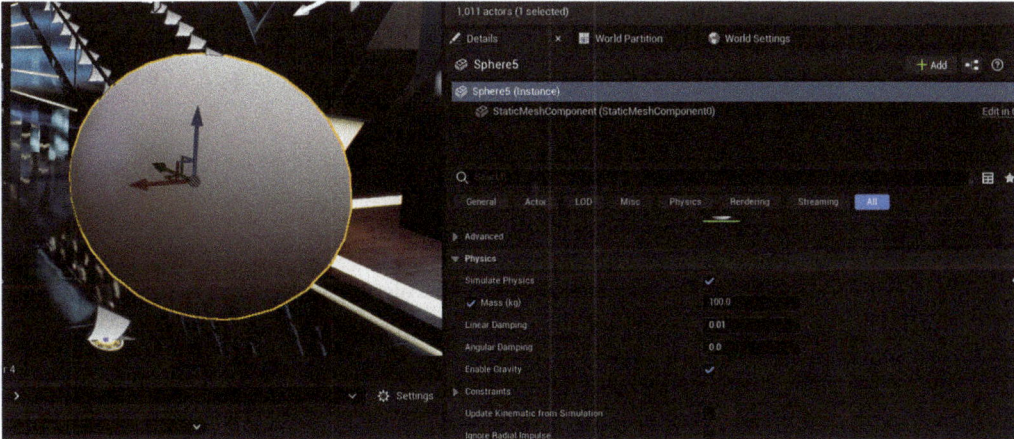

Figure 5.1: The Details settings for a Static Mesh Actor to be a physics object

Tip

If objects jitter or behave unpredictably, ensure the collision settings match the intended behavior. Unreal provides options such as **Simple Collision** for performance and **Complex Collision as Simple** for more accurate physical interactions. These settings can be found under **Collision Complexity** in your asset details.

Applying forces and impulses

To move or interact with Chaos rigid bodies dynamically, you can apply forces and impulses via Blueprints or C++:

- **Forces** are continuous influences that push or pull an object over time (e.g., gravity or wind).

- **Impulses** are instantaneous forces applied at a single moment (e.g., explosions).

To apply a force via blueprints, take the following steps:

1. Select the object and ensure **Simulate Physics** is enabled.

2. Open the Blueprint Editor for the object.

3. Use the **Add Force** node and specify the following:

    - **Force Vector**: The direction and strength of the force (e.g., **Z = 1000** applies an upward push within world space).

    - **Apply Location**: Whether the force applies at a specific point or the center of mass, done through **Bone Name.**

    - **Acceleration Change**: You should check this box if you want the force applied to be relative to the object's mass, making it accelerate or decelerate in a more realistic manner based on the object's mass (as discussed previously).

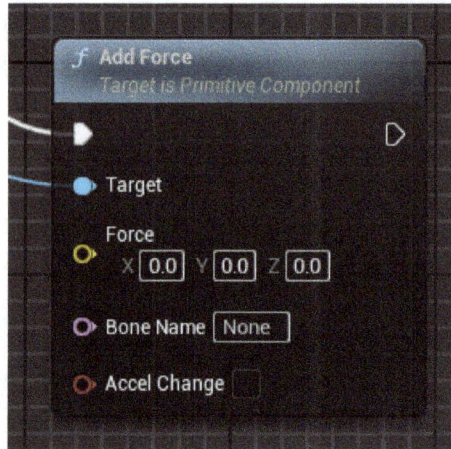

Figure 5.2: Add Force (a linear force from a location) node

Impulses work similarly but are best for short, sudden movements such as explosions or collisions. For example, if a player throws a grenade, the nearby objects should scatter realistically based on their distance from the explosion center. To apply impulses for instant motion, use the **Add Radial Impulse** node and set the following:

- **Impulse Origin**: The specific point where the impulse is applied.
- **Radius**: The size at which the force effect will be active.
- **Impulse Strength**: The magnitude of the push.

- **Falloff**: How quickly the **Strength** value falls off from the point of **Origin** based on **Radius**.

Figure 5.3: Add Radial Impulse (a radial fall-off force like that of an explosion) node

> **Important note**
>
> As you can see in the preceding screenshot, there are also **Falloff** and **Vel Change** settings. I haven't used these enough to speak on them here but have found that simply leaving them at their defaults achieves what I want in most instances. But I encourage you to do your own research if you'd like to experiment with those two values beyond what we have discussed here.

With forces and impulses covered, let's take things a step further by looking at how Chaos can be used to create dynamic destruction and breakable objects.

Chaos Destruction: Creating dynamic breakable objects

Destruction is a powerful tool in game development, enhancing realism and immersion by allowing environments to respond dynamically to player actions. Whether it's walls crumbling under explosive force or crates splintering upon impact, **Chaos Destruction** provides a solid and scalable system for breakable objects in Unreal. Let's learn how to implement it.

Enabling Chaos Destruction

Before using Chaos Destruction, ensure it's enabled in your project:

1. Go to **Project Settings | Physics** and enable **Chaos Physics** and **Chaos Destruction**.

2. You'll be prompted to restart the Unreal editor to apply changes.

> **Tip**
>
> Chaos Physics and Destruction should be active by default when you open a new project in UE5 and beyond, but in case it isn't, follow the preceding steps.

To make an object destructible, replace its standard Static Mesh with a Geometry Collection. Select the mesh, then open **Fracture Mode | New | Create Geometry Collection** in the toolbar.

This would convert the object into a physics-ready destructible asset.

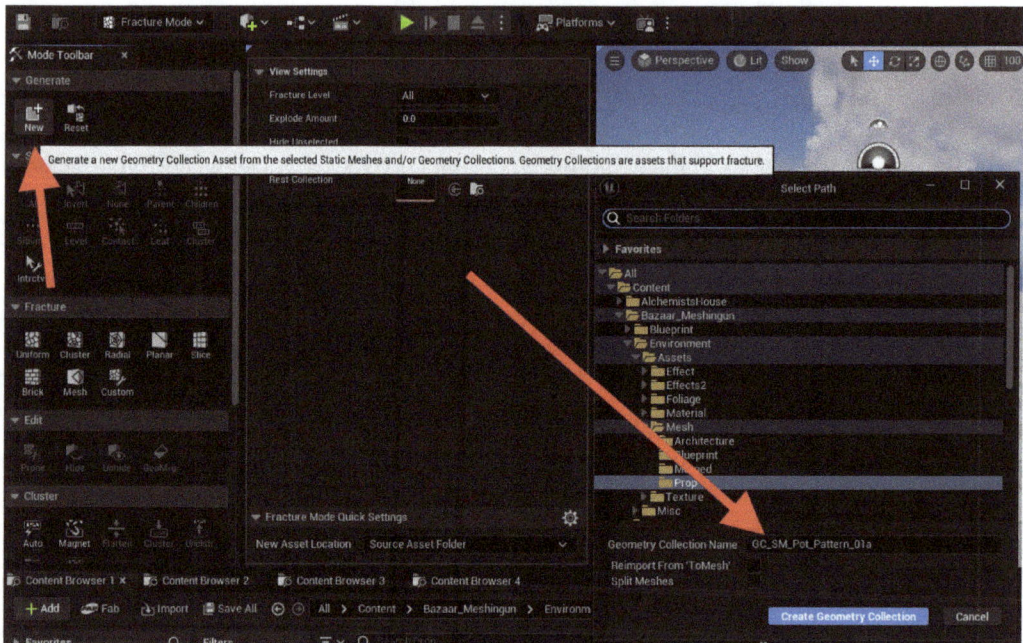

Figure 5.4: Creating a new Geometry Collection, naming the file, and saving it

Fracturing objects

The fracture editor allows precise control over how objects break apart:

1. Apply **Uniform, Radial, or Custom Fracture Patterns** to define breakable sections.

2. Adjust **Cluster Num Min & Max** to control fragment distribution—larger clusters break into bigger chunks, while smaller clusters produce finer debris.

3. Use **Explode Amount** to see how the object fractures.

> **Tip**
>
> Avoid excessive fragmentation in gameplay-critical assets to maintain performance and avoid visual bugs.

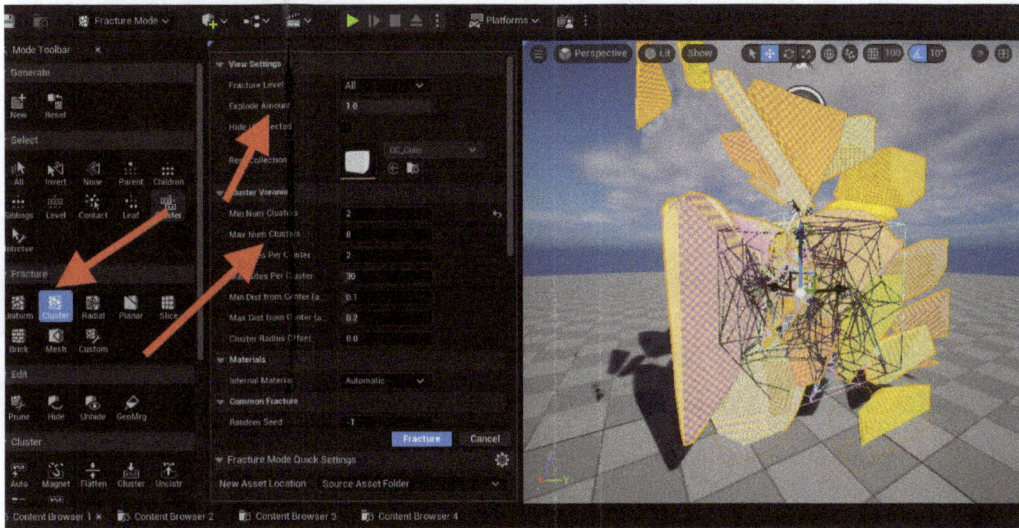

Figure 5.5: Different fracture types, cluster amount, and explode amount

Triggering destruction

To make destruction interactive, you can use Blueprints or C++ to activate fractures based on in-game events.

For breaking on impact in Blueprint, take the following steps:

1. Select the Geometry Collection and enable **Simulate Physics**.

2. In the Blueprint Editor, use an **On Hit** or **Apply Impulse** event to trigger destruction.

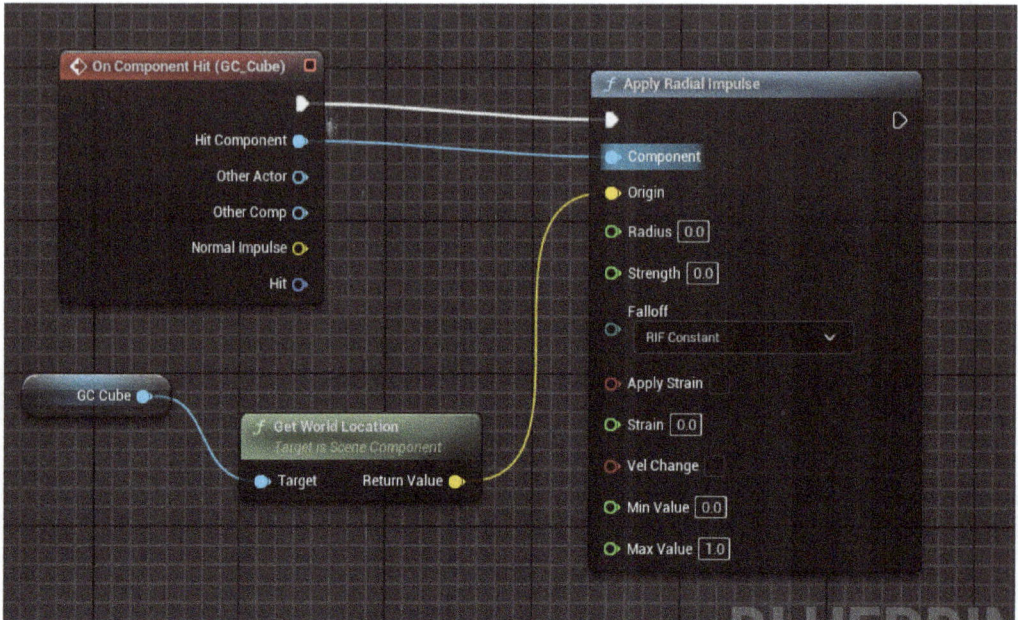

Figure 5.6: Simple setup for triggering an On Hit event for your Geometry Collection

Chaos enables dynamic and interactive breakable objects that enhance immersion. By fine-tuning the fracture settings and using Blueprints to control destruction triggers, you can create compelling physics-based interactions without sacrificing performance.

Now that we've explored how to trigger Chaos Destruction, let's shift gears and look at applying cloth physics to bring soft-body realism to our scenes.

Applying cloth physics

Adding **cloth simulations** enhances realism by making fabrics, flexible materials, and in some cases organic objects react naturally to forces such as gravity, wind, and collisions. Whether it's a character's cape flowing in the wind or a dress that deforms upon movement, **Chaos Cloth** in UE5 provides the tools to create convincing, physics-driven movement. Let's learn how to implement it.

Assigning cloth physics to a mesh

To apply Chaos Cloth to an asset, do the following:

1. Import or select a **Skeletal Mesh** in the **Content Browser**.

2. Open the **Skeletal Mesh Editor** and navigate to the **Cloth** panel.

3. Click **Create New Cloth Asset**, then paint cloth constraints onto areas that should be simulated (e.g., loose fabric on a character's robe).

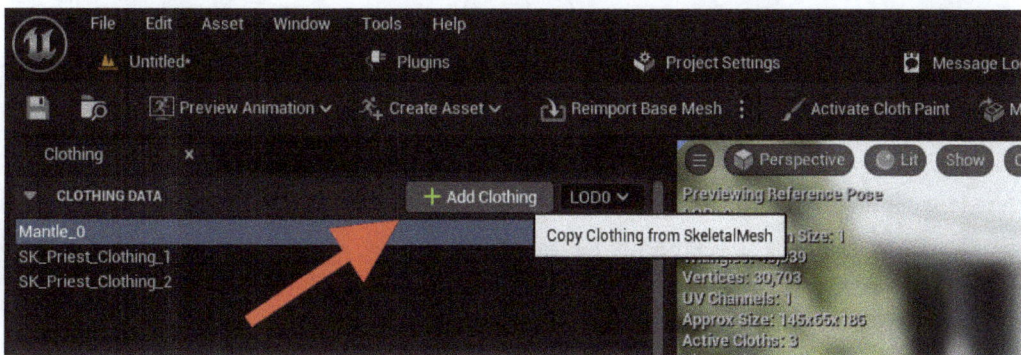

Figure 5.7: Where to add a new piece of clothing

When painting cloth, there are a few key things to keep in mind, which you can reference in *Figure 5.8*:

- *Red arrow* in *Figure 5.8*: **Paint Value** is basically how much the cloth can move: 100 indicates full movement, while 0 indicates no movement at all. This is much like weight painting on a character rig.

- *Pink arrow* in *Figure 5.8*: Shows the area on the character where no physics movement will take place.

- *White arrow* in *Figure 5.8*: Shows the area on the character where physics movement *will* take place.

- *Yellow arrow* in *Figure 5.8*: You need to press this button to access the cloth painting feature.

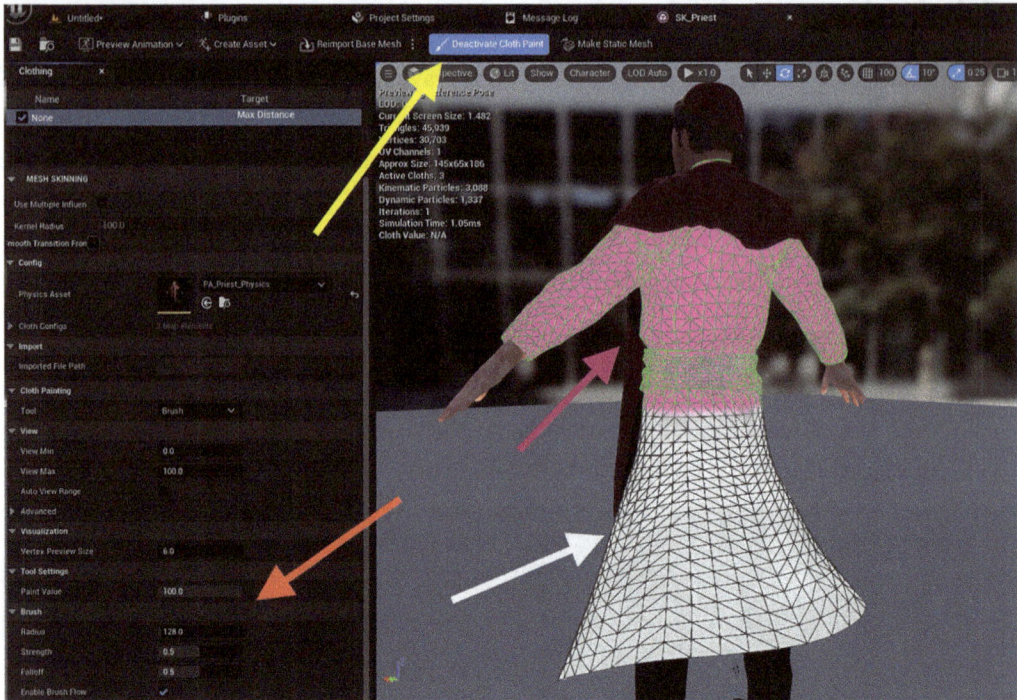

Figure 5.8: Arrow references for cloth painting

Tip

Keep certain areas you don't want simulated anchored with pinned points to ensure stability during the simulation. Pinned points are areas of the mesh that stay fixed in place during a simulation, acting as anchors. For example, this might be the waistband of pants or the seams where fabric connects to armor.

Configuring constraints for realistic deformation

Cloth physics requires proper constraints to behave realistically:

- **Bend and stretch constraints**: Define how flexible or rigid the fabric is.
- **Collision settings**: Ensure cloth interacts correctly with characters or objects.
- **Self-collision**: Prevents cloth from clipping through itself.

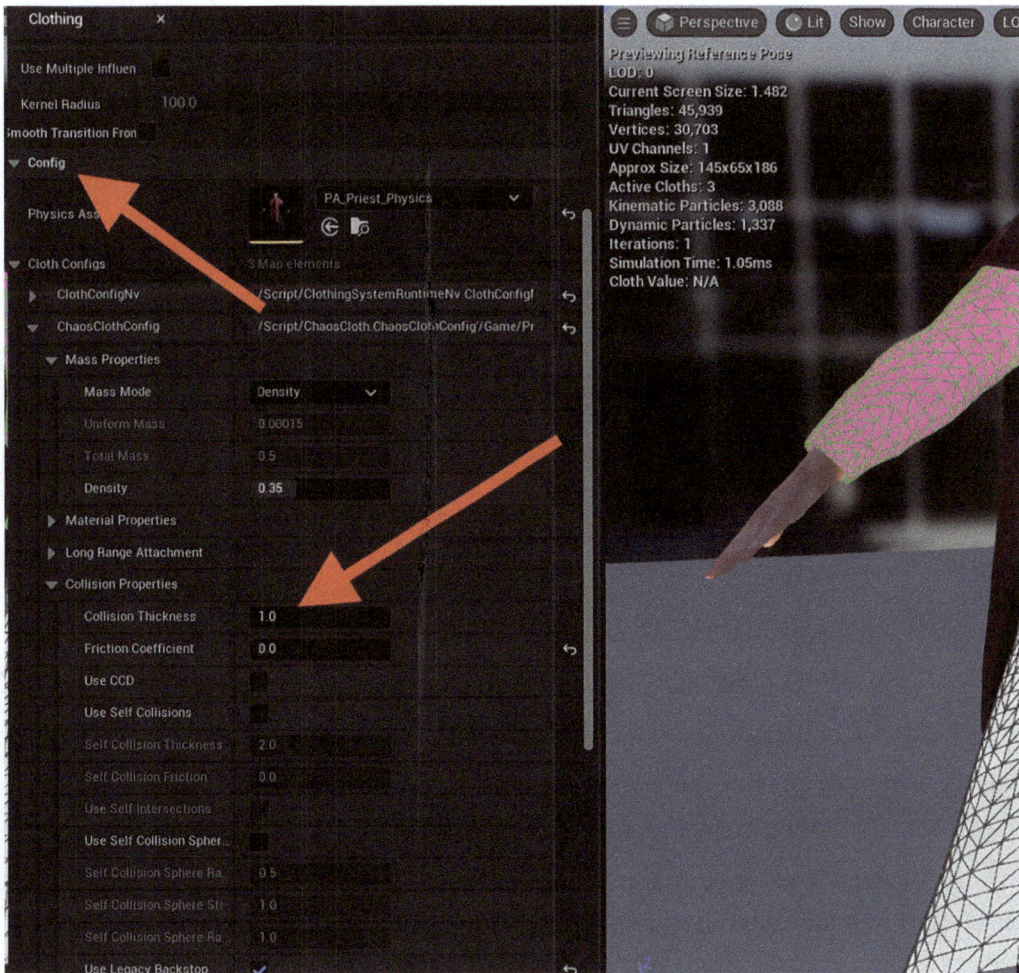

Figure 5.9: Where to find the config to edit the cloth physics settings

Adjust these settings in `ChaosClothConfig` to fine-tune how the material behaves under different forces.

Adjusting wind and environmental effects

To make cloth dynamic, apply environmental effects such as wind:

- Add a wind directional source to your level.
- Adjust **Wind Strength**, **Speed**, and **Direction** to affect cloth motion.

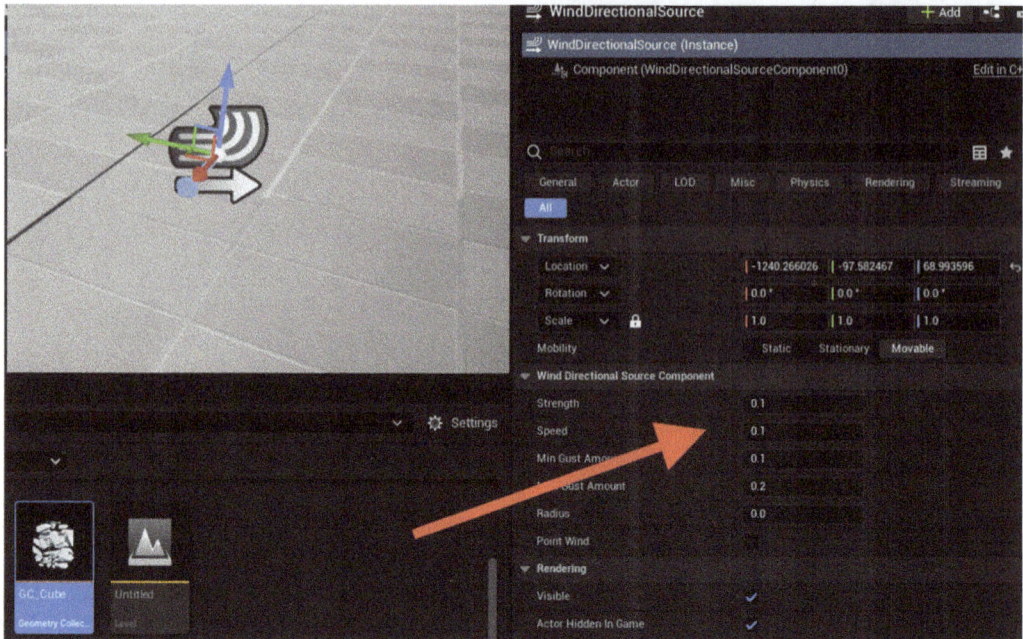

Figure 5.10: A simple showcase of the details for a wind directional source in a level

Cloth physics can transform static environments and simple characters into living beings and reactive worlds. By carefully configuring constraints, collision settings, and environmental influences, you can create dynamic assets that enhance immersion.

By combining rigid body physics, destruction mechanics, and cloth simulations, Chaos Physics enables highly dynamic and interactive game worlds. However, successfully implementing these systems requires a balance between realism and performance. In the next section, we'll summarize the key takeaways to help you get the most out of Chaos Physics in UE5.

Summary

Chaos Physics in UE5 provides developers with a robust and flexible system for creating dynamic, physics-driven gameplay mechanics. Whether it's realistic object interactions, destructible environments, or cloth simulations, Chaos Physics allows for interactive worlds that respond naturally to our players' actions.

However, while these features bring incredible realism, optimization is crucial (something we dive into deeper in future chapters) to ensure that performance remains stable across different platforms. A well-balanced approach to physics simulation enables both high-fidelity interactions and efficient performance.

Throughout this chapter, we explored the following principles and workflows behind chaos physics in UE5:

- **Chaos rigid bodies:** Enable realistic object interactions with forces, constraints, and collision responses.
- **Chaos Destruction:** Implements breakable objects to enhance environmental storytelling and player immersion.
- **Cloth simulations:** Add fluid, natural movement to fabrics, organic materials, and deformable objects.

By covering even these few principles of **Chaos Physics**, we developers can push the boundaries of interactivity and realism, crafting engaging, physics-driven worlds that feel truly alive. With Chaos Physics explored, the next chapter shifts focus to **responsive and adaptive worlds**—environments that react intelligently to player actions and evolving game states.

> **Important note**
>
> Like "design" in the previous chapter, "physics" is a monster of a discipline that could easily fill the pages of several books, and something even I am learning more about constantly with Epic's ever-changing updates to the system, so I also recommend reviewing the resources in the *Further reading* section to really understand this complex and nuanced discipline.

Further reading

This list of further readings is from other authors under the Packt Publishing label, and a few of my personal recommendations for getting a more advanced look into Unreal and game engine physics as a whole. The lessons taught in these books directly overlap with what we have discussed in this chapter and provide a great insight into the study of engine physics as a whole, whether in Unreal or otherwise.

- *Unreal Engine Physics Essentials.* Read more here: `https://amzn.asia/d/fMqM1BM`
- *Game Physics in One Weekend.* Read more here: `https://amzn.asia/d/5KC1CrW`
- *Game Physics Simulation with C++: Mastering real-time collision detection, response and optimization techniques for 2D and 3D game worlds:* Unreal uses C++, so this is a great resource for the more programming-savy reader. Read more here: `https://amzn.asia/d/cELXOif`

Subscribe to Game Dev Assembly!

We are excited to introduce **Game Dev Assembly**, our brand-new newsletter dedicated to everything game development. Whether you're coding, designing, animating, or managing a studio, we've got insights, trends, and expert advice to help you create, innovate, and thrive. Sign up now and get exciting benefits.

```
https://packt.link/gamedev-newsletter
```

Get This Book's PDF Version and Exclusive Extras

UNLOCK NOW

Scan the QR code (or go to packtpub.com/unlock). Search for this book by name, confirm the edition, and then follow the steps on the page.

Note: Keep your invoice handy. Purchases made directly from Packt don't require one.

6

Responsive and Adaptive Worlds

Modern game worlds are no longer static backdrops—they are living, breathing spaces that evolve, react, and respond dynamically to player actions. Whether it's a forest regrowing after a fire, **non-player characters (NPCs)** adapting to changes in terrain, or buildings collapsing realistically due to destruction, the ability to create truly dynamic environments elevates the sense of immersion and player engagement.

At its core, a responsive game world reacts meaningfully to the player's presence. This could be as simple as footprints appearing in the snow or as complex as an ecosystem that shifts based on in-game events. By leveraging UE5's procedural workflows and physics simulations, we as developers can craft adaptive environments that feel organic and unpredictable. These techniques not only enhance the visual and interactive appeal of a game but also deepen the player's sense of agency—making them feel like a true part of the world rather than just a visitor.

In this chapter, we will explore the key theories for building responsive and adaptive environments and provide you with the **threads** to explore beyond this book to implement this theory in practice, ensuring that every action the player takes has meaningful feedback in the world around them. I am taking an approach that I was taught during my master's degree. I assume you know the basics of what you are doing in Unreal and from previous chapters, so now I want to provide you with the path to expanding upon those skills and where to look.

This chapter acts as a kind of "halfway house" checkpoint for this book, going over many topics we have explored previously and making sure you know how to apply them logically within Unreal, and providing you with extra external tools on how to go beyond what is covered in the limited pages of this book. We will again look at **procedural systems** and **real-time environmental changes** that create emergent storytelling moments. Additionally, we'll examine how physics can be used to make interactions more intuitive, from destructible objects to dynamic weather effects.

In this chapter, you will learn about:

- Procedural generation to create evolving game worlds
- Implementing real-time environmental changes based on player actions
- Enhancing immersion with physics-driven world interactions
- Developing interactive world logic that alters environments based on gameplay choices

By the end of this chapter, you will have the knowledge to create game worlds that feel organic, interactive, and truly responsive to the player, but more importantly, you will know how to keep learning yourself to go beyond what is taught in this book; *I will be teaching you how to fish as opposed to giving you a fish.* Let's build on what we learned in the first few chapters of this book, dive deeper into these advanced techniques, and explore how to make game worlds feel more alive than ever before.

Fun fact!

NPCs are characters controlled by the game rather than the player, often serving as enemies, allies, merchants, or quest-givers. Their behavior is driven by **artificial intelligence** (**AI**), which determines how they react to the player and the game world. AI systems can control movement, decision-making, combat strategies, and even environmental interactions, making NPCs feel more lifelike and responsive.

Technical requirements

To follow along with this chapter, ensure you have:

- Unreal Engine 5.4 or later
- A system with real-time ray tracing support (optional but recommended)
- A solid understanding of the Unreal Engine interface

- Have read the previous chapters of this book, especially *Chapter 4*

- Optional: A project with pre-built assets for testing and practice (or start with Unreal's sample projects)

Procedural world generation: Creating dynamic environments

Creating large, detailed game worlds by hand is both time-consuming and usually impractical for modern game development, especially when aiming for expansive or highly interactive environments. **Procedural generation** allows developers to automate the creation of environments while still maintaining artistic control. This technique enables dynamic level layouts, terrain evolution, and object placement, making each playthrough feel unique while reducing manual workload.

By leveraging **UE5's procedural tools**, we can generate landscapes, distribute assets intelligently, and even craft entire levels in real time. This is particularly useful in open-world games, rogue-likes, and sandbox experiences where variety and adaptability enhance gameplay.

> **Important note**
>
> In this chapter, I'll introduce a strategy called **threads**—suggested paths for you to explore further in your own study. For example, if I say, *"Here are some threads to follow,"* try Googling the listed topics to discover insights that go beyond what we can cover in a single chapter. These threads serve as a guide—the adventure is yours to take!

With this brief introduction, let's look at some techniques for procedural generation.

Landscape auto-material systems

Instead of hand-painting terrain layers across massive landscapes, **landscape auto-materials** use procedural blending to apply textures dynamically based on slope, height, or biome rules. This ensures that cliffs, riverbanks, and grassy plains transition naturally without manual adjustments.

Here are some threads to follow:

- Procedural materials that *automatically blend textures* based on terrain properties in UE5

- **Erosion masks, height-based layering**, and **biome logic** to generate realistic surfaces in UE5

- Modify parameters dynamically, allowing for *seasonal shifts or weather-driven terrain changes* in UE5

- Try the following as a solid recommended starting point: *UE5 Landscape Auto Material tutorial by Unreal Sensei*

Rule-based asset spawning

Placing every tree, rock, or bush manually in a large environment is impractical. **Rule-based asset spawning** allows procedural tools to intelligently populate the world based on predefined logic. In Unreal, this is called **Procedural Content Generation** (**PCG**) and provides a flexible way to scatter assets while maintaining control over their placement.

Here are some threads to follow:

- How to use the **PCG framework** to distribute trees, foliage, or even interactive props dynamically

- How to set constraints in PCG to avoid unnatural placements of assets

- Try the following as a solid recommended starting point: *UE5 PCG Framework Documentation*

Blueprint-driven procedural level design

For games requiring dynamically generated levels, **Blueprint-driven procedural level design** allows us to create randomized dungeons, cave networks, or even full cities. By leveraging procedural logic, each level layout can offer a fresh experience without needing handcrafted variations.

Here are some threads to follow:

- Blueprints to generate random layouts for levels, rooms, or roads

- Modular construction in Unreal, where different assets and tiles connect dynamically

- Try the following as a solid recommended starting point: *Blueprint Procedural Level Generation by Mathew Wadstein*

Procedural generation *isn't just about efficiency*—it's about adaptability. Whether used for *expansive open worlds*, *interactive landscapes*, or *replayable levels*, it enhances the sense of immersion by making game environments feel dynamic and alive. By combining procedural techniques with handcrafted details, we as developers can strike a balance between efficiency and artistic intent, ensuring a polished and engaging experience for players.

After looking at procedural world generation, let's now explore how environments can change in real time based on player actions.

Real-time environmental changes based on player actions

A truly immersive game world is one that reacts dynamically to player input, making every action feel impactful. Whether it's a shifting time of day, weather changes that influence gameplay, or destructible environments that alter over time, adaptive environments create a sense of agency and realism.

Unreal provides powerful tools and systems that allow developers to make environments feel alive. By implementing real-time environmental changes, we can ensure that the game world is *not just a backdrop but an interactive and evolving space.* Let's learn some techniques for environmental adaptation.

Time-of-day systems: Dynamic lighting and sky transitions

A dynamic **time-of-day system** can transform a static world into a breathtaking environment. As time progresses, lighting, shadows, and even atmospheric conditions shift naturally, creating **immersive day-night cycles** that impact visibility, gameplay mechanics, and world aesthetics.

Here are some threads to follow:

- Use the Sky Atmosphere system to generate realistic sun and moon transitions, adjusting color gradients and fog density dynamically
- Implement Volumetric Cloud and Exponential Height Fog to shift weather effects with the time of day
- Link NPC schedules, enemy behaviors, or stealth mechanics to time cycles, making certain activities easier or harder at night
- Try the following as a solid recommended starting point: *Epic's Dynamic Sky Atmosphere Documentation*

Weather systems: Real-time rain, snow, and wind effects

While the weather can be just visual, it can affect gameplay in interesting ways. Dynamic weather systems allow developers to create worlds where rain makes roads slippery, snow accumulates, and wind alters projectile accuracy.

Here are some threads to follow:

- Use **Material Parameter Collections (MPCs)** to update shaders dynamically, allowing puddles to form during rain or frost to spread during snowstorms
- Implement **Niagara particle systems** for volumetric rain, snow, and fog, with real-time accumulation on surfaces
- Adjust player movement, AI perception, and physics interactions based on weather conditions
- Try the following as a solid recommended starting point: *Ultra Dynamic Sky*

> **Use case**
>
> A stealth-based game where heavy rain muffles player footsteps, making it easier to sneak past enemies, while strong winds cause projectiles to drift off-course, adding a layer of realism and challenge.

Destruction and reconstruction: Physics-driven environmental changes

A game world doesn't technically need to be destructible, but when it is, I feel it should go beyond even that—it should be modifiable based on player interactions. Whether it's buildings crumbling from an explosion or terrain shifting dynamically, real-time destruction and reconstruction create engaging and reactive gameplay moments.

Here are some threads to follow:

- **Chaos Physics** to enable destructible structures that break apart naturally upon impact
- Implement **Blueprints-based rebuilding mechanics**, allowing players to restore environments over time
- How to synchronize destruction events with AI behaviors and world progression, creating adaptive level design
- Try the following as a solid recommended starting point: *Chaos Destruction Overview – Unreal Docs*

Use case

I'm personally—like many others—really into *Marvel: Rivals* at the moment. This game is a perfect example of this philosophy. Go play it and observe how the maps can be both destroyed *and* rebuilt!

By combining these real-time environmental systems, we can create a world that feels alive and reacts meaningfully to player choices. Whether altering landscapes through magic, adapting to weather patterns, or influencing time-based mechanics, an adaptive environment enhances immersion and creates dynamic, player-driven storytelling.

While world adaptation through procedural generation and environmental changes creates immersive spaces, player interaction should also influence the world on a mechanical level. Next, we'll explore how physics-driven interactions make environments feel more tangible and alive.

Physics-driven world interactions

Again, a visually stunning world is only part of the equation—*true immersion comes from how that world behaves*. I know I've said this to you a few times now, but it is important. A responsive environment should not only react to the player's actions but also follow the laws of physics in a believable way, or at least be defined by the laws that make up a world's physics and movement; *Super Mario: Odyssey* is an example. Whether it's a swaying bridge, a rolling boulder, or the subtle ripples in water as a player walks through it, physics-based interactions bring environments to life in ways that simply go beyond static visuals. Let's learn how to implement them.

Physics Constraints for interactive objects — bringing structure and motion to static worlds

Physics Constraints allow for controlled movement and interactions between objects, simulating realistic motion while maintaining structure. This is useful for elements like hinges, ropes, suspension systems, and breakable connections.

Here are some threads to follow:

- Use Physics Constraints in Blueprints to create objects that move within defined limits
- Apply **hinges**, **springs**, and **sliders** for controlled physics-based motion
- Combine constraints with forces and impulses to create dynamic but stable structures
- Try the following as a solid recommended starting point: *Physics Constraints Documentation – Unreal Engine*

Dynamic object reactions — making the world feel alive

Players expect their actions to have visible, physical effects on the world. Whether it's water rippling when stepped in, foliage swaying when brushed past, or snow compacting underfoot, *small interactions contribute to a more immersive experience.*

Here are some threads to follow:

- Use Niagara particle systems to create real-time water ripples or dust clouds when objects move

- Implement **AnimDynamics** or **physics-based vertex animation** to allow vines, banners, and cloth to sway in response to player contact

- Utilize **material displacement maps** to create footprints in sand or snow that gradually fade over time

- Try the following as a solid recommended starting point: *Interactive Grass & Foliage Tutorial (YouTube)*

Weight and force mechanics — simulating realistic object behavior

Objects in the world should react appropriately to their weight and applied forces—a light crate should be easy to push, while a massive boulder should require significant effort to move. Proper weight and force simulation can make *puzzle-solving and traversal mechanics more engaging.*

Here are some threads to follow:

- Assign mass values to objects to determine how they react to forces in Unreal

- Use **Add Force** and **Add Impulse** nodes in Blueprints to apply realistic motion when objects are pushed or impacted

- Implement **Physics Materials** to fine-tune surface properties such as friction and restitution (bounciness)

- Try the following as a solid recommended starting point: *Physics Asset and Physics Materials Docs – Unreal Engine*

By integrating physics-driven interactions, your world becomes more than just a set piece—it turns into a dynamic and interactive playground. From the smallest ripples in water to large-scale destruction mechanics, well-implemented physics heightens immersion and makes every player interaction feel meaningful.

Now that we've covered physics-based interactions, let's take it a step further and explore **AI-driven world logic**, where game environments intelligently react to NPC behaviors and procedural decision-making.

Environmental AI and adaptive world logic

While the player's direct actions can result in what feels like a truly responsive world, it can also evolve further based on autonomous AI systems. AI-driven logic can influence everything from world reconstruction to weather-driven gameplay mechanics, making the game feel more alive and reactive. By combining procedural systems with AI, we can create environments that adapt, change, and tell a story over time.

Let's take a dive into some key AI-driven environmental techniques.

AI-driven world adaptation — NPCs shape the world over time

Our world doesn't stay "static" after destruction—we *rebuild*, *evolve*, and *react* dynamically based on the event. AI-controlled systems can handle **world restoration**, **settlement growth**, and **post-destruction recovery** in a similar way in virtual worlds, ensuring that player actions leave a lasting but flexible impact.

Here are some threads to follow:

- NPCs **trigger rebuilding animations, path clearing**, or **defensive structure placement**
- Implement **timed world changes** where areas slowly return to their pre-destruction state unless the player intervenes
- Try the following as a solid recommended starting point: *UE5 AI Perception and Environment Query System (EQS) Tutorial*

Procedural storytelling elements — a world that evolves over time

AI-driven procedural storytelling creates a living world narrative by modifying environmental elements in response to player choices. This allows the game world to feel organic and evolving without relying on pre-scripted events.

Here are some threads to follow:

- Use **procedural foliage systems** to regrow vegetation over time after destruction or deforestation.

- Implement **structure degradation mechanics**, where abandoned buildings collapse or become overgrown after extended periods of neglect.

- Have *NPCs react dynamically to world changes*, recognizing shifts in terrain or story events.

- Try the following as a solid recommended starting point: *GDC Talk: "Between Tech and Art: The Vegetation of Horizon Zero Dawn"*

Use case

If a player abandons a village for too long, roads become overgrown, buildings start crumbling, and nature reclaims the area, creating a sense of time passing in the game world.

Real-time weather influence on gameplay — AI-driven environmental challenges

AI-controlled weather systems can introduce strategic changes to traversal, combat, and survival mechanics.

Here are some threads to follow:

- How *AI adjusts NPC behaviors based on weather conditions* (e.g., villagers take shelter during storms, merchants close their shops)

- **Physics-based weather effects**, such as muddy roads slowing movement or strong winds affecting projectile accuracy

- **AI-driven weather forecasting**, where NPCs warn the player of incoming storms or change their routines accordingly

- Try the following as a solid recommended starting point: *Dynamic Weather AI Reactions in UE5 (YouTube)*

Use case

A heavy snowstorm rolls in, causing enemy patrols to take alternative routes, bridges to freeze over, and fire-based attacks to become less effective, forcing the player to adapt their strategy.

By leveraging AI-driven environmental logic, developers can craft worlds that react naturally and evolve beyond scripted events. We've explored how procedural generation, physics-based interactions, and AI-driven behaviors contribute to responsive worlds, and where to start looking to expand your knowledge base. Now, let's look at real-world case studies where these techniques can and have been successfully implemented.

Case study 1: Games with responsive and adaptive worlds

In many modern open-world games, immersion goes beyond stunning visuals, and they create an organic, self-sustaining ecosystem that responds to the player's actions and the passage of time. By using AI-driven systems, PCG, and physics-based interactions, these games' developers have crafted worlds where the environment isn't just a backdrop but an active participant in gameplay.

Creating a living world

One approach to world dynamism is simulating an interconnected ecosystem. Animals hunt and migrate, forests recover from deforestation, and NPC factions respond to environmental changes. Instead of static environments, these mechanics create an ever-changing world where the player's presence feels like just one piece of a larger system.

The following are examples:

- **Wildlife AI** follows survival instincts—predators track prey, while herbivores flee when sensing danger.
- **Flora regrowth** systems allow felled trees to sprout new saplings over time, impacting resource availability.
- **Weather and seasonal shifts** influence animal behaviors and NPC behavior cycles.
- **Resource:** *GDC Talk – Creating Ecosystems in RDR2*

Games such as *Red Dead Redemption 2* and *Horizon Forbidden West* showcase ecosystems where animals and NPCs interact independently of the player, giving the world a sense of depth and realism.

In *Primordials Legends: Hollow Hero*, we use a similar approach to animals in the world (see *Figure 6.1*).

Figure 6.1: A screenshot of Primordials Legends: Hollow Hero showing some of the creatures in the world and their different states (image source: Primordials Legends: Hollow Hero, by Toybox Games Studios)

In **Small Animal Behavior Pack**, we have a pack that has basic small animal logic set up for us to deconstruct and experiment with. See the following screenshot from the pack.

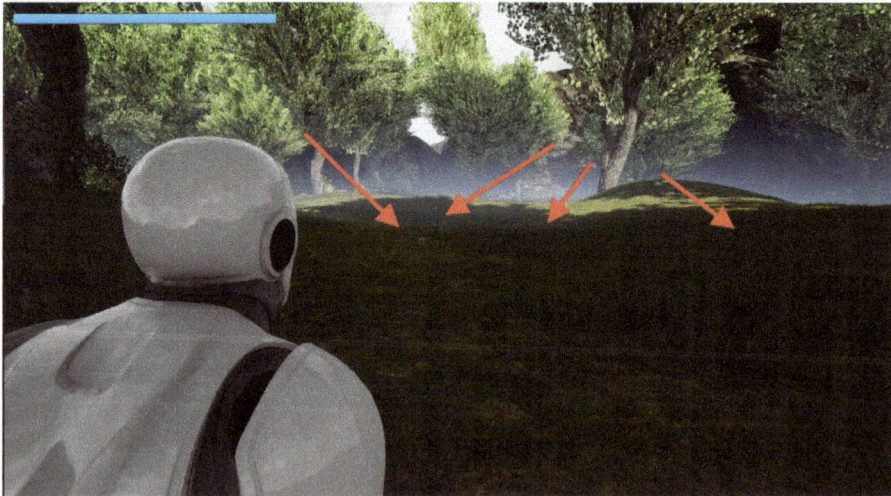

Figure 6.2: An in-engine screenshot of Small Animal Behavior Pack, a great system for quick AI prototyping (image source: Small Animal Behavior Pack by Living Systems | FAB.com)

Responsive and adaptive worlds thrive on systems that feel alive—ecosystems where AI, flora, and NPCs behave independently of the player, creating a sense of authenticity and unpredictability. By simulating cycles such as hunting, regrowth, and weather-driven changes, you transform environments from static backdrops into living, breathing spaces.

Now that we've looked at ecosystems that adapt and evolve, let's shift focus to another powerful form of world reactivity—**destructible battlefield environments**, where the terrain itself becomes part of the action.

Case study 2: Destructible battlefield environments

In combat-heavy games, destruction isn't just for spectacle—it can be a gameplay tool that forces strategic adaptation. By leveraging physics, AI-driven decision-making, and procedural destruction, battlefields can evolve in real time, presenting new challenges and opportunities.

Tactical destruction as a gameplay mechanic

Unlike static environments, destructible worlds require players to adjust their strategies dynamically. Cover that was once reliable can be blown apart, structures can collapse under fire, and terrain shifts mid-battle, creating unpredictable combat scenarios.

The following are examples:

- *A player fires an RPG into a building*, collapsing part of the structure and exposing enemies inside.
- *AI enemies react accordingly*, changing their pathfinding, finding new cover, or even retreating to safer ground.
- *Destroyed environments persist*, shaping the battlefield for the remainder of the mission/game.
- **Resource:** *Rainbow Six Siege Destruction System Breakdown (GDC)*

Games such as *Marvel: Rivals* and *Rainbow Six Siege* integrate real-time destruction, forcing players to rethink positioning, cover, and movement mid-fight.

In *Primordials Legends: Hollow Hero*, real-time destruction is used for breakable walls, floors, and secret passages.

Figure 6.3 shows an in-game screenshot of *Hollow Hero*, just after the player has destroyed a wall.

Figure 6.3: An in-game image showing the map destruction possible in Hollow Hero (image source: Primordials Legends: Hollow Hero – by Toybox Games Studios)

Figure 6.4 shows an in-engine screenshot of Epic's Content Examples. This is a great project for understanding several of Unreal's features, but it is especially good for Chaos-based destruction principles that are beyond the scope of this book!

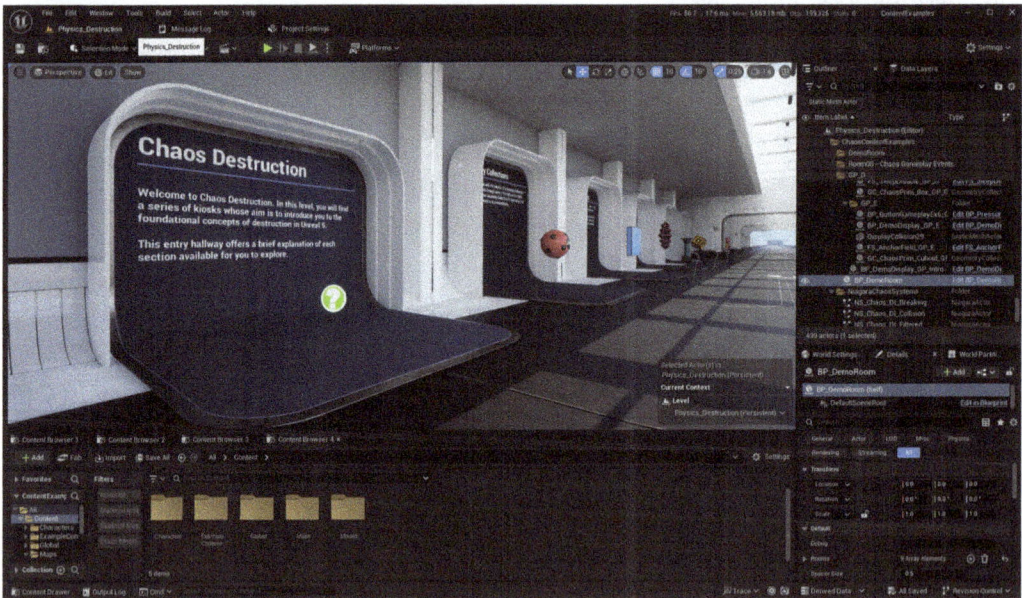

Figure 6.4: An in-engine screenshot of Epic's Content Examples (source: FAB.Com – Content Example – by Epic Games)

Destructible environments bring a heightened sense of immediacy and impact to gameplay. By using physics-driven destruction systems, players can alter the battlefield itself—toppling structures, collapsing cover, or carving new pathways in real time. These mechanics not only add spectacle but also create tactical depth, forcing players to adapt strategies as the world reshapes around them.

With battlefields that can shatter and reshape mid-game, we've seen how destruction transforms player interaction. Let's finish this chapter up with a quick summary of what we have discussed.

Summary

Modern game worlds are no longer just static backdrops; they need to feel alive, responsive, and interconnected. In UE5, and games in general, this is achieved through a combination of procedural generation, real-time environmental adaptation, physics-driven interactions, and AI-powered world logic. By implementing these systems effectively, we as developers can create immersive and dynamic environments that adapt to player actions and evolve over time, keeping everything fresh and interesting.

From auto-generated landscapes and procedural content placement to interactive destruction and AI-driven behaviors, the threads explored in this chapter and the learnings from previous chapters provide a toolkit for crafting adaptive worlds and beyond. Whether it's a forest that regrows, AI that reacts intelligently to battlefield destruction, or weather systems that influence gameplay, the key to a compelling world is making it *feel responsive*.

Throughout this chapter, we explored the following principles and threads:

- **Procedural generation**: Utilize PCG tools and Blueprint-driven logic to generate dynamic terrain, biomes, and level layouts that create unique gameplay experiences.
- **Environmental adaptation**: Implement real-time weather changes, time-of-day shifts, and destructible environments to make the game world react to player choices.
- **Physics-based interactions**: Use Chaos Physics, soft body simulations, and real-time. object constraints to add realistic movement, destruction, and weight to in-game objects
- **AI-driven adaptation**: Design NPC behaviors, pathfinding adjustments, and dynamic interactions so that the world reacts intelligently to evolving scenarios.

By mastering these systems, we can push beyond static game design and create living, breathing worlds that evolve alongside the player, enhancing both immersion and engagement.

This acts as the halfway point of this book, and a major change in direction as we move away from world-building and toward cinematics and storytelling in Unreal, before we finally finish up with some of my favorite tips and tricks with regard to optimization and project management.

> **Important note**
>
> I highly, highly recommend exploring the **threads** outlined in this chapter in order to explore and evolve your existing learning base. My intention with this book isn't just to show you how to do things, but to teach you how to think about finding solutions yourself. It's why we have included *Further reading* sections, and in this context, I want you to *pull on the thread* and see what you unravel and find in your own journey to Unreal and game dev mastery.

Further reading

This list of further readings is from other authors under the Packt Publishing label, and a few of my personal recommendations for getting a more advanced look into Unreal, AI, and evolving worlds in games. These are meant to supplement the *threads* I have already recommended in this chapter, and also have their own paths they will send you down as you grow in your respective field.

- *Unreal Engine Physics Essentials*. Read more here:https://amzn.asia/d/fMqM1BM
- *Blueprints Visual Scripting for Unreal Engine 5*. Read more here: https://amzn.asia/d/5ycEJwN
- *Mastering AI Game Development with Unreal: Unleash creativity, empower gameplay, and transform player experiences with advanced AI techniques in Unreal Engine (English Edition)*. Read more here: https://amzn.asia/d/9mUjP9x

Subscribe to Game Dev Assembly!

We are excited to introduce **Game Dev Assembly**, our brand-new newsletter dedicated to everything game development. Whether you're coding, designing, animating, or managing a studio, we've got insights, trends, and expert advice to help you create, innovate, and thrive. Sign up now and get exciting benefits.

https://packt.link/gamedev-newsletter

Join our community on Discord

Join our community's Discord space for discussions with the authors and other readers:

https://packt.link/unrealengine

Part 3

Crafting Immersive Cinematic Storytelling

In this part, we'll shift our focus to storytelling through the cinematic lens. You'll learn how to use Unreal's cinematic tools to design cutscenes, build narrative-driven environments, and craft adaptive sequences that react dynamically to gameplay. Whether you're aiming for tightly scripted drama or branching player-driven experiences, these chapters will show you how to bring stories to life with clarity and impact.

This part of the book includes the following chapters:

- *Chapter 7, Designing High-Quality Cinematic Sequences*
- *Chapter 8, Environment as Narrative and Storytelling*
- *Chapter 9, Adaptive Cutscenes and Interactive Paths*

7

Designing High-Quality Cinematic Sequences

Games often showcase that they are more than just interactive experiences—they're full-fledged storytelling platforms. These stories can profoundly impact people's lives and are why gaming, as an art form of entertainment, is so universally loved. For me, after playing and completing *Halo 3* in 2007, I was so emotionally moved by the experience that, in that moment, I decided I was going to become a game developer. This decision has been a driving force for me ever since.

Whether you're building a narrative-driven title, an emotional short film, or an epic cutscene for an action game, **cinematic storytelling** in UE5 allows you to achieve visuals and moments that rival the silver screen. The line between real-time and offline rendering continues to blur, and UE5 puts powerful cinematic tools directly in our hands as artists, designers, and developers.

From precise camera control to photorealistic lighting, and animated performances to high-fidelity rendering pipelines, UE5 gives you everything you need to design emotionally rich, technically sound, and visually striking sequences that leave a lasting impact. These cinematics can be used for marketing trailers, in-game narrative beats, pre-rendered sequences, or even branching real-time story moments that adapt to player choice.

But building a great cinematic is more than just dragging in a camera and pressing record. It requires a blend of **film grammar**, **technical knowledge**, and **creative instinct**. In this chapter, we will explore not just the tools but how to use them effectively—how to compose shots with purpose, light scenes for tone, move the camera with intention, and render sequences with production-ready polish.

In this chapter, you will learn:

- The fundamentals of cinematic design in UE5: How to think like a filmmaker using the tools of a game developer
- How to build and manage scenes using Sequencer, Unreal's powerful timeline-based editing system
- Tips for cinematic composition, framing, and camera motion—including how to apply classical film theory in real-time scenes
- Lighting techniques and environmental storytelling strategies to guide mood, clarity, and narrative tone
- Exporting high-quality sequences using Movie Render Queue, including render settings and post-processing strategies
- Best practices for working with animation, characters, audio, and visual effects across both real-time and pre-rendered cinematic workflows.

By the end of this chapter, you'll have the skills and knowledge needed to plan, build, and polish your own high-quality cinematics in Unreal—whether for *games, short films, marketing trailers,* or *interactive storytelling experiences*. Let's dive into the craft of real-time storytelling—and learn how to build sequences that look incredible and feel unforgettable!

Technical requirements

To follow along with this chapter, ensure you have:

- Unreal Engine 5.4 or later
- A system with real-time ray tracing support (optional but recommended)
- A solid understanding of the Unreal Engine interface
- Have read the previous chapters of this book
- Optional: A project with pre-built assets for testing and practice (or start with Unreal's sample projects)

Cinematic design fundamentals

Before launching Sequencer or animating a single camera, it's essential to first understand what makes a scene *feel* cinematic. Unreal offers powerful tools for creating visually striking sequences—but the artistry lies in how those tools are used to serve a story.

When you're building cutscenes, trailers, or in-game moments of narrative importance, strong cinematic design relies on intentional choices in *framing*, *pacing*, *lighting*, and *emotional tone*. This section will guide you through these fundamentals so you can craft scenes that do more than just look good—they *resonate*.

So, what makes a scene cinematic?

- **Visual clarity and intent**: Every frame should communicate something—emotion, story progression, or world-building. If a shot doesn't serve a purpose, it can dilute the viewer's engagement.

> **Example**
>
> In *The Last of Us Part II*, wide establishing shots often show the ruined cityscapes overgrown with nature. These aren't just pretty images—they reinforce themes of decay, resilience, and humanity's small place in the world. Indoors, however, the camera tightens into closer, more confined shots. This shift creates a sense of claustrophobia and tension, making players feel the fear and uncertainty of exploring dark, hostile spaces.

- **Emotional tone**: Lighting, color grading, and pacing shape a viewer's emotional response. A soft, desaturated palette may signal melancholy, while dramatic contrasts and shadows can build suspense or tension.

- **Spatial awareness**: Cinematic storytelling plays with proximity—knowing when to pull back and when to zoom in. Wide shots provide context, mid shots show relationships, and close-ups deliver emotional intensity.

- **Movement and rhythm**: Camera movement, whether subtle or dramatic, helps establish energy and flow.

> **Example**
>
> In *God of War (2018)*, the near-constant "one-shot" camera moves seamlessly between action and dialogue, creating intimacy and momentum. By contrast, *Uncharted 4* often uses sweeping, cinematic pans during set-piece chases and collapses, amplifying excitement and scale while keeping the player oriented within the chaos.

Tip

As discussed in *Chapters 1* and *2*, we can use **Post Process Volumes** to adjust the tone dynamically throughout our scenes to help bring a cinematic look to our shots.

Figures 7.1, 7.2, and *7.3* show three renders with cameras using a wide, mid, and close-up shot of the same scene to help show the difference in perspective and how they are used.

The wide shot establishes the location and tone:

Figure 7.1: Wide shot

The mid shot highlights character interaction and body language:

Figure 7.2: Mid shot

The close-up shot focuses on emotional expression or key details:

Figure 7.3: Close-up

With the fundamentals of cinematic design in mind, let's turn to the practical side and see how Sequencer in Unreal Engine brings those ideas to life.

Sequencer overview

At the heart of UE5's cinematic capabilities is **Sequencer**—a powerful, non-linear timeline editor that lets you direct, animate, and fine-tune every aspect of your scene. Whether you're crafting complex character performances or orchestrating large-scale environment shots, Sequencer is where your cinematic vision comes to life.

It functions similarly to professional video editing software, but with the added bonus of full real-time 3D control, animation, and interactivity—all from within the Unreal Editor. Sequencer is also fully extensible, supporting everything from keyframe animation to Control Rig-driven performances, VFX timing, and dynamic audio integration.

Setting up your first sequence

Getting started with Sequencer is quick and intuitive. Here's how to set up a basic scene:

1. Create a Level Sequence asset:

    a. Right-click in the Content Browser and select **Cinematics | Level Sequence**.

    b. Give it a clear, descriptive name (e.g., Intro_Cinematic_Shot01).

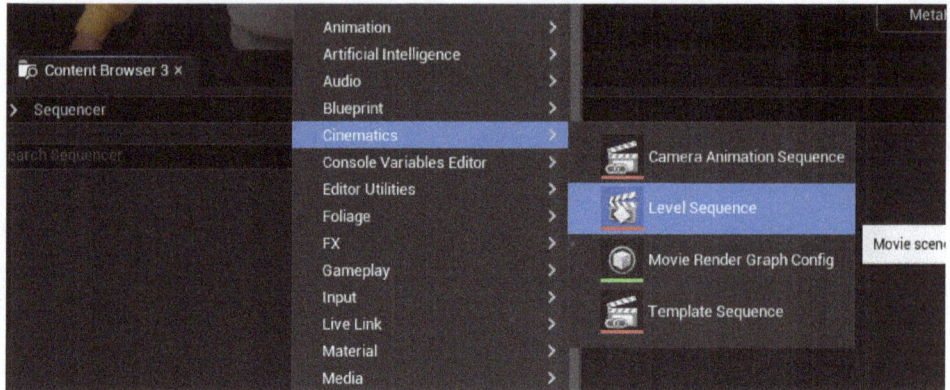

Figure 7.4: Selecting Cinematics | Level Sequence

2. Add a Cine Camera Actor:

    a.   Drag in a Cine Camera Actor from the **Place Actors** panel.

    b.   Position and rotate the camera to your desired shot framing.

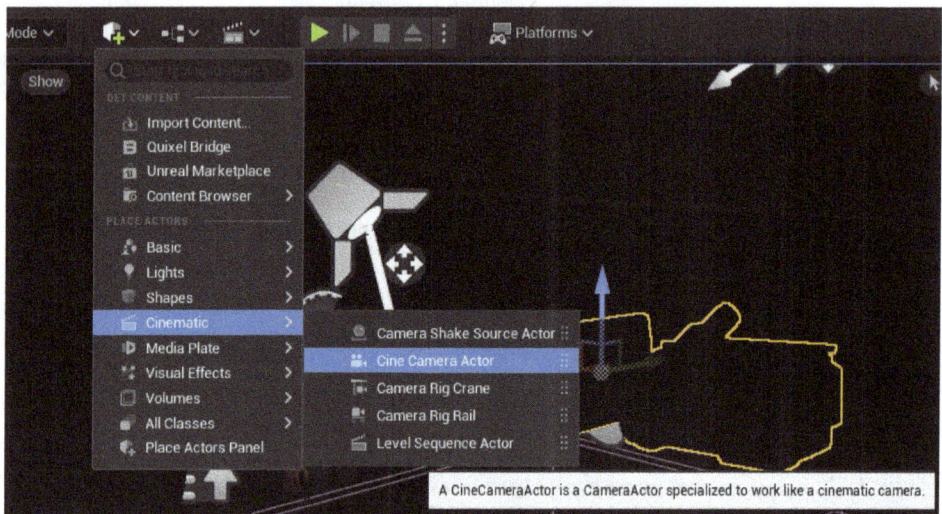

Figure 7.5: Where to find a Cine Camera Actor

3. Open Sequencer and populate the Timeline:

    a.   Double-click your Level Sequence to open it in the Sequencer Editor.

    b.   Click the **+ Add** button to add your camera under the **Actor to Sequence** option, and any Actors, props, lights, or sound you want to animate.

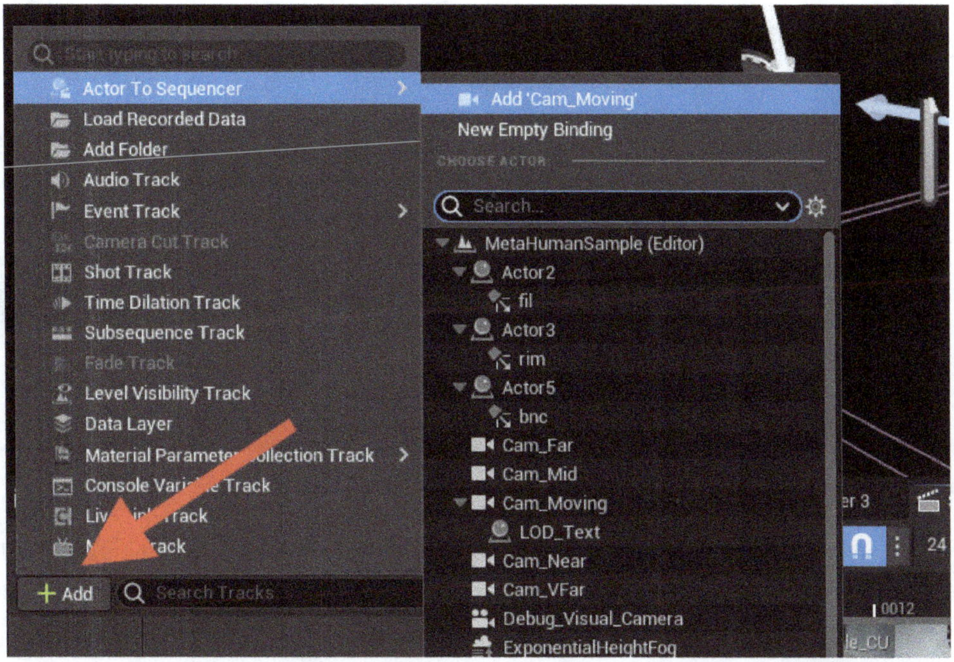

Figure 7.6: + Add button

4. Begin keyframing:

    a. Move the Timeline scrubber and begin setting keyframes for **Transform** (position and rotation), **Camera Settings** (focal length and aperture), **Material Changes**, **Animation Clips**, and more.

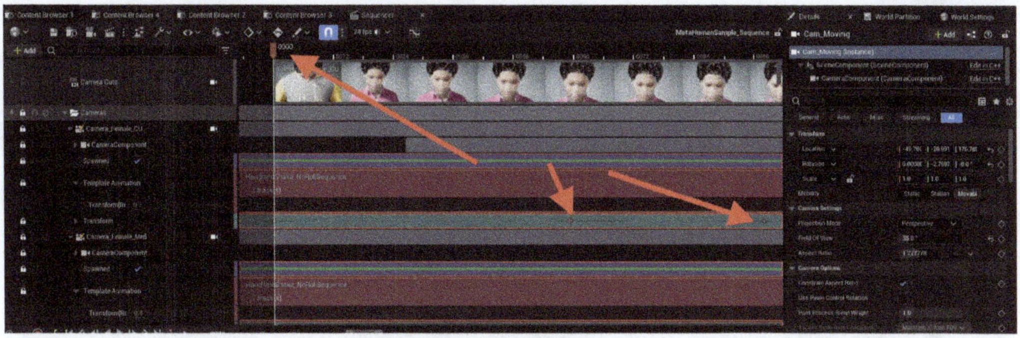

Figure 7.7: Sequencer Editor showcase

With our first sequence set up successfully, let's take a deep dive into the key features of Sequencer.

Key Sequencer features

Sequencer offers an impressive level of control over your cinematic Timeline. Here are some of the most essential features for creating polished, professional-quality cutscenes:

- **Camera cuts and blends**: Use the Camera Cuts Track to switch between multiple cameras. You can also blend between shots smoothly for more cinematic transitions.

Figure 7.8: Camera Cuts Track location

- **Keyframe automation**: Animate Actors, props, or environment elements with traditional keyframes or curves. Adjust easing and interpolation using the curve editor for smooth motion.

Figure 7.9: Curve Graph Editor button

- **Track versatility**: Animate everything from light intensity and color, material parameters, audio triggers, and visibility toggles to particle system activations.

Figure 7.10: An example of the extensive things that can be controlled on different Actors through Sequencer

- **Control Rig integration**: For character animation, Sequencer supports **Control Rig**, allowing precise skeletal control inside the engine. You can keyframe facial expressions, gestures, and even entire performance captures directly within your Timeline.

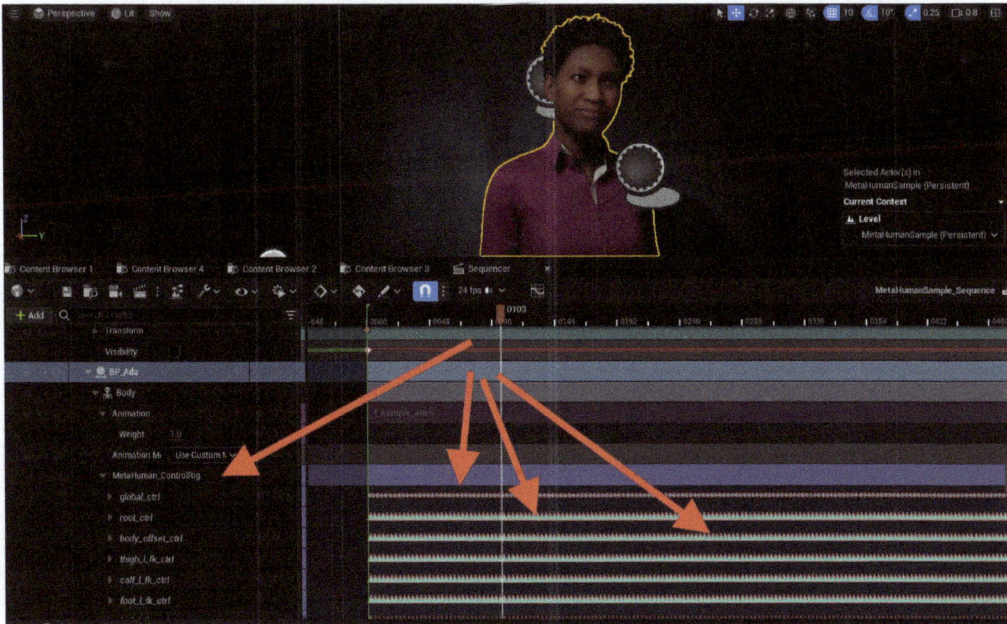

Figure 7.11: A Control Rig setup in Sequencer

Next up, we can move on to a more hands-on breakdown of cine cameras, including how to set up lenses, depth of field, and framing techniques. Let me know when you're ready!

Camera work and cinematic composition

When it comes to high-quality cinematics, camera work is everything. It's the lens through which your audience experiences the story—literally. In Unreal, **Cine Camera Actors** provide the tools to replicate real-world cinematography with a high degree of control over lens settings, depth of field, focus, and movement. But great cinematics go beyond just technical accuracy—they also require an understanding of how to compose a shot emotionally and visually.

By blending the technical power of UE5's camera system with time-tested composition principles from film and photography, you can create sequences that are deeply impactful.

Using Cine Camera Actors in UE5

The Cine Camera Actor is designed to simulate the look and feel of a real camera, complete with adjustable lenses, physical apertures, focus tracking, and more. These tools allow you to control the visual language of your scene and fine-tune how each shot feels.

Here's a list of key camera settings:

- **Filmback (sensor size)**:

    - Choose from presets such as **Super 35mm**, **Full Frame**, or **Custom settings**. This affects your camera's field of view and how focal length behaves.

    - Larger filmbacks offer wider shots with a shallower depth of field—ideal for sweeping landscapes or character-focused close-ups.

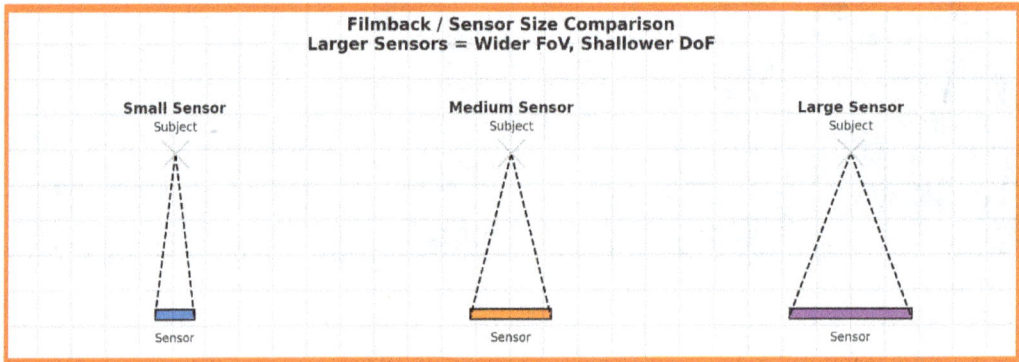

Figure 7.12: Filmback comparison diagram

- **Focal length and zoom**:

    - Controls how much of the scene is visible and the level of image compression. Use shorter lenses (18 mm–35 mm) for wide establishing shots, and longer lenses (85 mm–135 mm) for dramatic close-ups with strong background blur.

- **Aperture (f-stop)**:

    - Affects depth of field. Lower f-stops (e.g., f/1.4) create a creamy background blur (bokeh), while higher values (e.g., f/8) keep more of the image in focus.

- **Manual and tracked focus**:

    - Adjust focus distance manually or enable focus tracking to dynamically follow characters or objects as they move through the scene.

- This can be used for dramatic *focus pulls*, where the depth of focus shifts from one subject to another mid-shot.

Tip

Turn on **Draw Debug Focus Plane** to see exactly where the focus distance for your camera is! This can be found under the **Focus Settings** dropdown shown in *Figure 7.11*. You can also search for individual properties in the search bar present at the top of the details panel.

- **Camera tracking and constraints**:
  - Attach your camera to splines or motion paths, or use **Lookat Tracking** to keep characters or objects in frame.
  - For more natural handheld movement, consider using camera shake or procedural movement modifiers.

Figure 7.11 shows three arrows corresponding to the *key camera settings* we just discussed: green for **Lookat Tracking,** red for **Filmback** and **Sensor Settings**, and blue for **Focus Settings**.

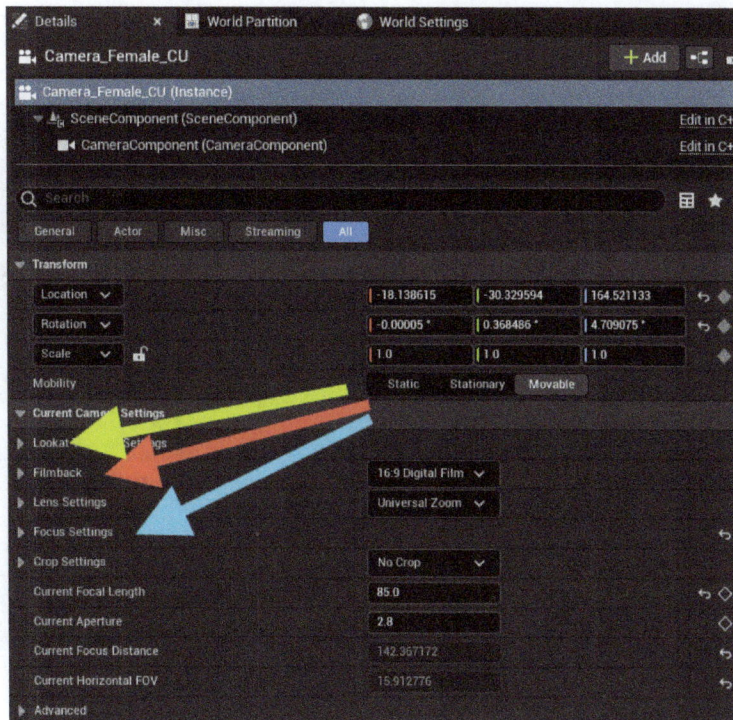

Figure 7.13: The details panel for a cinematic camera, with respective arrows for different values to change

We've covered the basics of camera work and composition. Let's dig deeper into specific cinematic composition techniques that can elevate your shots even further!

Cinematic composition techniques

A beautiful shot isn't just about lens settings—it's about visual storytelling. Composition is what guides the viewer's eye, sets the mood, and conveys meaning, often without a single word being spoken. Here are some foundational principles to use when framing shots:

- **Rule of thirds**:
  - Divide your frame into a 3x3 grid. Position key subjects along the intersections or lines to create balanced and pleasing visuals.
  - For example, place a character's eye at the upper-left grid point, or align the horizon along the lower third for landscape shots.

The rule of thirds is used with cameras because it helps create balance and visual interest in a shot. By placing key subjects or points of focus along the grid lines or their intersections, the viewer's eye is naturally guided to them without the frame feeling static or flat. It's a simple guideline that makes shots feel more dynamic, natural, and engaging than if everything were centered.

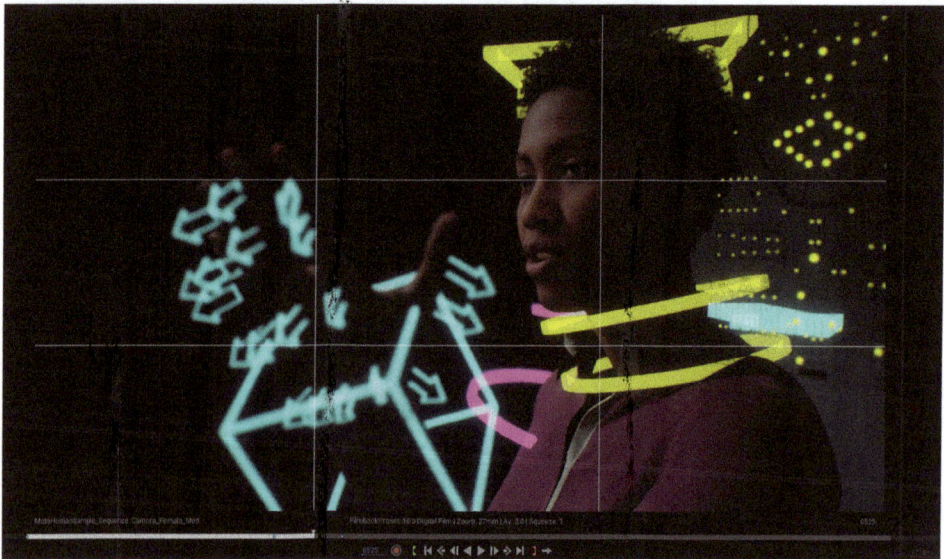

Figure 7.14: A Cinematic Camera with a "rule of thirds" grid active

> **Important note**
>
> The following link to Epic Games is another thread for you to follow and goes over various properties and caveats for the various framing and grid patterns available in Unreal. I highly recommend reading the documentation to better understand the preceding principles and general viewport controls:
>
> https://dev.epicgames.com/documentation/en-us/unreal-engine/cinematic-viewport-controls-in-unreal-engine

- **Leading lines:**
  - Use roads, hallways, railings, or architecture to draw the viewer's gaze toward the subject (see *Chapter 4*).
  - This creates visual momentum and can subtly direct attention without forcing it.
- **Foreground, midground, and background:**
  - Layering your shots adds depth and realism.
  - Introduce environmental elements such as fog, foliage, or debris in the foreground to create separation and depth between planes (see *Chapter 2*).
- **Contrast and silhouetting:**
  - Strong lighting contrast can be used to silhouette characters or highlight action within the frame.
  - This is especially effective during emotionally charged moments or reveal shots.

Next, we'll look at Sequencer in action, diving into how to block scenes, animate shots, and time your edits for maximum storytelling impact.

Blocking, animating, and timing cinematic shots in Sequencer

Now that we've explored the building blocks of cinematography—camera setup, composition, and visual storytelling—it's time to bring it all together in motion. Cinematic scenes don't exist in a vacuum; they are *built*, *choreographed*, and *timed* through meticulous direction and planning. This is where Sequencer shines.

Sequencer isn't just a timeline tool—it's your virtual director's chair. It allows you to define camera movement, animate Actors, sync with audio, and control everything from facial expressions to light flickers. Whether you're crafting a short cutscene or an extended in-engine cinematic, understanding *how to block a scene, animate your cameras*, and *cut effectively* is essential to creating emotional impact and narrative clarity.

Blocking a scene: Directing the action

Blocking refers to planning the movement and positioning of Actors and cameras within a scene— similar to stage choreography in theater or pre-visualization in film.

Here are some key blocking considerations:

- Where is the character entering from?
- What is their emotional state and goal?
- What does the camera need to emphasize during this moment?

To block a scene in Sequencer:

1. Begin by placing your characters and key props in the scene.
2. Use **Transform keyframes** to animate character or object movement paths.
3. Introduce basic staging early—decide who is foregrounded, who is in the background, and how these elements shift over time.

> **Important note**
>
> Props and characters can be static or "T-posing" at this point; it's just to get an idea, much like grayboxing a Level or environment as we discussed in previous chapters.

> **Tip**
>
> Use reference footage to guide natural character movement and blocking. Even basic animation is elevated when it follows human principles of timing, anticipation, and follow-through.

Animating shots in Sequencer

Camera movement tells just as much story as dialogue. A slow dolly-in can heighten tension. A handheld camera adds chaos. A sweeping crane shot evokes scale and wonder.

Here's a list of cinematic camera movement types you can animate in Sequencer:

- **Static composition**: No movement, purely framed composition. Great for dialogue or tension-filled moments.
- **Dolly and trucking shots**: Smooth forward/backward or side-to-side movement.
- **Panning and tilting**: Rotational movement to follow or reveal subjects.
- **Crane shots**: Vertical movement, often used to transition between locations or highlight scope.
- **Handheld feel**: Add subtle shake or sway using camera shake modifiers or by manually keyframing motion curves.

Timing and editing for storytelling

One of the biggest cinematic pitfalls in game development I see is *misjudging pacing*. Even beautifully animated sequences can fall flat if they're too slow or confusing. Sequencer gives you frame-level control over the rhythm and timing of your shots.

Think like an editor:

- **Start strong, end stronger**: The first and last frame of a shot should convey emotion or plot progression.
- **Hold beats for impact**: Let emotional moments breathe—don't cut away too fast.
- **Cut on action**: If a character turns or reaches, cut to another angle mid-motion for smoother transitions.
- **Match motion direction**: Keep continuity between shots by maintaining screen direction (e.g., left-to-right movement stays consistent).

Here's an example workflow:

1. Start with a wide establishing shot to show the scene.
2. Cut to a mid-shot as the character begins speaking or moving.
3. Shift to a close-up for emotional delivery or reaction.

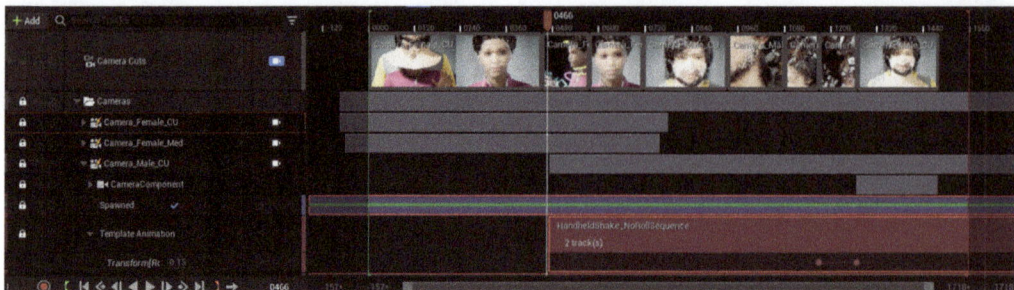

Figure 7.15: Showcase of Camera Cuts Track with multiple camera cuts

Now that we have a solid feel for handling a camera, let's explore how to light scenes for mood, build atmospheric depth, and then prepare stunning outputs with **Movie Render Queue (MRQ)**.

Lighting for cinematics

We have already discussed in detail the importance of lighting in video games, and cinematics are no different. **Cinematic lighting** is one of the most potent storytelling tools in a cinematic sequence. In the hands of a skilled artist, it communicates emotion, draws focus, enhances atmosphere, and adds visual depth. In UE5, lighting for cinematics blends traditional film lighting principles with the powerful real-time rendering technologies the engine offers.

I don't want to spend too much time on this topic again; if you need a lighting refresher, go back to *Chapters 1* and *2*. Instead, I want to cover the general lighting practices I use as a lighting artist that overlap heavily with cinematic lighting principles, so you know where to focus your own practice.

Artistic lighting principles

Even in digital cinematography, we draw from the classic **three-point lighting system** as a foundation for scene composition:

1. Key light:

    - The main source of illumination.

    - It defines the subject's shape, form, and mood.

    - Often positioned at a 45° angle to one side of the camera to create depth and contrast.

2. Fill light:

- Softens the shadows cast by the key light.

- Helps control contrast and visibility, especially on faces.

- Usually placed on the opposite side of the key and kept lower in intensity.

3. Rim light (back light):

- Placed behind the subject to create a light edge or "rim."

- Helps separate the subject from the background, enhancing the silhouette and clarity.

Figure 7.16 showcases individual lights (fill, key, and rim) that lead to the complete three-point lighting setup in *Figure 7.17*:

Figure 7.16: Individual lights (fill, key, and rim)

Figure 7.17: A complete three-point lighting setup

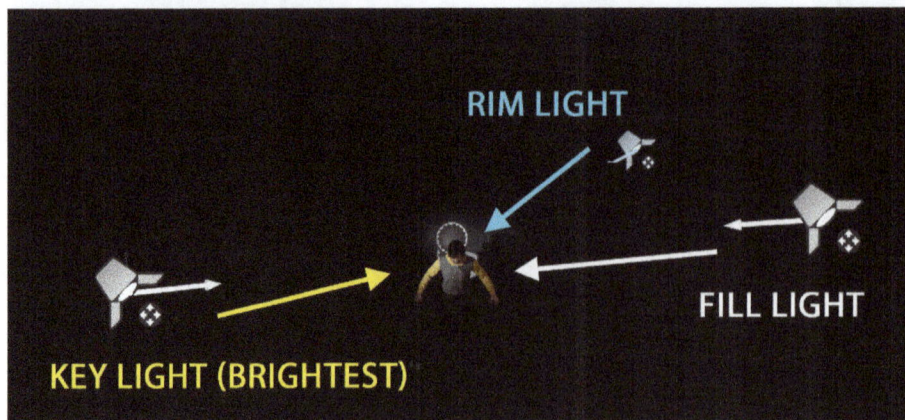

Figure 7.18: A complete three-point lighting setup from above

Tips

Use shadow intentionally. Darkness can add mystery or tension—don't feel like you need to over-light everything.

Warm versus cool lighting drastically shifts the tone. Consider using warm key lights against cool fill/backdrops or vice versa.

Practical tips for lighting in UE5

Now that you understand the lighting principles, here are some tips to implement them in UE5:

- **Light cards**: Used in virtual production and controlled lighting, light cards are large softbox-like surfaces used to sculpt lighting in a scene—especially useful for portrait-style close-ups or reflective surfaces.

- **IES lights**: These use real-world photometric data to shape the beam and falloff pattern of a light, adding realism and nuance.

- **Post Process Volume**: This is your digital grading suite. It controls the final color, contrast, bloom, exposure, and tonality of your image—just like a film colorist.

- **Creating visual drama with lighting**: Some cinematics demand a theatrical touch—harsh silhouettes, dramatic color shifts, or extreme contrast. This is where you can experiment and push visual storytelling with intention.

Examples are a villain's reveal with a single backlight and red accent fill, a dream sequence with blown-out whites and high bloom, or an intimate conversation with low fill light and strong rim separation.

With lighting for cinematics established, the next step is learning how to bring those polished scenes out of Unreal using MRQ.

Movie Render Queue (MRQ)

While real-time rendering in UE5 is powerful, sometimes your cinematic needs demand the *absolute highest visual fidelity*—whether for marketing shots, trailers, cutscenes, or pre-rendered film-quality sequences. This is where MRQ enters the equation.

Introduced as a replacement for the older **Matinee Movie Capture** system, MRQ gives creators full control over output resolution, sampling, and render passes—allowing for photoreal results, layered VFX workflows, and precise image sequences that easily rival traditional offline renderers.

Fun fact!

During my time as a cinematic lighting artist, I worked on several game trailers using both Unreal Engine and Redshift via 3ds Max. While Redshift offered superior visual output to the trained eye, we quickly realized that the general audience was largely unaware of the subtle, micro-level differences between the two rendering solutions. As a result, we increasingly leaned toward Unreal—primarily because what Redshift could achieve in 3 hours, Unreal could deliver in just 10 minutes of render time.

High-quality render setup: Step by step

Let's walk through the basics of rendering a high-quality cinematic using MRQ:

1. Accessing MRQ:

    a. Go to **Window** | **Cinematics** | **Movie Render Queue** to open the interface.

    b. Create a new render job by selecting your Level Sequence.

Important note

MRQ is a plugin and is disabled by default. You can enable it by going into **Edit** | **Plugin** | **Movie Render Queue** | **Movie Render Queue Additional Render Passes**.

2. Basic output configuration (settings):

   a. **Output Directory**: Choose where your frames will be exported

   b. **File Format**: Select PNG or EXR for lossless, frame-by-frame output (recommended for post-production)

   c. **Resolution**: For high-end trailers or marketing assets, target 3840x2160 (4K) or higher

   d. **Game Overides**: This is great for overriding Unreal's optimization setting to allow for crisp (but expensive) renders at the highest possible quality

3. Anti-aliasing and temporal sampling:

   a. **Anti-aliasing method**: Stick with **Temporal Super-Resolution (TSR)** for Unreal's out-of-the-box solution. Alternatively, override the **Anti-Aliasing Method** setting and increase the **Temporal Sample Count** value for more cinematic smoothness.

   b. **Temporal sample count**: Increase the sample count for ultra-smooth motion and reduced flicker. This setting is critical for glass, particles, motion blur, and other complex image details.

In the past, I have gone all the way up to 64 sub-samples, but this appears to have diminishing effects the higher you go and dramatically increases the render time.

Advanced MRQ features and tips

Once your base job is set, explore these advanced render features to elevate your cinematic workflow:

- **Render passes**: Enable additional **render layers** for post-production compositing:

  a. **Beauty**: Final color image

  b. **Ambient Occlusion, Depth, World Normals**, and **Lighting Only**: Great for VFX teams or stylized effects

  c. Exporting render passes requires **deferred rendering**

> **Important note**
>
> Deferred rendering is the default rendering path in Unreal Engine. Instead of shading every object directly as in **forward rendering**, it first stores surface data (such as color, normals, roughness, and depth) into screen-space buffers called the **G-buffer**. Lighting is then applied as a separate pass across the whole scene. This matters in a rendering context as you would only ever really use forward rendering for VR, mobile, or projects needing very few lights and maximum performance.

- **TAA/upsampling tweaks**: To enhance image sharpness, do the following:

  a. Use the **Anti-Aliasing Overrides** setting in **MRQ Settings**.

  b. Enable **Override Anti-Aliasing** and fine-tune the **Screen Percentage** value for supersampling (e.g., set it to 200%).

- **Motion blur and camera settings**: MRQ will use your Cine Camera Actor's motion blur, shutter speed, and focal settings—but make sure to double-check the exposure and DOF settings in both your Sequencer and Post Process Volume to ensure accuracy.

> **Tip**
>
> Set **Priority** on your camera or **Post Process Volume** to make sure it always determines what values are being used, depending on your preference.

Tips for reliable renders

Getting a cinematic ready for final output can be tricky, and small oversights often lead to frustrating re-renders. To save time and ensure consistent results, here are a few practical tips that will make your renders more reliable:

- *Always render to image sequences, not video.* This protects against crashes and allows for per-frame adjustments.

- Under **Settings | Warm Up Frames**, set a few frames (e.g., 10) to allow effects such as particles or lighting to settle before capture begins.

- Turn off **Auto-Exposure** in your **Post Process Volume** for consistent brightness across frames.

- Use **Console Variables (CVars)** via **Command Line Arguments** in MRQ for fine-grained tweaks (e.g., **r.TemporalAA.Upsampling 1** or **r.MotionBlurQuality 4**).

> **Important note**
>
> There a literally hundreds of CVars in Unreal that do all manner of things, so I recommend googling them as the need for something you want arises and seeing whether there is a CVar solution.

Figure 7.16 shows five arrows corresponding to the MRQ settings we just discussed: green to add a Render, red for **Sequencer** and **Level settings**, pink to add settings for your render, blue for the **Anti-aliasing** location, and yellow for where to set your output.

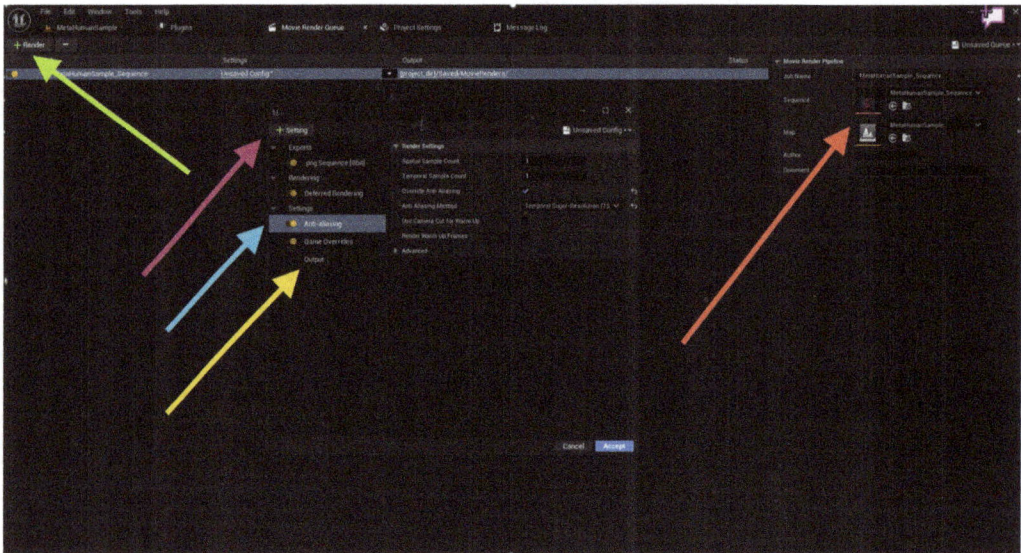

Figure 7.19: The details panel for a Cinematic Camera, with respective arrows for different values to change

In the next section, we'll zoom out and explore basic **cinematic production workflows**—how to keep your scene manageable, structured, and optimized for iteration and feedback.

How to manage the movie

As your cinematic project grows, so does the complexity of managing it. What starts as a single Level Sequence can quickly balloon into dozens of shot cameras, characters, audio tracks, and lighting events. Without clear organization, even the most promising scene can become unwieldy, trust me.

Luckily, Unreal gives us all we need to manage large-scale sequences—from Subscene and Shot Tracks to folders, color coding, and metadata tagging.

Modular sequencing with Master and Sub-Sequences

Just like game levels, cinematics should be modular. Use **Master Sequences** to organize your film or cutscene into digestible parts.

A **Master Sequence** acts like a container that links together multiple Level Sequences (often called **Sub-Sequences** or **Shot Tracks**). Each Sub-Sequence can represent a single shot or camera setup.

The following setup helps:

- Keep individual shots isolated for easy editing.
- Allow multiple artists to work on separate shots simultaneously.
- Enable quick reordering or replacement of entire scenes.

This is how you can set up a Master Sequence:

1. Create a Master Level Sequence (this is just a Level Sequence that you want to be the master, not a different kind of sequence).
2. Add Shot Tracks to it.
3. Insert or create Sub-Sequences within each Shot Track (each with its own camera, animations, and timing).
4. Use the Camera Cut Track to switch between cameras in each Sub-Sequence.

Think of it like working in an editing program such as Premiere Pro or DaVinci Resolve: each Sub-Sequence is its own shot, and the Master Sequence acts as the full timeline where those shots are arranged, cut, and played back in order. In other words, it's Sequencer inside Sequencer—shots nested together to form your complete cinematic.

Organizing your Sequencer timeline

Once you're working with multiple cameras, characters, VFX, audio, and lighting tracks, it's easy to get overwhelmed. Staying organized in Sequencer is key.

Tips for Sequencer organization

- *Use folders* to group similar tracks (e.g., all character animations, audio cues, or lighting keyframes).
- *Color-code tracks* for readability (e.g., red for cameras, blue for animation, and yellow for lighting).
- Use *track labels and notes* to mark important moments such as "climax," "beat change," or "reaction close-up."
- *Collapse inactive tracks* to keep your workspace clean.

Sequencer tools for large scenes

UE5 includes several quality-of-life tools to manage large sequences:

- **Track filters**: Filter by Actor, type (e.g., camera or skeletal), or animation to isolate what you're working on.
- **Ripple editing**: Shift all subsequent keyframes when adjusting timing—great for retiming sequences without breaking sync.
- **Markers**: Add Timeline markers for narrative beats, shot notes, or timing references.
- **Slomo and Time Dilation**: Use Sequencer's **Play Rate** settings or time dilation tracks for slow motion or dramatic pacing shifts.

Collaboration and version control

If you're working in a team or on a large cinematic project, do the following:

- Use **Multi-User Editing** to allow multiple artists to contribute to the same scene collaboratively.
- Version control systems (such as **Perforce**) are crucial for handling shared sequences and preventing overwrites.
- Name your sequences clearly using a consistent naming convention (e.g., `Cutscene_A_Shot03_CameraTrack`).

Important note

Perforce is a version control system widely used in game development and other large-scale creative projects. It allows teams to manage, track, and collaborate on files—such as code, assets, and Levels—by storing them in a centralized repository. With Perforce, developers can roll back changes, resolve conflicts, and ensure that everyone on the team is working with the most up-to-date content. It's especially useful in Unreal Engine projects, where large binary files and complex asset dependencies require robust and reliable source control.

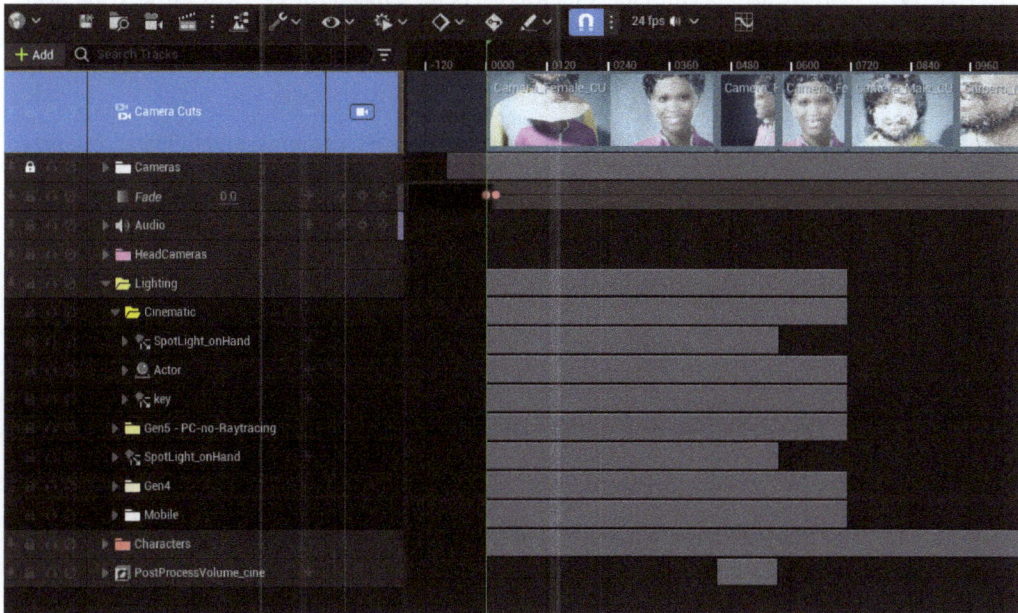

Figure 7.20: An image showing a solid, color-coded setup for cleanliness and efficiency

Once your Sequencer timeline is organized, the next step is to look at some best practices that will help streamline your overall cinematic workflow.

Best practices for cinematic workflows

Continuing on from Sequencer management, at the end of the day, a clean, efficient workflow becomes just as important as the creative process itself.

These best practices, tips, and tricks will help you stay organized, agile, and production-ready—whether you're building a short film, a gameplay cutscene, or a complex narrative sequence:

- **Keep sequences modular**: Instead of building one long, unwieldy sequence, break your scenes down into manageable shots or chunks. This makes editing, debugging, and re-ordering shots much easier.

- **Name every track and keyframe clearly**: Naming conventions may seem tedious, but they become invaluable over time:

    - Avoid generic names such as `Camera_01` or `Track_3`.
    - Instead, use specific labels such as `HeroCam_CloseUp` or `Villain_WalkCycle_Start`.
    - This reduces confusion in larger teams and helps during version reviews or revisions.

- **Use folder structures in the Outliner**: Keep your Actors, cameras, and lighting organized in the Outliner with clear folders and labels:

    - Create folders for `Cameras`, `Lighting`, `Props`, `Characters`, and so on.
    - This makes the scene easier to navigate and helps avoid duplication or misplacement of key elements.

- **Always version and back up your work**: Sequencer is powerful—but complex timelines and heavy assets can cause unexpected issues:

    - Save incremental versions frequently (e.g., `Shot_05_v02`, `Shot_05_v03`).
    - Use source control such as Perforce or Git for team collaboration and to safeguard against data loss.

- **Other handy tips**:

    - Lock camera cuts using the Camera Cuts Track to prevent accidental overrides.
    - Mute tracks temporarily to troubleshoot animation or lighting.
    - Use markers in the Timeline to denote key narrative or visual beats.

        a. To add markers, right-click on the Timeline and select **Add Mark**.

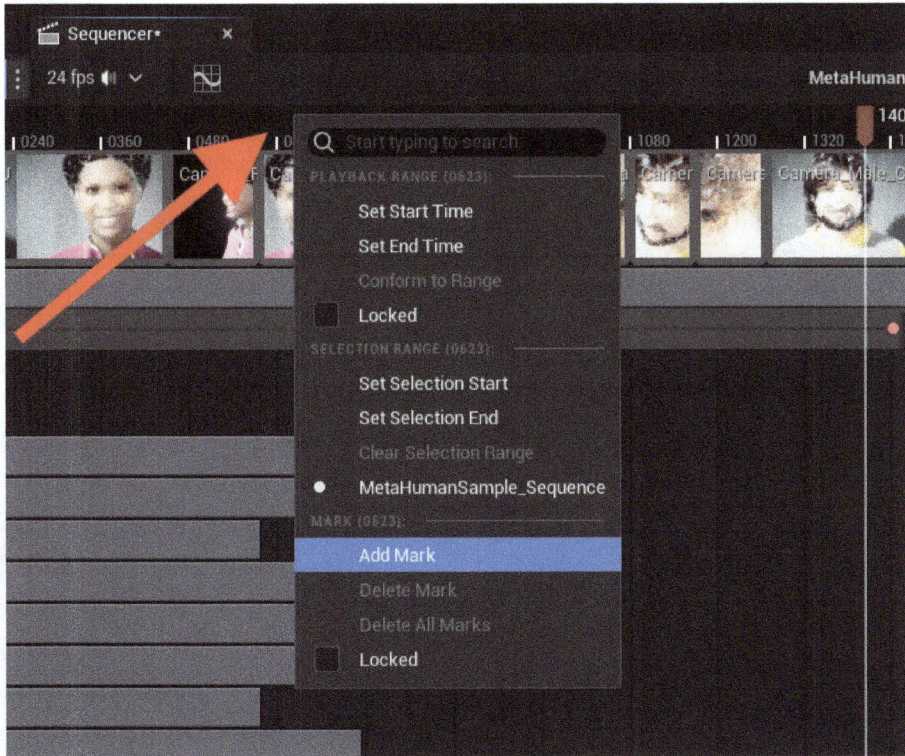

Figure 7.21: Adding markers

Bonus section: Audio and music integration

I want to add this very short section here as a love letter to the audio folks I have worked with in the past, but also as a chance to let you know to take the time to learn the basics of having audio in your cinematic scenes. I am not a musician, and can't teach you how to make beautiful music, but audio plays such a pivotal role in all my cinematic work that I thought I should add just a quick section here to make sure we don't forget this often-overlooked art form.

Cinematic storytelling is just as much about what you hear as what you see. In fact, powerful audio can elevate an average sequence into an unforgettable moment. UE5 unsurprisingly, then, provides strong support for audio integration directly within Sequencer, making it easier than ever to synchronize dialogue, music, and sound effects with camera cuts, animations, and visual beats.

"Sound is 50% of the experience." – George Lucas

Adding audio tracks in Sequencer

Sequencer lets you treat sound like a first-class citizen in your cinematic pipeline. You can drag and drop **audio tracks** directly into your Timeline and line them up with character performances, camera shifts, and environmental changes. Here's how to get started:

- **Add audio tracks**: Drop .wav or .cue files into the Timeline for immediate playback and synchronization.

- **Dialogue syncing**: Align character lip sync or facial animation with recorded dialogue using audio waveform previews.

- **Environment matching**: Use attenuation and reverb volumes to spatialize sounds based on the cinematic environment—for instance, a character's voice echoing in a cave versus a clean studio sound.

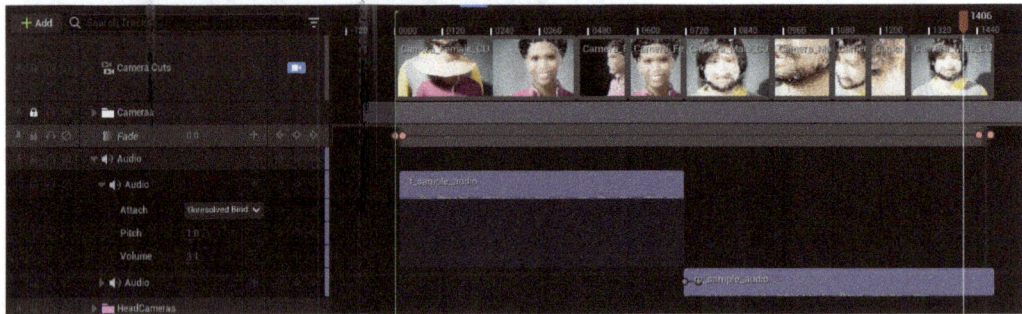

Figure 7.22: How audio tracks look in Sequencer

Sound cues for emotional impact

Music and sound design drive emotional tone, often more than visuals alone. A slow string swell can heighten drama; a sudden percussive beat can intensify tension. In Sequencer, sound cues can be timed precisely to do the following:

- **Match action to music**: Line up music beats with cuts, impact moments, or character actions to amplify rhythm and flow (great for trailers).

- **Foley and ambient layering**: Add subtle environmental details like footsteps, cloth movement, or wind rustle to ground the world in realism.

- **Emotional transitions**: Gradually fade audio or change musical keys to match tonal shifts in the story—melancholy to hopeful, calm to chaotic.

Example

In a hypothetical dramatic standoff scene, the music slowly builds tension as two characters exchange glances. At the moment of the draw, a bass-heavy beat lands exactly with the cut to a close-up, punctuated by a sharp gust of wind and subtle leather creak from the character's movement. The sequence feels powerful, not just because of what you see but because of how you hear it.

With audio and music layered into your cinematics, you now have the tools to engage not just the eyes but the ears—creating sequences that feel complete and emotionally resonant.

Summary

Creating cinematic sequences and cutscenes in UE5 is a powerful intersection of artistry and technical execution. With tools such as Sequencer, Cine Cameras, and MRQ, you have everything you need to bring film-quality storytelling to life in real time.

By applying classic principles of **composition**, **lighting**, **camera movement**, and **pacing**, and combining them with Unreal's rendering features, you can deliver emotionally resonant narratives that stand shoulder-to-shoulder with AAA productions.

Whether you're crafting in-game cutscenes, marketing trailers, or creating full animated shorts, what matters most is intentionality: every frame should serve the story.

Throughout this chapter, we explored the following principles:

- **Sequencer** is your core tool for managing animation, cameras, and scene direction.
- **Cine Cameras** offer deep control over focal length, aperture, and focus to mimic real-world cinematography.
- **Lighting** guides emotion and visual clarity—use it with purpose.
- **MRQ** delivers top-tier visuals with high-resolution output, advanced render passes, and compositing flexibility.
- **Management and planning** are essential—strong scenes start with clear intent and structure.

Mastering these tools and workflows allows you to create cinematic moments that elevate your game's (or film's) narrative and deeply engage your audience on a completely new emotional level.

Further reading

This list of further readings is from other authors under the Packt Publishing label, and a few of my personal recommendations for getting a deeper understanding of both Sequencer in Unreal and the cinematic process. These are meant to aid you in general film theory, camera principles, and so on, to help overlap and elevate your cinematic work within Unreal.

- *Virtual Filmmaking with Unreal Engine 5*: A step-by-step guide to creating a complete animated short film. Read more here: `https://amzn.asia/d/9JS143F`
- *Unreal Engine 5 Character Creation, Animation, and Cinematics*. Read more here: `https://amzn.asia/d/d6Vguf9`
- *Film Theory: An Introduction through the Senses*. Read more here: `https://amzn.asia/d/4TowzqV`
- *Capturing Cinematic Moments: The Art and Science of Motion Picture Cameras and Lenses*. Read more here: `https://amzn.asia/d/gubQxg0`

Subscribe to Game Dev Assembly!

We are excited to introduce **Game Dev Assembly**, our brand-new newsletter dedicated to everything game development. Whether you're coding, designing, animating, or managing a studio, we've got insights, trends, and expert advice to help you create, innovate, and thrive. Sign up now and get exciting benefits.

`https://packt.link/gamedev-newsletter`

Get This Book's PDF Version and Exclusive Extras

UNLOCK NOW

Scan the QR code (or go to packtpub.com/unlock). Search for this book by name, confirm the edition, and then follow the steps on the page.

Note: Keep your invoice handy. Purchases made directly from Packt don't require an invoice.

8

Environment as Narrative and Storytelling

We know by now that game environments are more than some set dressing or a pretty vista; they are carefully crafted designs by which we guide a player to our desired goal. So, while it is important to make sure that the design of an environment always remains readable and consistent from a gameplay perspective, I also believe a well-crafted space needs to do more than provide a visual layer over the design that just looks "pretty"; it needs to say something. It should communicate tone, reveal history, and shape the player's emotional journey without a single word being spoken. In many games, the environment can be, and is, the narrator.

In earlier chapters, we touched on **atmospheric effects**, **lighting**, and **mood-setting**: tools that support a scene's visual storytelling. In this chapter, we'll go further. We'll explore how **space**, **structure**, and **interaction** combine to create environments that *tell* a story, not just support it. This means layering meaning into every architectural decision, every prop placement, and every bit of negative space. It's the art of showing rather than telling, something games can do better than any other medium.

Whether you're building a grand fortress whose collapsed walls hint at a lost war, or a quiet bedroom filled with subtle clues about a character's past, this chapter will guide you in designing spaces that speak, without a single word being uttered. You'll learn how to embed narrative into design and layout, use environmental rhythm to pace a player's journey, and bring intentionality to every piece of visual information.

In this chapter, you will learn:

- How to design game environments that support and tell a story
- Techniques for visual storytelling through architecture, props, and lighting
- How to guide players through emotion and intent using spatial design
- Practical examples of environmental storytelling in Unreal Engine 5
- Advanced-level design best practices that reinforce narrative themes

By the end of this chapter, you'll have the knowledge and practical tools to craft environments that do more than just look good; they'll communicate meaning, mood, and story. You'll have a more advanced understanding, building on what we have discussed previously, of how to lead the player's eye with intent, reinforce narrative arcs through environmental cues, and build emotionally resonant spaces that leave a lasting impression. Whether you're designing quiet, character-driven vignettes or sweeping worlds filled with lore, this chapter will help you create environments that *speak for themselves*.

Technical requirements

To follow along with this chapter, ensure you have:

- Unreal Engine 5.4 or later
- A system with real-time ray tracing support (optional but recommended)
- A solid understanding of the UE Interface
- Some experience with level and environment design
- Read the previous chapters of this book
- Optional: A project with pre-built assets for testing and practice (or start with Unreal's sample projects)

Understanding environmental storytelling

Before we dive into the how, let's take a moment to understand the *why*. **Environmental storytelling** is the art of conveying narrative through space, through what players see, sense, and explore. Unlike cinematic cutscenes or written dialogue, environmental storytelling happens passively, inviting the player to observe, interpret, and emotionally connect with a space on their own terms.

A well-crafted environment doesn't shout its story; it *whispers* it. It invites curiosity and rewards attention. Whether it's a battlefield frozen in time, a vandalized monument, or a cozy room filled with subtle signs of past life, environments can carry emotional weight, worldbuilding depth, and narrative intention.

The language of space

Environments speak a visual language. As designers and artists, our job is to shape that language into meaning.

- **Tone and mood**: Every environment immediately communicates a feeling; this could be foreboding, safety, sadness, or nostalgia. This is done through lighting, palette, architecture, and atmosphere. The moment a player enters a space, their emotional response begins before a word is said.

- **Environmental clues**: Props, clutter, decay, and scale provide context. A dead soldier surrounded by slain aliens would hint at an epic final struggle. A broken door could suggest someone escaped or broke in. These cues add layers of history and make the world feel lived-in and real.

- **Implied narrative**: Sometimes, what's *missing* tells the story. An empty crib, a meal left uneaten, or a deserted town. All of these invite the player to imagine what came before.

> **Use case**
>
> A derelict house with a child's toy still sitting on a bed says more than a cutscene ever could in the same short moment. Without dialogue, we know something happened here. Something sudden, perhaps tragic. It stirs the imagination, allowing the player to connect the dots emotionally.

Now that we've covered the power of space as a narrative tool, let's break it down further by examining the key ingredients that make environmental storytelling truly effective.

Core elements of environmental narrative

With the fundamentals of environmental storytelling covered, let's explore the individual building blocks that bring it to life. Think of each environment as a **composition,** and that every asset placed, every light cast, and every texture aged has narrative potential.

When done well, these elements don't just create visual interest; they build a living, believable world full of untold stories waiting to be discovered. Let's look at some of these *building blocks*.

Architecture as history

Architecture isn't just structural, it's temporal. The way a building is constructed, altered, or damaged can tell a story of the past, often better than dialogue ever could.

- **Design reflects purpose**: Think about how function is embedded in form: industrial complexes are vast and utilitarian, while temples are ornate and reverent. Shape, material choice, and layout all imply a specific cultural or historical role.

- **Wear and decay**: Cracked walls, water damage, collapsed roofs: these visual details hint at the passage of time or catastrophic events. For instance, a fortified bunker overrun by nature implies abandonment, possibly even defeat.

- **Alterations as clues**: Barricaded doorways, makeshift repairs, or new additions built into old architecture can reveal desperation, adaptation, or evolution within the world.

Architecture usually makes up a large majority of an environment, depending on the scene, and its history can be a perfect way to achieve both design and narrative intent. A collapsed pillar could block a door, but make a hole in the wall, providing a way for the player to escape. *Design, art*, and *narrative*, working together!

Props as personal clues

Props are some of the most direct ways to build personal stories into a space. They function like **environmental dialogue**, intimate, silent, and full of character. Let's look at how:

- **Clutter tells a life story**: The way objects are arranged speaks volumes. A messy workbench might tell of an inventor lost in thought; a perfectly arranged dining table might suggest tradition, or obsession.

- **State of objects**: Burned papers, broken glass, or a still-burning candle suggest recent activity or sudden conflict. Use props to subtly reveal events without explicit storytelling.

- **Personal details**: A child's drawing on the wall, a worn-out teddy bear, or a set of keys left on the counter all anchor the environment in humanity. These micro-narratives make players emotionally invest and make a world feel lived in and believable.

Figure 8.1 offers a powerful example of this in action: a crashed plane resting on the ocean floor. The wreckage itself is more than scenery; it immediately tells a story of disaster, loss, and time passed, inviting players to imagine what happened long before they arrived.

*Figure 8.1: Showcasing a crashed plane underwater (asset source: Ocean Floor Environment
by Anil Isbilir | FAB.com)*

These techniques also go hand in hand with the lighting foundations discussed in *Chapter 1* and *Chapter 4*. Here, we extend those principles toward narrative application, crafting scenes where light can be more than visibility; it can be voice, feeling, and story.

Next, let's look at how spatial layout and player movement can also be used to guide emotional responses and reinforce storytelling without words.

Leading the player through the story

Once the core elements of your environment are telling a story, the next step is to guide the player through that narrative in a meaningful and engaging way. This is where **spatial storytelling** and subtle **signposting** become essential tools.

Unlike traditional films or literature, games allow players to move at their own pace, so the challenge lies in crafting environments that gently lead them through narrative beats without forcing direction or breaking immersion. It's important to note that I am not referring to the design of a level; that should be done before this point and tested appropriately, as we have discussed. I am talking about how we can use the environmental story to encourage the player's "want" to move through the level, sparking their curiosity, and so on. So, let's look at how we might achieve that.

Spatial storytelling

The way a player moves through a space can, and should, be a storytelling experience in itself, so how do we achieve this?

- **Narrative unfolding through space**: Design your environments so that the story reveals itself over time, almost like chapters of a book. A charred battlefield leading into a quiet church can tell of a desperate last stand. A broken bridge detouring through an overgrown back alley might shift tone from action to introspection. Games such as *A Plague Tale* are a wonderful example of this.

- **Pacing and discovery**: Think about *when* players learn something, not just *what* they learn. Do they stumble across a reveal early, or is it reserved for a dramatic moment? Use visual layering (foreground, midground, background) to stage narrative reveals based on distance and angle.

- **Control the player's eye**: Guide attention through sightlines, elevation, and motion. If you want players to notice a collapsed statue or a key item, don't place it in a cluttered area; instead, frame it in a way that makes it stand out naturally within the space.

Figure 8.2 shows an in-engine example of the preceding *Control the player's eye* concept, showing a scene designed and lit to clearly show the statue as the key element.

Figure 8.2: An example of spatial storytelling with a stone statue (asset source: Temples of Cambodia by Scans Factory | FAB.com)

Environmental signposting

Good level design nudges the player toward discovery without pointing a neon arrow at it. The goal is to guide without overt instruction or handholding, as we have discussed previously.

- **Drawing the eye with light and contrast**: Use warm tones against cool environments, shafts of light in shadowy interiors, or even movement such as swaying cloth or sparking wires to grab attention. Players are naturally drawn to contrast whether they know it or not.

- **Color as a narrative beacon**: Consistent use of color can build associations. A red banner might mark the path of an enemy faction, while cool blue lighting could indicate safety or technology. These cues help players associate spaces with certain emotional or narrative expectations.

> **Use case**
>
> Have you ever reached a big door in a game, seen a fallen ally nearby, and noticed a pile of green health items on the ground? You probably thought, *"Uh-oh...boss fight!"*
>
> This is a great example of a design signpost as it gives you supplies to get ready, lets you take a breath, and also tells you through the environment narrative that something big is about to happen.

- **Encouraging organic exploration**: Avoid making your guidance too overt. Instead, design scenes where the environment naturally encourages curiosity. A slightly ajar door, a trail of footprints, or a cracked wall with light seeping through all suggest places worth investigating without a single word of dialogue.

> **Use case**
>
> A flickering light in a dark hallway draws the player's eye toward a forgotten side room. Inside, they find a dusty table, scattered papers, and a faded photo. These elements offer a critical backstory that rewards observation without ever forcing interaction.

Now that we've explored how to guide players through narrative space, let's dig deeper into how emotional tone and environmental symbolism can be layered in to add further meaning to your scenes.

Environmental layers and discovery

Once the player is moving through your world with intention, the next layer of storytelling comes from what they discover *along the way*. A truly rich environment offers depth, subtle narrative threads hidden in corners, small details that reward curiosity, and changes that reflect the passage of time or consequence.

These layers create a world that feels alive, reactive, believable, and filled with meaning just below the surface. Let's look at adding these layers and how we can influence player curiosity.

Designing for player curiosity

Environmental storytelling is most effective when it doesn't shout but *gently invites*. Think of your level as a canvas, and every extra detail as an invitation for the player to lean in and connect the dots.

- **Layered detail for explorers**: Great environments reward those who look more closely. A cluttered desk may reveal a scientist's obsession, providing more context for the character, or a trail of blood might lead to a forgotten bunker. These quiet moments don't need to be essential to gameplay, but they deepen the world for players who are paying attention.
- **Secondary worldbuilding**: Use props, overheard conversations, graffiti, broken-down machines, and time-of-day changes to tell stories in the background. Even something as subtle as a half-eaten meal or a recently extinguished fire can hint at recent activity, loss, or life interrupted.
- **Environmental dialogue**: You don't always need an NPC to tell the story. A smashed vending machine next to a scavenged backpack tells us about desperation. A shrine built under a broken statue might hint at reverence for a fallen figure. This is storytelling without exposition; let the scene speak for itself.

World-state changes as storytelling

A powerful way to deepen narrative impact is to let your digital world *respond*. This expands on the dynamic systems we explored in *Chapter 6*, adaptive environments, but with a stronger narrative intent.

- **Player impact made visible**: Let the environment reflect the consequences of the player's actions. If a player chooses to help a town early in the game, show it thriving later, with windows repaired, gardens blooming, and children playing. If they ignore it, the same town might become desolate or overrun. Check out **Obsidian's** *Avowed* for some wonderful examples of this.

- **Storytelling over time**: Environmental changes can also be paced slowly. Maybe a settlement becomes more militarized as tensions rise, or a city slowly succumbs to a spreading infection. Use evolving visuals to support long-form narrative arcs.

With the world now layered with systems to encourage player curiosity, we are really starting to see the concepts of our world coming together; but there is one final piece of this puzzle we should discuss, and that is usually what makes the really memorable moments in games—**story beats** and **set pieces**! Anyone who's played any *Call of Duty* campaign knows what I am talking about here!

Environmental story beats and set pieces

With so much solid narrative foundation, let's explore one last key principle: how to use environments to deliver *highly impactful narrative* moments—what we call environmental **story beats**. These are the climactic, emotional, or revealing moments where the player learns something meaningful purely through the world itself.

Great environments are immersive at the core, but I find the truly incredible ones have something else; they're *memorable*. These moments of clarity or emotion are often built into the world itself, without the need for exposition or dialogue.

- **Set pieces**: A *set piece* is a bespoke space designed to serve a specific narrative or emotional function. This might be a ruined temple that reveals the game's core mystery, or a cozy cabin that humanizes a long-forgotten character. These areas often feature unique architecture, lighting, music cues, or interactable elements that reinforce their significance.
- **Pacing**: Storytelling through environments doesn't always need to be loud or dramatic. In fact, contrast is key. A silent, untouched bedroom in the middle of a war zone can be just as powerful as a collapsing tower. Think about how these **beats** land within the flow of the game, and reserve your most powerful reveals for moments when the player has space to absorb them.

Use case

Game studio **Naughty Dog** is a master of this kind of narrative moment, with games from their hit series *Uncharted* basically being built entirely of awesome set pieces, and so on. I highly recommend playing this series or at least YouTubing a walkthrough to see how *Naughty Dog* weaves narrative into every aspect of its games—the environment especially.

Figure 8.3 shows a screenshot from *Uncharted 4*, showcasing the team's exceptional use of all the environmental principles we have just discussed.

Figure 8.3: Screenshot from Uncharted 4 showcasing environmental principles (image source: Cave Descent by Matt Morgan | Uncharted 4 ©Sony Computer Entertainment | ArtStation.com)

Tip

Treat your environment like a character in its own right. It should have an emotional arc, rising action, reveals, and reflection, mirroring the player's journey. Ask yourself: "What does this space feel like? What does it reveal now that it didn't before?"

With the world now brimming with *story beats*, layered with hidden meaning and reactive systems, set up with guidance and signposts, and bolstered by the core principles of environmental narrative, we have covered the important foundational theory behind what makes a great environmental story. So now, let's explore what this book is all about: how we can achieve all this in Unreal!

Building a narrative space in UE5

Once you've crafted the narrative intention behind your environment, it's time to bring that story to life using Unreal Engine 5's powerful suite of tools. In this section, we'll break down some workflows and techniques that will help you translate abstract narrative goals into concrete, explorable spaces.

Practical workflow in Unreal

UE5 enables highly modular and iterative world-building, while still supporting deeply layered storytelling. Whether you're working solo or as part of a team, the following techniques can help you maintain both consistency and narrative depth across your project.

Modular kits for narrative architecture

Modular construction is not just about efficiency; it's also a great storytelling tool. As we discussed in *Chapter 6*, **kits** or **Blueprints** can radically improve work output, and by designing and using reusable components that carry visual storytelling detail, you can build environments that feel authentic and lived-in, relatively easily.

Here are some workflow tips:

- Design modular pieces with wear-and-tear variants:
  - Create alternate versions of walls, floors, and doors: clean, cracked, burned, reinforced, and so on.
  - Use Material instances or decal layers to swap damage types procedurally.
- Assemble rooms with historical context in mind:
  - Ask questions while placing: "Was this space fortified? Was it looted? Did someone hide here?"
  - Show evidence of repurposing (e.g., dining hall turned into a medical triage room).
- Add narrative signifiers subtly:
  - A barricaded door might hint at a previous threat.
  - A pristine hallway in a ruined base suggests someone is still maintaining it

Tip

Use the **Merge Actors** tool once a section is complete to optimize performance while preserving story geometry.

Figure 8.4 shows where to access the **Merge** tool and some key settings to consider.

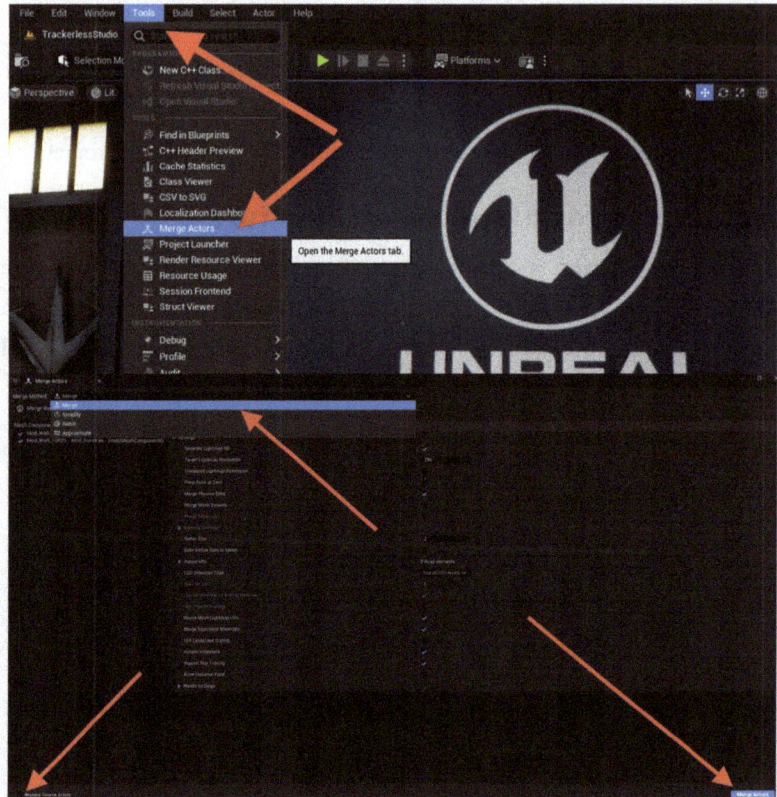

Figure 8.4: Screenshot of Merge tool in UE5

Blueprint-driven prop placement systems

Blueprints can massively streamline set dressing while adding narrative richness—especially in larger environments where hand-placement becomes unsustainable.

Here are step-by-step instructions for randomized prop placement in Blueprints:

1. Create a new Actor Blueprint (e.g., `BP_PropScatterer`).
2. Add a **Static Mesh Array** variable for your props (books, mugs, tools, etc.).

3. Use **Construction Script** to do the following:

    a. Loop through a defined area (Box Volume or grid).

    b. Randomly spawn props from the array using the **Add Static Mesh** component.

    c. Offset transform and rotation with randomness to avoid uniformity.

    d. Use tags or exposed variables such as **Clutter Level** to tune density.

4. Add logic for environment-aware placement:

    a. Use traces or collision checks to detect valid surfaces.

    b. Trigger higher clutter near damaged areas or story-critical actors.

5. Optimize using **Instanced Static Mesh** components if you're placing high numbers of props.

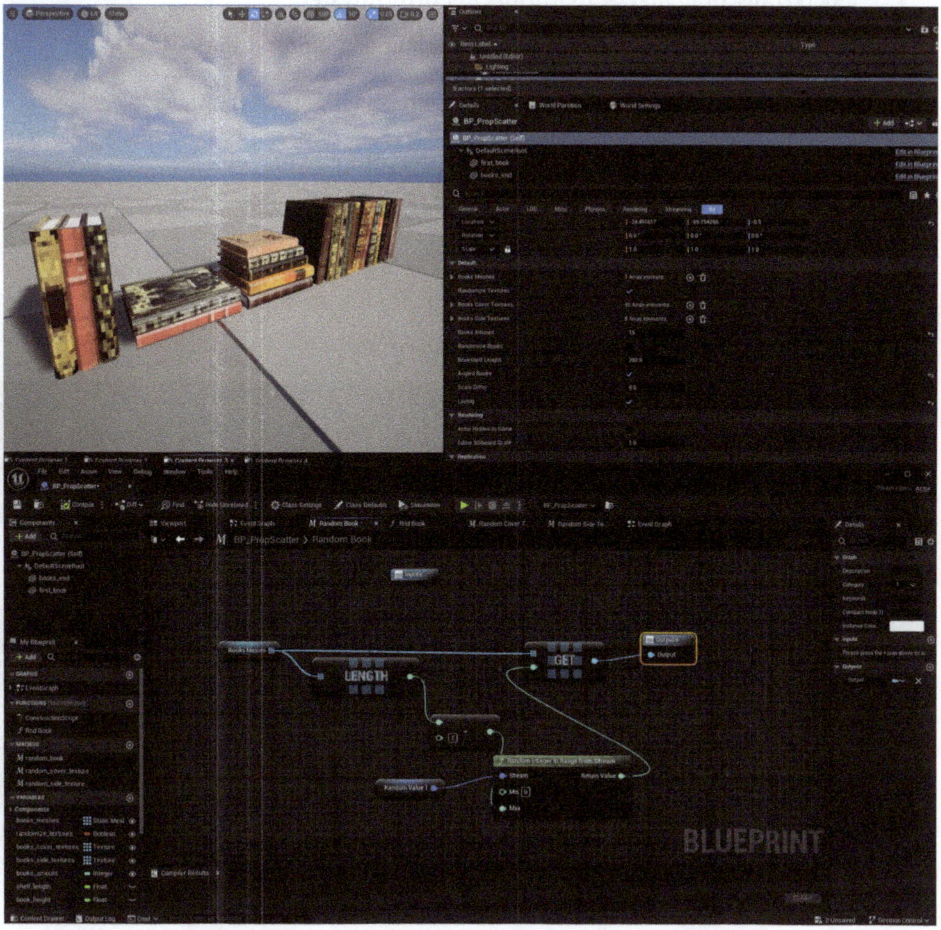

Figure 8.5: Screenshot of a Book Scattering Blueprint in UE5

> **More information**
>
> Check out *Populate Books* by RadbarZaremba on the Fab marketplace for a great example of a prop placement Blueprint.

Spline tools for organic storytelling elements

Splines are ideal for injecting dynamic, non-grid storytelling elements such as cables, vines, or trails of destruction.

Some use cases are as follows:

- Power cables and piping in industrial or sci-fi spaces
- Blood trails, drag marks, footprints in horror/mystery
- Vines or overgrowth in abandoned or reclaimed environments

Here are step-by-step instructions on adding spline-based story elements:

1. Create a new Actor Blueprint with a **Spline** component.
2. Add a **Spline Mesh** component using your mesh (e.g., vine segment or cable).
3. Expose parameters such as segment mesh, random scale, or material.
4. Add logic for adapting to surroundings or environment states.
5. Place and edit control points for organic layout.

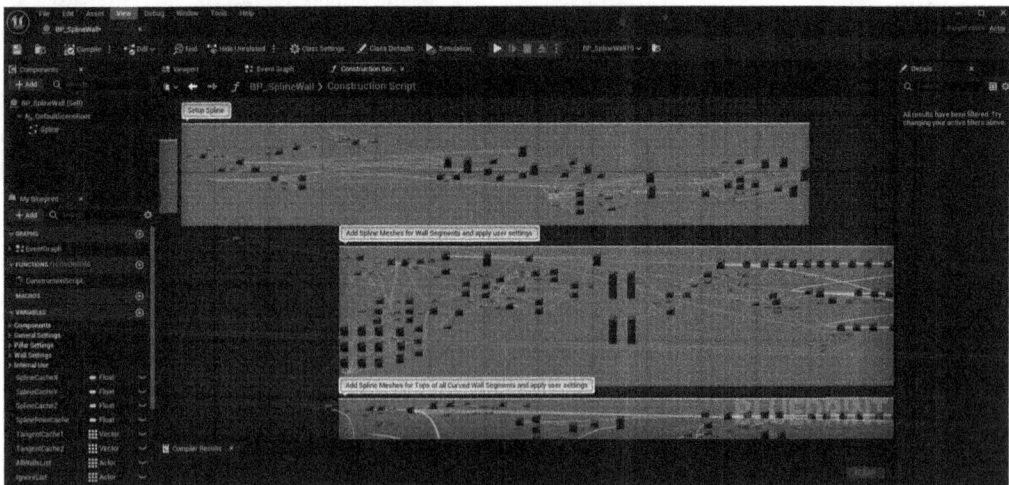

Figure 8.6: Screenshot of a more complex Wall Spline Blueprint in UE5

> **Thread**
>
> Check out *Procedural Spline Walls System* by Karl Mullera on the Fab marketplace for a great example of a spline system.

Handcrafted asset placement and set dressing

While modular workflows and Blueprint tools are powerful for scalability and consistency, there's no substitute for good old-fashioned artistic placement when it comes to scene polish and emotional storytelling.

Sometimes, the best way to tell a story is to manually place each object with intention. This can communicate human presence, emotional weight, or cinematic staging far more effectively than procedural methods alone. My suggestion? Use both. Start with procedural placement and then refine manually afterwards with the more *important* details.

Follow these best practices for manual placement:

- **Work in narrative layers:** Start with structural or architectural elements, then add narrative props (e.g., overturned chairs, packed bags, unfinished meals), and finish with micro-details such as dust, papers, or light shafts.
- **Use asset scale and orientation to guide emotion:** A crooked portrait, a chair turned away from the door, or scattered medication on a counter can all silently reinforce character moments.
- **Use negative space intentionally:** Sometimes what isn't placed is just as powerful. A lone photo frame on an empty shelf can raise more questions than a fully decorated wall.

> **Tip**
>
> It's often worth setting aside dedicated time for final pass dressing; this is where emotion lives.

Quick refresher: placing assets in UE5

This is an advanced book; I've assumed a lot of you and expected you to have a general idea of how to use Unreal already. So, I'll assume you're already familiar with dragging assets from the Content Browser into the Level Editor, using the **Translate, Rotate,** and **Scale** tools, and working with **Snapping** for precision. However, here are a few power tips:

- Use *Alt + drag* to quickly duplicate and scatter variations
- Use the **Foliage** tool for organic asset painting (works well for debris or rubble)
- Use **Hierarchical Instanced Static Meshes (HISM)** when repeating detailed clutter for performance
- Group or parent items (*Ctrl + G*) for cleaner scene management

Figure 8.7 is a fun image to include as it is a screenshot from my upcoming indie game, *Primordials Legends: Hollow Hero*. I am adding it here as I think it shows well how both procedural and hand-placed disciplines can co-exist, with background elements such as plants being procedurally placed, and key design and narrative elements such as the creature, statue, and mushrooms being manually placed.

Figure 8.7: Screenshot showcasing the use of procedural and manual set dressing in "Primordials Legends: Hollow Hero"

With these practical workflows in place, you're ready to push narrative meaning even deeper, using some traditionally cinematic tools in unique and interesting ways.

Real-time storytelling tools in UE5

Cutscenes and cinematics are awesome. I love watching and making them, and they absolutely have a unique place in game development, but in many cases, the most impactful moments can be the ones that unfold dynamically, as the player explores, observes, and uncovers pieces of the narrative organically. UE5 offers a great toolkit for creating these kinds of in-world moments (some we have already explored) that preserve immersion while still delivering dramatic narrative beats.

Cinematics versus environmental moments

Not every narrative needs to be tightly choreographed. Knowing when to use Sequencer and when to let the player drive the moment is key to pacing and immersion.

Use Sequencer in the following situations:

- You need *precise control* over the camera, animation, VFX, and timing.
- You want a *guaranteed emotional beat*, like a character death or revelation.
- You're delivering a *cinematic transition*, flashback, or cutscene (see *Chapter 7* for full Sequencer workflows).

Use in-world triggers in the following situations:

- You want to *maintain player control*.
- You want the player to feel like *they discovered something*.
- The moment is *contextual* or reactive—light reveals, sound cues, or environmental shifts.

> **Tip**
>
> In some cases, you can actually use Sequencer to achieve an in-world moment—simply build the sequence as you imagine, and then remove the camera! That way, the player can move freely, but the actions of your Sequencer scene will still play out.

In my game, *Hollow Hero*, we use triggers placed on the player path to activate environmental moments that are sequencers in nature. You can see an example of a highlighted trigger and its placement in *Figure 8.8*.

Figure 8.8: Screenshot showcasing the use of in-world narrative triggers in "Primordials Legends: Hollow Hero"

Let's put the idea of the preceding trigger system into practice by walking through the step-by-step process of creating story events directly in your world.

Creating in-world story events step by step in UE5

Here's how to set up a *real-time narrative reveal* using Blueprint and level elements.

Imagine the following scenario: "The Sealed Door Reveal."

The player opens a sealed blast door. Lights flicker on. A distant sound echoes. A blood trail is revealed.

Here's the step-by-step setup:

1. Place a Trigger Box in front of the door.

2. In the Level Blueprint or Actor Blueprint, do the following:

   a. Use **OnActorBeginOverlap** to detect the player.

3. Trigger a series of events:

   a. Play *a light-flicker timeline* using **Set Intensity** or **Set Visibility** on point lights.

   b. Use **Play Sound at Location** to emit a scream or machinery noise.

   c. Have a pre-placed decal Actor (e.g., blood trail).

    d.   Optional: Temporarily lock doors behind the player to focus attention forward.

    e.   dd a cinematic camera that briefly triggers with a blend if you want to emphasize a key reveal but return to player control quickly.

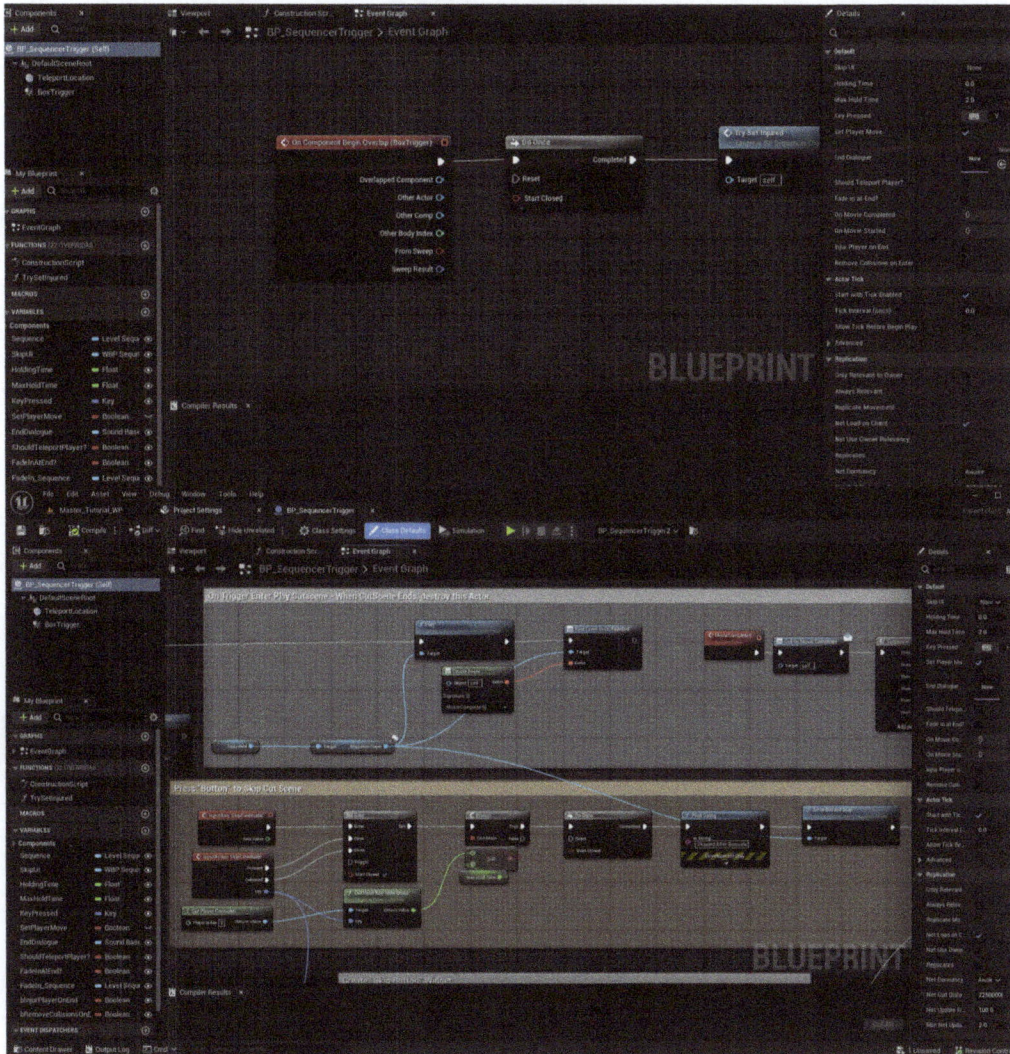

Figure 8.9: Screenshot of some key elements in setting up a trigger-based event Blueprint in Unreal

Now that you've built a story event end to end, let's use **Data Layers** and **Level Streaming** to control when, where, and for whom it appears.

Using Data Layers and Level Streaming

UE5's **Data Layers** and **Level Streaming** tools allow environments to evolve based on player actions, creating powerful narrative shifts without cutscenes or loading screens. We'll touch on this again in *Chapter 11*, but let's go over the basics.

Data Layers (for state-based variation)

Use **Data Layers** to hold different versions of the same space: intact versus destroyed, dark versus lit, peaceful versus hostile.

Here's the workflow:

1. Open the **Data Layers** panel in the Level Editor.
2. Assign actors to specific data layers (e.g., Hideout_Clean, Hideout_Destroyed).
3. In **Blueprint** or **Level Blueprint**, do the following

     a. Use **SetDataLayerVisibility** or **ActivateDataLayerByLabel** at runtime based on story progression.

4. Combine with trigger volumes to swap layers when a player returns to a space.

Level Streaming (for spatial or memory efficiency)

Use **Level Streaming** to control what parts of your environment are loaded in or out based on player location or story triggers.

Here's the step-by-step workflow:

1. Divide your level into *streamable sub-levels* (e.g., Hideout_Calm, Hideout_Destroyed).
2. In the Level Blueprint or **World Partition** settings, define streaming logic:

     a. Load/unload using **Load Stream Level** and **Unload Stream Level**.
     b. Use player overlap or trigger volumes to initiate.

3. Consider using Blueprint Interfaces to coordinate transitions from multiple systems, lighting, audio, and FX—at the same time.

> **Tip**
>
> Streaming is especially valuable for large, memory-heavy maps where you want to change visuals and tone without full reloads. However, you may need to use HLODs to make sure key assets (such as a large tower) are always visible from a distance.

Figure 8.10 shows how to convert non-world partition maps using Unreal's simple and easy-to-use tool.

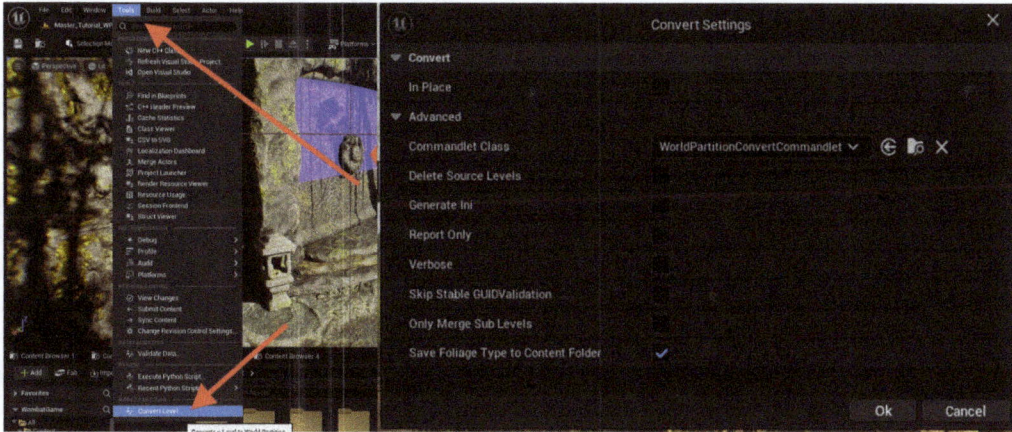

Figure 8.10: Accessing a level for World Partition and recommended settings

Be careful when converting large existing maps, as data (such as Blueprints) can be lost in translation!

Now let's look at a practical workflow about returning to a changed (edited) space to see how these techniques play out in action.

Example workflow: returning to a changed space

For this example, imagine the following scenario: The player returns to a previously safe base, only to find it now ruined and abandoned.

We will apply the following narrative impact techniques:

- **Data Layers**: Activate damaged props, flickering lights, graffiti, or ambient FX (dust, sparks).
- **Level Streaming**: Unload the peaceful version and load the damaged one seamlessly.
- **Audio Cues**: Replace ambient music with ominous wind or silence.
- **Lighting Shifts**: Change warm lighting to cold blue tones using exposed parameters on Light Actors.

Here's the implementation stack for these techniques:

1. Trigger Zone → Blueprint Logic → Activate new Data Layer or Streamed Level.

> **Thread**
>
> Check out **Epic's** *Valley of the Ancient Free Demo* for excellent examples of the preceding use of Data Layers—and then hop on YouTube for a breakdown. There are lots of excellent tutorials under the search *Changing Environments with Data Layers in UE5* that you can follow for a greater understanding of how to change spaces dynamically.

2. Change Post Process → Adjust lighting or apply lens FX (e.g., desaturation).

3. Play ambient soundscape → Fade in low hum, distant echoes, water drips.

4. Enable new decals, VFX → Blood smears, flickering signs, broken furniture.

> **Tip**
>
> These changes are more powerful when the player remembers what the space once felt like; don't overplay them in earlier passes.

Figure 8.11 shows how a scene can change from a familiar and safe room on a ship that the player can come to know, and then later how it is destroyed in an attack, with blood scattered on the walls for dramatic effect, and to show the intensity of the conflict.

Figure 8.11: The before and after of a space after an attack on the ship (asset source: Modular Scifi Bundle by Jonathan Frederick | FAB.com)

With these real-time tools and storytelling techniques, you can now build narrative spaces that evolve, respond, and *stick* with the player—all without breaking immersion. Next, let's have a quick look at the other side of the environmental narrative coin, audio.

Environmental audio as storytelling

I've said it before, and I'll say it again, **sound** is one of the most underrated tools in storytelling, but when used with intention, it becomes a powerful narrative layer. In UE5, audio is not just background texture; it's an active participant in setting tone, hinting at past events, and guiding emotional response. Let's explore how sound can speak volumes.

Telling stories through sound

Well-placed audio reinforces the story being told through space and visuals. Use it to create tension, suggest activity, or communicate something just out of view.

- **Ambient loops**: Wind howling through broken windows, distant thunder, or mechanical hums can reinforce tone and suggest location.
- **Diegetic sound**: In-world audio sources such as radios, flickering lights, footsteps in a quiet hallway, or dripping water provide realism and narrative hints. What's making that sound? Why is it still playing?

These sonic elements help the player *feel* a space's story before they fully *see* it. Let's see how we can add sound in UE5.

Adding audio to a level in UE5

Here is a quick step-by-step on how to get some audio into your environment. I'm by no means an expert in this field, but these steps alone will help get a great sense of sound in any environment.

1. Import your audio:

   a. Go to the Content Browser.

   b. Right-click and choose **Import to /YourFolder/**.

   c. Select your `.wav`.

   UE will convert it into a Sound Wave asset.

2. Create a Sound Cue (recommended for flexibility):

    a. Right-click the imported sound and select **Create Cue.**

    b. Open the new **Sound Cue** asset:

        a. Add nodes such as **Modulator**, **Random**, or **Looping** to create variation or control playback.

        b. Connect the nodes to **Output.**

> **Tip**
>
> Use Sound Cues instead of raw Sound Waves for more control (e.g., randomized ambiance, volume modulation, etc.).

3. Place audio in the level:

    a. Drag your Sound Cue into the level viewport.

    b. It creates a Sound Cue Actor in the world.

4. Set sound properties:

    a. With the Sound Cue Actor selected, in the **Details** panel, do the following:

        a. **Auto Activate: ON** (if it should play when the level loads).

        b. **Looping: ON** (for ambient loops).

    b. **Attenuation Settings:** Use or create an **Attenuation** asset to control falloff, spatial blend, and range.

5. Trigger audio with Blueprints (optional for events):

    a. Use a Trigger Box to detect player overlap.

    b. In the Level Blueprint or a custom Actor Blueprint, do the following:

        a. Use **Play Sound at Location** or **Play Sound Attached** to trigger one-shots or ambient loops.

        b. Add delays, fade-ins, or logic based on player progression or environment state.

With the basics of adding audio to UE5 under our belt, let's now move on to something advanced.

Advanced audio techniques for storytelling

Beyond dialogue and music, audio can be shaped in powerful ways to support storytelling. By using tools such as reverb, filters, and audio volumes, you can make sound react to spaces and situations, deepening immersion and reinforcing the player's emotional experience.

- **Reverb volumes**: Add to rooms to simulate acoustic spaces (e.g., echo in caves)
- **Audio volumes**: Dynamically adjust ambient mixes across zones
- **EQ and filters**: Use Blueprint logic to change how sound is perceived (e.g., muffled underwater)

Figure 8.12 shows a simple setup I use regularly to achieve basic randomization in sound. This setup is especially good for general foley or storm sounds.

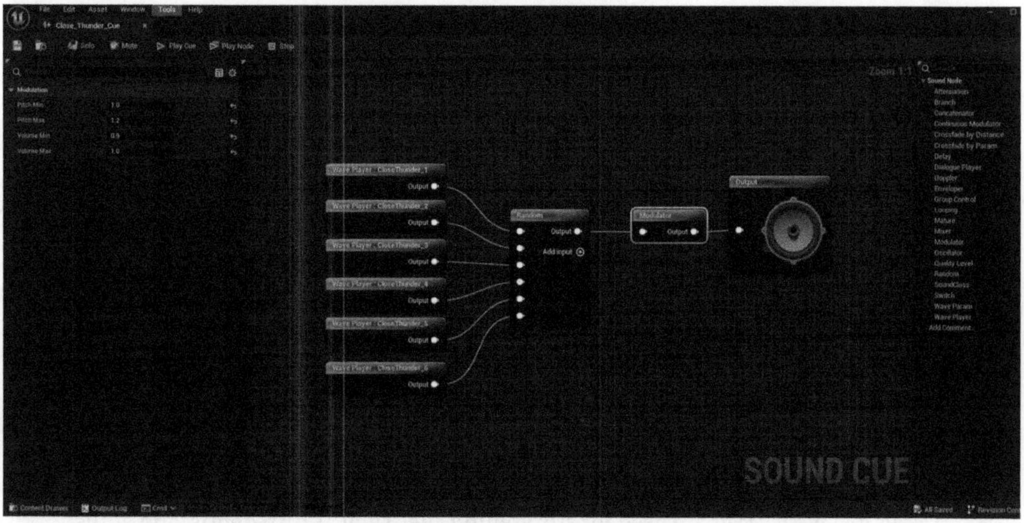

Figure 8.12: Screenshot of a Sound Cue randomizer for lightning

Next, we'll go through a case study that brings all the principles we have discussed together into a single cohesive environment.

Case study: Telling a story through space

To bring all these principles together, let's look at a practical example of how space can be designed to *communicate narrative* without dialogue or cutscenes. This case study demonstrates how atmosphere, layout, lighting, and prop placement can guide a player through an emotionally rich experience told entirely through the environment.

The abandoned apartment

Set in a long-abandoned building that is becoming overcome with ever-encroaching plant life, this abandoned apartment was once home to a family who loved football. Now, it stands silent, *a visual autopsy of what could have gone wrong.*

Environmental narrative highlights

- A **football** deflated and with plants growing out of it shows a valued possession that was left behind.
- A **table** covered in clutter from the old family, and maybe a mix from new people who camped here for a while.
- A **collapsed roof** caused by the event, or the result of no upkeep? For the player to decide or discover.
- The **absence** of human life is deliberate, leaving players to imagine the final moments themselves.

Narrative flow

1. The player enters through a broken door and gradually explores the apartment.
2. Environmental storytelling unfolds *sequentially*—as they move through the space, more of the building collapses, providing new areas to explore.
3. Small discoveries—*an uneaten meal, a deflated football, a cooking pot over rubble*—build an emotional arc, showing multiple stories in a single scene.

Development notes

- *Decals and mesh decals* are used for storytelling cues such as dirt, debris, and spills.
- *VFX* (subtle dust motes) support mood and visibility hierarchy.
- *Blueprint interactions* drive story beats:
    - Walls crumble when approached.
    - Wind blows in response to player proximity.

Environmental audio shifts dynamically to reflect deeper story layers.

Figure 8.13 depicts a scene from the case study:

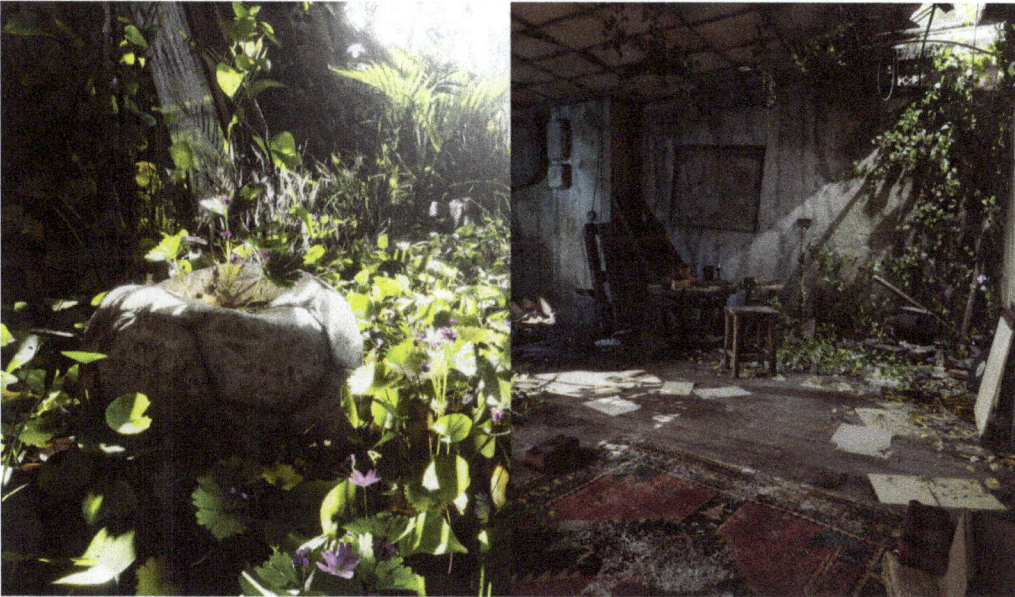

Figure 8.13: Screenshot of the above-mentioned case-study (asset source: Megascans Abandoned Apartment by Quixel | FAB.com)

As we've seen, great storytelling through space is as much about *what you choose to show* as it is about *how you reveal it*. Let's close this chapter with a few guiding principles to keep your narrative environments grounded, emotional, and impactful.

Best practices for environmental narrative design

Designing narrative-rich environments requires more than visual polish; it demands clear intent, restraint, and a deep understanding of how players absorb story through space. These best practices serve as some final guiding principles for building emotionally resonant, story-driven levels in Unreal Engine 5.

- *Build narrative goals into your blockout*: Don't wait until the polish phase to think about storytelling. From your very first geometry, identify what story each area is meant to tell. Is this a place of safety, loss, mystery, or tension?

- *Avoid "lore clutter"*: Every environmental detail should have a purpose. Too many notes, props, or disconnected details can overwhelm or dilute your story. Focus on meaningful objects and story signals.

- *Think like a cinematographer*: Consider how players will approach, view, and move through a space. Use composition, leading lines, and silhouette to guide the eye and emphasize narrative elements. The camera may be player-controlled, but your design still frames the experience.

- *Balance clarity with mystery*: Great environmental storytelling often invites curiosity. Don't explain everything outright; create visual questions. Let players infer and imagine the rest. This builds emotional investment and rewards exploration.

- *Create a short checklist*: Before finalizing a narrative space, do the following:

    - What is the emotional goal of this area?

    - What does the environment tell the player that the dialogue or UI does not?

    - Is anything redundant or visually noisy?

    - Will a player remember this space?

To wrap up, let's reflect on how all of these techniques combine into a complete storytelling toolkit, and how you can continue to evolve your approach as your project grows.

Summary

Environmental storytelling is one of the most powerful and immersive tools in a developer's toolkit. When used with care and purpose, it transforms static scenes into dynamic narratives, allowing players to engage with the world on their own terms. It's not about telling them what happened; it's about letting them *discover* it.

From architectural choices and lighting to spatial pacing and reactive environments, every element can serve the story. Whether your world whispers its history through a shattered picture frame or shouts it from a crumbling skyline, remember: in great level design, the environment is never just a backdrop, it's the storyteller.

Throughout this chapter, we explored the following principles:

- **Tell the story through space, not just the script**: Every object, light, and corner has the potential to communicate narrative.

- **Use Unreal Engine's toolset to craft rich, reactive worlds**: From Blueprints and data layers to sound cues and visual effects, UE5 empowers environmental storytelling.

- **Plan with emotion, design with intention**: Think beyond layout; focus on feeling. Build scenes that resonate, surprise, and invite players to ask questions.

When combining these tools with strategies from other chapters in this book, you will begin to have a full "big picture" overview of how to approach stories within your own projects and be able to create story moments that elevate your game's environments in a way that will stick with gamers forever.

Further reading

This list of further reading is from other authors under the Packt Publishing label, and a few of my personal recommendations for getting a deeper understanding of both 3D design in Unreal and general storytelling. These are a bit old at this point now, but still absolutely solid reads for anyone serious about environmental storytelling within Unreal and beyond.

- *3D Game Design with Unreal Engine 4 and Blender.* Read more here: `https://amzn.asia/d/eyVBBfE`

- *Video Game Storytelling: What Every Developer Needs to Know about Narrative Techniques.* Read more here: `https://amzn.asia/d/j2GVnAA`

- *Procedural Storytelling in Game Design.* Read more here: `https://amzn.asia/d/4AF51yf`

Subscribe to Game Dev Assembly!

We are excited to introduce **Game Dev Assembly**, our brand-new newsletter dedicated to everything game development. Whether you're coding, designing, animating, or managing a studio, we've got insights, trends, and expert advice to help you create, innovate, and thrive. Sign up now and get exciting benefits.

`https://packt.link/gamedev-newsletter`

Join our community on Discord

Join our community's Discord space for discussions with the authors and other readers:

`https://packt.link/unrealengine`

9

Adaptive Cutscenes and Interactive Paths

Cutscenes have long been a pillar of narrative delivery in games, but traditionally, they've served as fixed, passive moments. They pause gameplay to deliver a story to the player. But modern storytelling, especially in narrative-rich or choice-driven experiences, can often demand more.

With UE5, you can design cutscenes that are *contextual*, that react to who the player is, what they've done, and where they are in the world. These are called **adaptive cutscenes**, and they transform passive storytelling into active engagement. Whether the player's moral choices shape which character appears in a scene or their inventory status alters the pacing of a cinematic event, UE5 gives you the tools to make storytelling deeply personal.

You can even go further, blending **player-controlled moments**, **triggered environmental reveals**, and **branching dialogue paths** into your cinematic structure. Adaptive storytelling isn't just about *choosing your own adventure*; it's about *reflecting the state of the world to the player* in subtle, emotionally resonant ways.

This chapter picks up where *Chapter 8* left off and also draws techniques and principles from a few other previous chapters by diving into *how to make those moments dynamic*, without losing immersion or creative control.

In this chapter, you will learn about the following:

- How to build branching cutscenes using Sequencer and Blueprint
- How to create in-game events that respond to player choices or world states
- Best practices for blending cinematic storytelling with player control

- How to use UE5 tools such as Actor tags to make cutscenes dynamic
- Practical techniques for adaptive camera transitions, shot logic, and seamless integration

Now that we've framed what cutscenes can be, and what we'll cover to empower you to make them interactive and reactive, let's begin by building a solid foundation. We'll cover some *terminology*: these definitions will be essential before we dive further into the chapter. Let's get started!

Technical requirements

To follow along with this chapter, ensure you have:

- Unreal Engine 5.4 or later
- A system with real-time ray tracing support (optional but recommended)
- A solid understanding of the Unreal Engine interface
- Some experience with Level and environment design
- Read the previous chapters of this book
- Optional: A project with pre-built assets for testing and practice (or start with Unreal's sample projects)

A note on terminology: Cutscenes versus cinematics

Before we go deeper into adaptive storytelling, it's important to clarify a distinction I make throughout this book, particularly between **cutscenes** and **cinematics**. While many developers (and players) use these terms interchangeably, I intentionally draw a line between them based on context, purpose, and production style.

When I refer to *cinematics*, especially in *Chapter 7*, I'm typically referring to high-quality, often pre-rendered sequences, trailers, marketing assets, or scripted scenes that emphasize polished animation, high-end lighting, and film-grade visuals. These are usually tightly orchestrated and follow more traditional filmmaking principles, even if rendered in real time.

On the other hand, *cutscenes*, as I define them, are built using similar tools but are more directly integrated into gameplay. They often *cut* from live player control but use the in-game world, real-time characters, and runtime lighting, VFX, and performance optimizations. Cutscenes tend to prioritize seamlessness and immersion, allowing storytelling to occur without disrupting the flow of play.

With modern game technology, especially in UE5, the visual gap between the two is shrinking fast. The fidelity of real-time rendering means that many in-game cutscenes rival cinematic sequences in quality. However, I still find it useful to separate them conceptually:

- **Cinematics**: Tightly crafted, often higher-budget scenes focused on presentation, some-times detached from player agency.

- **Cutscenes**: In-world, gameplay-adjacent sequences that are more flexible and reactive to player-driven events.

It's also worth noting that in Unreal, both experiences are typically built using **Sequencer** and act more like a timeline or container for visual storytelling. Sequencer refers to the type of file and system, not the style or fidelity of the scene. Whether you're creating a cinematic intro or a reactive mid-game cutscene, it's likely all happening within Sequencer.

Understanding this distinction will help as we move forward, particularly in this chapter, where we focus on adaptive cutscenes that respond to our players' actions and game state, built on top of the very same tools introduced in earlier chapters.

Now, with the semantics out of the way, let's dive into **adaptive cutscenes**, pushing the advanced features of your project. It all starts with how we *think* about a cutscene.

> **Important note**
>
> In this chapter, we'll be using the *Chapter 6* strategy again—**threads**! Again, I'll provide suggested paths for you to explore further in your own study. For example, if I say, *"Here are some threads to follow,"* try Googling the listed topics to discover insights that go beyond what we can cover in a single chapter. This chapter relies on a lot of code support, so keep that in mind when reading this chapter.

Rethinking the cutscene

Cutscenes are often seen as the non-playable rewards for reaching key points in a game. In tra-ditional pipelines, they're locked sequences, animated, voiced, and framed with precision, but ultimately disconnected from gameplay. No matter how you arrived at that moment, the cutscene plays out the same way. While this approach can absolutely deliver polish and control, for the most part, it doesn't reflect the interactivity that defines games as a medium.

But what if your cutscenes could respond? What if they could feel *aware* of what the player did, how the world has changed, or even how the player is feeling?

What is an adaptive cutscene?

An **adaptive cutscene** is designed to adjust based on gameplay context, player choices, or dynamic variables tracked during play.

This doesn't always mean complex branching logic or dialogue trees. Sometimes, the most impactful adaptivity is subtle:

- **Camera shifts** when the player's health is critical, as well as tight framing, hand-held shakes, or desaturated LUTs.

- **Facial expressions or character tones** that change based on earlier choices: supportive, suspicious, or even silent.

- **Environmental changes** reflected mid-cutscene, such as dynamic lighting shifts or storm systems rolling in during a character's speech.

- **Custom assets** can change based on what weapons or items the player has on them, and they can appear in the cutscene.

- **Custom characters** can go even further, where the player can change their appearance at will in the game. This is a form of adaptation for a cutscene.

These adaptive layers make the story feel personal, like it's *acknowledging* the player's journey.

Adaptive cutscenes in practice

Let's break down a few ways you can introduce adaptivity into an otherwise-linear scene:

Scenario	Adaptive Technique	Tools Used
Player arrives at a village in different conditions (day/night, rain/clear)	Change sky, lighting, and NPC behavior in cinematic	Data Layers, Blueprint triggers
A character reacts differently if they were previously saved or ignored	Alternate animations or dialogue tracks	Sequencer variants + Blueprint switches
Show unique camera angles based on stealth approach or loud combat	Use Sub-Sequences and conditional camera triggers	Sequencer + game variable query

Table 9.1: A table showing a hypothetical scenario, a respective adaptive technique, and the tools used to achieve the technique

Tip

Even a 10-second camera tilt or voice inflection change can make a scene feel hand-crafted for the player.

Now that we have looked at cutscenes from a different perspective, in order to create these moments, we first need a strong cinematic foundation. In the next section, we'll revisit how to build a flexible cutscene in Sequencer and lay the groundwork for branching logic and runtime variation.

Let's build the baseline before we make it dynamic.

Foundations: Building a Sequencer-driven scene

Before we can create dynamic, reactive cinematics, we first need a solid cinematic foundation. In UE5, Sequencer is the primary tool for crafting in-game cutscenes, from simple camera pans to full dialogue scenes with animation, audio, and lighting control.

If you've already worked through *Chapter 7*, much of this will be familiar. But here, we'll revisit a few key Sequencer techniques with a specific focus on *preparing your scenes for interactivity and adaptation*.

Sequencer refresher

Here's a quick overview of the core steps for building a cinematic in UE5 using Sequencer:

1. Create a new Level Sequence:

    a. Open your **Level** and go to **Cinematics | Add Level Sequence**.

    b. Name and save your sequence asset.

    c. Drag it into the Level or attach it to a Level Blueprint or Trigger Volume for in-world activation, or simply set the sequence asset to **Auto Play**.

2. Place and animate a cine camera:

    a. Use the Cine Camera Actor for advanced filmic controls, such as focal length, aperture, and tracking.

    b. Animate transforms, focal changes, or cuts between cameras using keyframes or **camera cut tracks**.

    c. Use **binding overrides** to enable Actor switching later—ideal for adaptive shots.

3. Animate characters and props:

    a. Drag characters or props into Sequencer.

    b. Use the following:

        - **Transform tracks** for movement.
        - **Animation tracks** for skeletal actions (e.g., from the AnimBP or imported FBX).
        - **Control Rig** for procedural rigging and posing.

    c. You can also blend between idle poses or have different versions of a character with different outfits, expressions, or animations.

4. Add sound, lighting, and FX:

    a. Drop in ambient or dialogue audio via Audio Tracks.

    b. Trigger particles such as smoke, sparks, or light flickers using Niagara with visibility tracks.

    c. Keyframe lighting intensity, temperature, and color for emotional tone shifts.

> **Note**
>
> While now a legacy system, you may run into a situation where you need to use the old Cascade Particle Systems. For the most part, there is a lot of overlap in the basic functions in Sequencer, such as visibility and keyframe controls, but it lacks some more advanced features that Niagara provides.

Figure 9.1 shows an in-engine example of how Sequencer can be laid out with the previous foundations considered.

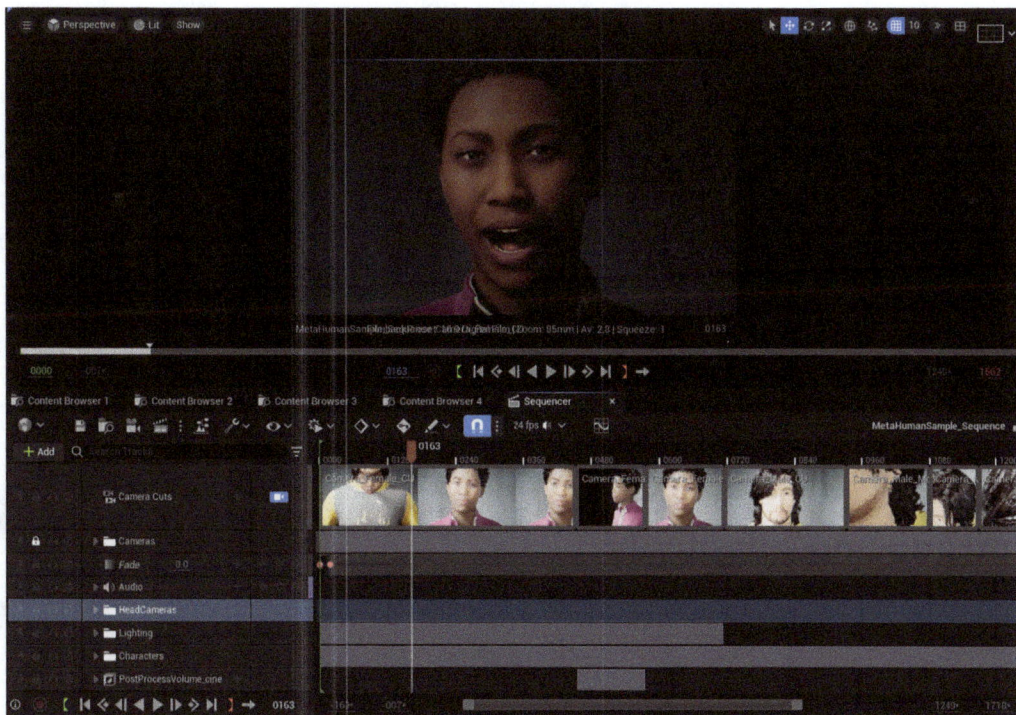

Figure 9.1: A screenshot showing a basic Sequencer setup with these track types: character, animation, camera cut, audio, and light intensity

Building for future adaptivity

Even in this foundational phase, it's worth thinking ahead about how your scene may *branch or adapt* later. You don't need to implement logic yet, but consider how your Sequencer can remain modular:

- *Structure shots in short subsequences*, which makes it easier to swap in/out later.

- *Use camera cuts sparingly early on* if you want player input to influence flow.

- *Name your tracks clearly* (e.g., Hero_LowHealth_React versus Hero_NormalReact).

- *Use Actor binding IDs* instead of hard-referenced Actors. This will allow you to reuse Sequencers dynamically across characters or game states.

> **Tip**
>
> Think of your cinematic as a toolkit, not a timeline. You're not locking in a story; you're preparing flexible beats that you can deploy based on what the player has done.

In *Chapter 7*, we covered the following:

- Cinematic lighting setups
- Camera movement and blocking for dramatic effect
- Movie Render Queue for final output

If you're new to cinematic design in Unreal, that chapter provides deeper guidance on **visual composition**, **lensing**, and **render quality**. Here, the focus shifts: we're aiming not just for visual fidelity, but *contextual responsiveness*.

With this base scene in place, we can now explore how to make it *adaptive*.

In the next section, we'll dive into the **logic layer**, building Blueprint systems that determine what your cinematic shows based on real-time variables and player choices.

Introducing adaptivity

Now that you've built a simple cinematic scene using Sequencer, it's time to unlock one of UE5's most powerful storytelling tools: **adaptivity.**

Linear cutscenes serve many purposes, but in interactive mediums such as games, your story can become far more immersive when it reacts to the player's past choices, current state, or in-world variables. Whether that means triggering one of several alternate cutscenes or subtly changing a single shot's tone or content, adaptive cinematics transform *passive watching* into *active participation*.

The role of Blueprint in adaptive cutscenes

Unreal's **Blueprint system** is your control hub for cinematic logic. It allows you to drive sequences based on variables, world states, or gameplay triggers. You don't need to rebuild your cinematics, just control *when* and *how* they're played.

Let's take a look at three core adaptivity techniques using Blueprint.

Switching between entire sequences

Let's say your story can branch into two major emotional outcomes: a peaceful resolution or an all-out war. Each has a dedicated cinematic, `LS_Peace_Cutscene` and `LS_War_Cutscene`.

Here's the Blueprint workflow:

1. Create both cutscenes using Sequencer.

2. In the Level Blueprint, check for a game variable (e.g., `PlayerMadePeace`).

3. Use a simple `If/Else` node setup to play the corresponding cinematic.

> **Important note**
>
> I am assuming here that either you or a programming teammate has provided code support to allow for player-affected game variables such as `PlayerMadePeace`. The systems behind game systems are a monster of a skillset beyond the scope of this book, and we are just focusing on how to set up your Sequencers while assuming this logic exists in your project.

Figure 9.2 shows a basic Blueprint setup of the preceding Blueprint workflow:

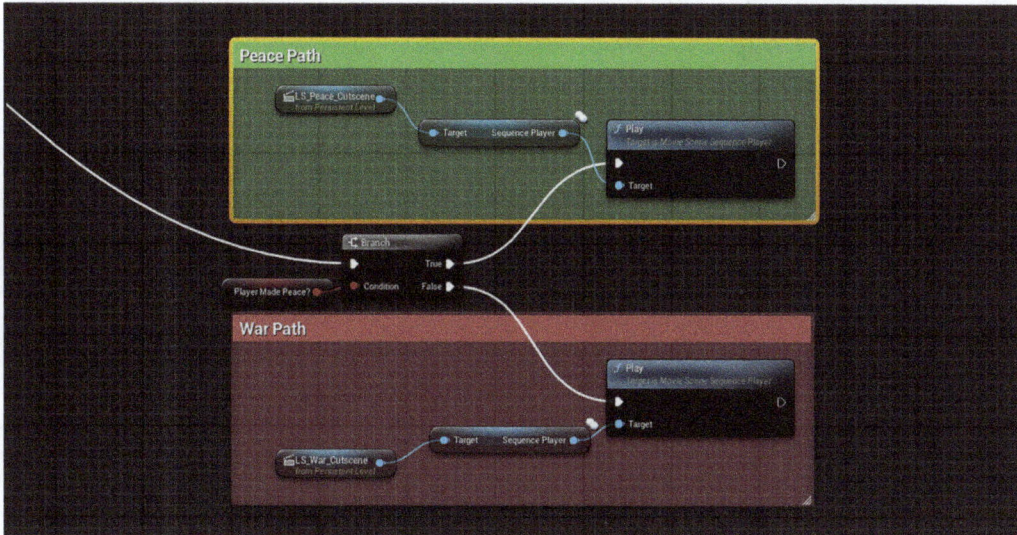

Figure 9.2: Basic Blueprint setup

> **Tip**
>
> You can use this setup for dozens of conditions, such as faction alignment, reputation, companion status, and even time of day or player health.

Branching camera shots within one sequence

Sometimes, you don't need entirely different cutscenes, just *different perspectives* or *emotions* based on the current state.

You can create one cinematic in Sequencer, then switch camera angles or character behavior dynamically using **visibility tracks, possessables**, or **Blueprint-controlled bindings**.

> **Use case**
>
> Show the player character limping if health is below 25%, use a high-angle "dominant" shot if the NPC is angry or a low-angle empathetic shot if they're sad, or hide or show a companion character depending on whether you've completed their "companion quest."

> **Tip**
>
> Use **Actor tags** or Blueprint-exposed variables to determine which camera track or character animation should be visible during the cutscene.

Conditional expressions and animation blends

Facial performance is a subtle but powerful storytelling tool. You can drive emotion adaptively by doing the following:

- Swapping in different facial animation tracks using control rigs.
- Switching between "neutral," "happy," and "angry" expressions based on decisions.
- Triggering idle behaviors (such as fidgeting or sighing) based on internal stats (e.g., stress level or fatigue).

You don't have to animate these entirely by hand. For this chapter, we're bringing back the *threads* strategy from *Chapter 6*. Here are some threads to follow for help with dynamic animation:

- Animation blueprints to blend poses.
- Control Rig Blueprint nodes to drive facial bones at runtime.
- Live Link Face or MetaHuman facial curves with adjustable inputs.

Figure 9.3 shows a more detailed, but still simple, step-by-step setup for an adaptive cutscene switch in the Level Blueprint:

1. Create a Boolean variable in your **Game Instance** or **PlayerController** (e.g., bBetrayedCompanion).

2. Add both sequences to the Level and disable autoplay.

3. In the Level Blueprint, do the following:

   a. Use a **BeginOverlap** or **Input Trigger** node.

   b. Add a **Branch** node to check the Boolean.

   c. Connect **True** to one **Play Level Sequence** node, and **False** to the other.

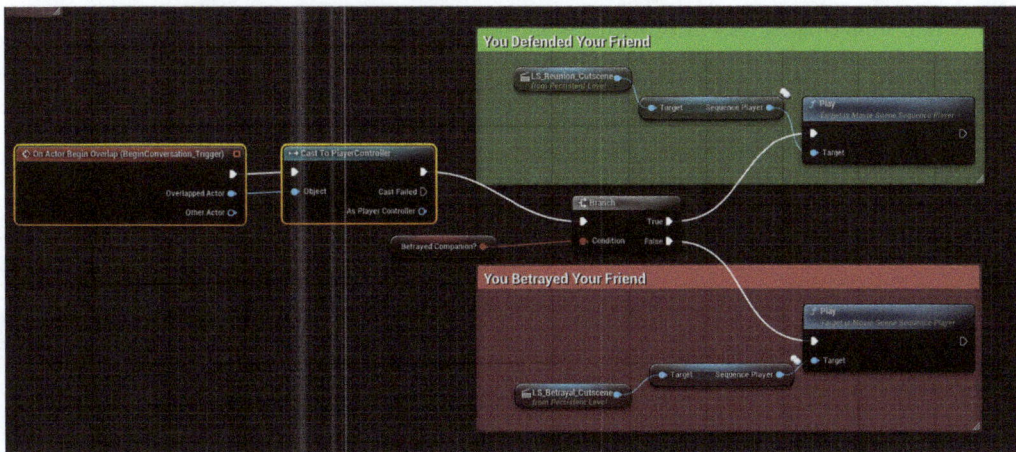

Figure 9.3: A screenshot of a blueprint for a basic adaptive cutscene trigger

Now that you understand how to *drive cinematic logic* using Blueprint, let's take it further.

Next, we'll look at how to blend these cutscenes seamlessly into gameplay, so the player never feels the "cut" between story and control.

Let's step into interactive cinematic integration.

Working with subscenes and nested sequences

As your cutscenes become more adaptive, you'll quickly find yourself managing more content, alternate versions of moments, conditional sequences, and player-driven outcomes. To keep your workflow clean, scalable, and modular, **subscenes** (nested Level Sequences) become essential.

Rather than trying to manage all your logic inside a single massive sequence, breaking your content into *smaller, self-contained pieces* allows you to build, test, and reuse content with far greater flexibility.

Why use subscenes?

Subscenes, also known as *nested sequences*, are Level Sequences that can be embedded inside a Master Sequence. Think of them as cinematic building blocks. You can use them to do the following:

- Modularize your cutscene logic.

- Reuse shared intros, outros, or transition moments.

- Branch to entirely different outcomes without duplicating shared content.

- Maintain cleaner timelines with fewer overlapping tracks.

Setup: Shared intro with diverging outcomes

Let's say you have a moment where the player confronts a traitor. The intro is always the same, dialogue begins, tension rises, but the ending changes depending on past choices.

Here's a step-by-step workflow:

1. Create a Master Sequence (e.g., `LS_Confrontation_Master`).

2. Within that sequence, add the following:

   - `LS_Confrontation_Intro_Subscene`: Shared setup dialogue and camera moves.

   - `LS_Confrontation_Betrayal_Subscene`: If the player turned on the faction.

   - `LS_Confrontation_Loyalty_Subscene`: If they remained loyal.

3. Use Blueprint to determine which subscene plays (via visibility tracks, binding overrides, or separate playback logic).

> **Tip**
>
> Using subscenes instead of branching inside a single timeline reduces clutter and makes it easier to iterate and test specific segments in isolation.

Managing visibility and timing

To ensure only the correct content plays, do the following:

- Use visibility tracks in your Master Sequence to hide/show Actors or cameras based on context.

- Alternatively, *trigger only the correct subscene* from Blueprint rather than embedding all options.

- Use *binding overrides* in Sequencer to reassign which in-scene Actor is referenced at runtime (great for NPC variants or swapped props).

Event Tracks: Calling Blueprint logic from Sequencer

You're not limited to visuals in Sequencer. With **Event Tracks**, you can trigger Blueprint events at specific points in your Timeline, as follows:

- Triggering a particle effect right when a weapon is fired

- Updating a quest state mid-cutscene

- Fading in a UI element or subtitle

- Starting a camera shake or slow-motion moment

Here's how you can set up event tracks:

1. In your Level Sequence, add an Event Track to any Actor.
2. Add a keyframe and name the event (e.g., `TriggerExplosion`).
3. In your Level Blueprint or bound Actor Blueprint, implement an event with that exact name.

> **Use case**
>
> You can use an Event Track to call a Blueprint function that fades the environment to red at a dramatic turning point

Reusable building blocks = smarter workflows

Using subscenes is not just about modularity; it's about *designing cinematics such as gameplay systems*. With this setup, you can do the following:

- Reuse the same intro across five different story paths.

- Mix and match endings without re-authoring core moments.

- Allow narrative designers to iterate on specific branches without disturbing others.

> **Tip**
>
> Treat subscenes like prefabs in narrative design. The more atomic and self-contained your scenes are, the easier it is to scale your story without breaking your pipeline.

Figure 9.4 shows a screenshot of a Master Sequence with three subscenes stacked sequentially on the Timeline, the blue arrows show the subscene tracks, and the red arrow is where you need to go to add them or create a new one via **Insert Shot**.

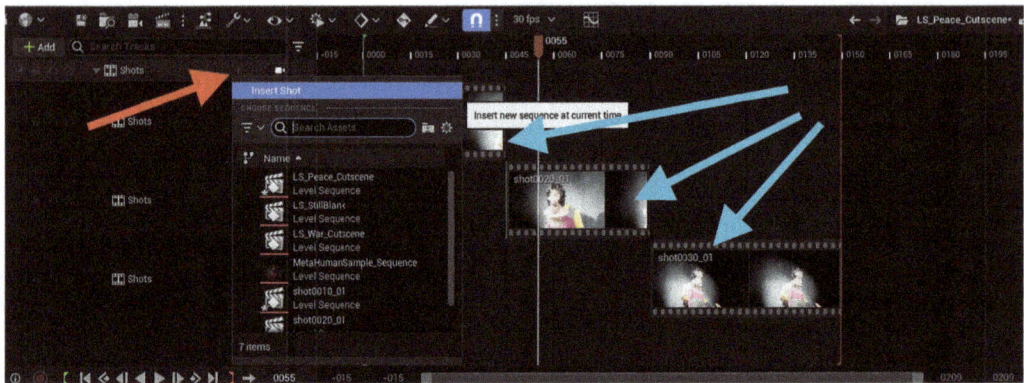

Figure 9.4: Screenshot of a Master Sequence with three subscenes stacked sequentially on the Timeline

Now that you've modularized your cutscene content, it's time to make that content responsive in real time. In the next section, we'll dive into **Blueprint Communication**, how to connect gameplay logic to your cinematics dynamically using events, triggers, and interface calls.

Let's explore how Unreal's Blueprint system makes your cutscenes *listen and react*.

Driving cutscenes with gameplay data

One of Unreal's greatest strengths is its ability to *connect live gameplay systems with cinematic content*, allowing your cutscenes to feel like an extension of player action rather than a break from it.

In this section, we'll explore how to use gameplay data, such as variables, flags, inventory, or character state, to shape cutscene content dynamically, creating branching or reactive outcomes that feel earned and personal.

Using gameplay state to influence cinematics

Whether it's a subtle detail or a major narrative branch, cutscenes can adapt based on a wide range of player-driven factors. These might include the following:

- **Inventory/resources**: Do they have ammo, the key item, a health pack?
- **World decisions**: Which faction did they side with? Who's alive?
- **Alignment/morality**: Have they acted mercifully or aggressively?
- **Player stats**: Are they low on health or fully buffed?
- **Environmental variables**: Is the area on fire or intact?

These variables can be *read in real time* to influence how a cutscene plays out.

Example: Contextual cutscene variant

Let's say you're triggering a scene where a character offers help during a tense moment.

Here is the in-game scenario:

- **Condition A**: If the player has *no ammo*, the NPC says, *"Here, take this!"* and tosses the player a weapon.
- **Condition B**: If the player is *fully loaded*, the NPC says, *"You look ready. Let's go,"* and they move on together.

This creates a sense that the world and its characters are *noticing and responding* to the player, without requiring complex branching paths.

Thread: Data-driven cinematic variants

To set up data-driven cinematic variants, do the following:

1. Track gameplay variables:

    - Store key values using the Game Instance, the player state, or a save system blueprint.
    - For one-off story moments, you can use Level Blueprint variables or tags.

2. Check conditions in Blueprint:

    - Before playing the cutscene, check the variable (e.g., ammo count).

    - Route to the appropriate Level Sequence or modify the sequence contents.

3. Drive visibility or animation logic:

    - Use visibility tracks to swap camera shots or props.

    - Switch animation sections based on input from the game state.

> **Tip**
>
> For more granular control, pass gameplay variables directly into the Level Sequence
> via Blueprint interfaces or Sequencer's custom events.

Thread: Centralizing state with game instance

To ensure consistent narrative branching across Levels and scenes, store persistent variables in the Game Instance. This allows you to do the following:

- Track long-term decisions or stats.

- Reference those decisions even after loading new maps.

- Avoid excessive duplication of logic.

For example, `PlayerChoseMercy = True` could influence dialogue, cutscenes, and even combat reactions across the entire game.

Figure 9.5 shows a basic flow chart of how a dynamic cutscene could play out based on the preceding example of `PlayerChoseMercy`.

BEFORE THE BATTLE FLOW CHART

Player Enters Trigger

Sequencer Blends from **Gameplay** to **Cinematic**

Player = No Ammo	Player - Has Ammo

Unique Dialogue Bonus - Recieves Ammo	*Unique Dialogue* Bonus - Donate Ammo to Companion

Previous Gameplay - Oppurtunity to Kill Thief
Q: Player Chose Mercy?

NO - The Thiefs Son swears revenge! *The next battle is harder - but provides unique loot!*	**YES** - Thief has become a companion over time! *The next battle is easier...*

Cutscene ends with a fade to black.
The Battle Begins...

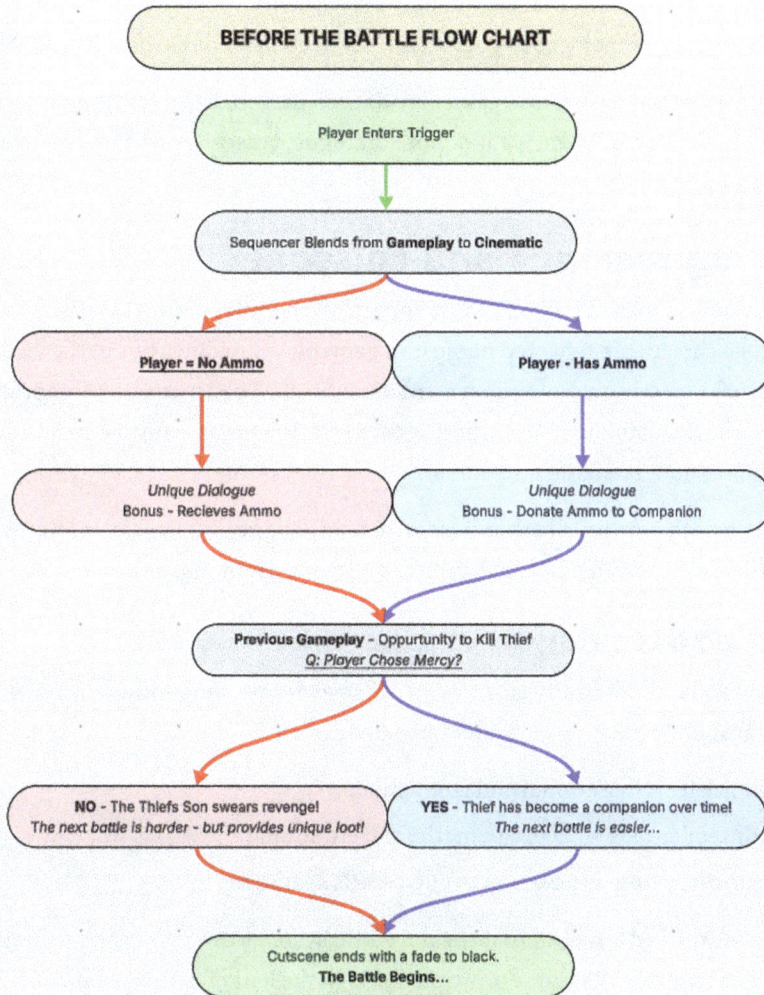

Figure 9.5: A cutscene flow chart showing one base cutscene with multiple dynamic outcomes

---

Tip

I recommend flow charts for planning out your dynamic cinematic/cutscene flows as it can be easier to manage your branching paths, especially as they become more complex.

his type of logic can be scaled to dozens of micro-variations without bloating your Timeline, as long as you, or your code team, keep your state-driven conditions clean and readable.

Now that you've learned how to use gameplay data to personalize your cinematics, let's take it a step further. In the next section, we'll explore **dialogue**, cutscenes where the player isn't just a spectator but a participant.

Integrating dialogue and cutscenes

Cinematic storytelling in games is at its most impactful when players feel that their choices matter, and when those choices are reflected not just in gameplay outcomes but in the visual language of the game world. By tying a **dialogue system** directly into Sequencer and **Blueprint-triggered cutscenes**, you can create moments where a conversation organically evolves into a cutscene, and vice versa, without breaking immersion.

In this section, we'll have a brief look at the **narrative dialogue system**, cinematic responses, and how to sell those moments using facial animation, camera framing, and visual feedback.

Dialogue as the catalyst for cinematic branches

When designing adaptive narratives, it's often a *dialogue choice* that initiates a major narrative or environmental shift. The key is to ensure the following:

- The choice feels intentional and contextual.
- The consequence is visible, cinematic, and emotional.
- The transition from interaction to cutscene is seamless.

In *Chapter 6*, we explored how game states and world systems can reflect player decisions in real time. Here, we're applying that same principle through the lens of cutscenes and dialogue-driven branching.

Thread: The Narrative plugin

Developing a robust dialogue and quest system from scratch can be a daunting task. Fortunately, the **Narrative** plugin offers a comprehensive, ready-to-integrate solution for your UE5 projects, and is a solution I use every day as a professional.

Narrative is a node-based plugin designed to facilitate the creation of complex quests and dialogues without the need for extensive custom development. It provides the following:

- **Node-based editors**: Intuitive visual editors for crafting branching dialogues and quest lines.
- **State Machine architecture**: Enables the creation of non-linear quests with multiple outcomes.
- **Cinematic tools**: Integrates with Unreal's cinematic features for immersive storytelling.
- **Save/load functionality**: Built-in systems for persisting player progress.
- **Multiplayer support**: Server-authoritative networking allows for shared quests in multiplayer settings.
- **MetaHuman compatibility**: Seamless integration with MetaHuman characters for high-fidelity interactions.

> **Important note**
>
> I am in no way affiliated with Narrative and have no monetary or personal stake in it or its success. This is purely my personal opinion/recommendation for a tool that I use daily in my professional career that can greatly improve the dialogue quality of your game.

Implementing Narrative in your project

To integrate Narrative, do the following:

1. **Download the plugin**: Acquire Narrative from the Fab marketplace.
2. **Enable required plugins**: In Unreal Engine, navigate to **Edit | Plugins** and enable both **Narrative 3** and **Narrative Common UI**. Restart the editor if prompted.
3. **Utilize the tutorial template**: Start with the provided **Narrative Tutorial Template**, which includes pre-configured settings and assets.
4. **Create quests and dialogues**: Use the node-based editors to design your narrative structures.
5. **Test and iterate**: Playtest your content, making use of the built-in debugging tools to refine the player experience.

For detailed guidance, refer to the Narrative Tales documentation and the Quick Start Video Guide, both found in the store details.

Figure 9.6: A screenshot from the Narrative store, highlighting some of the key features available as part of the suite of plugins. Source: narrativetools.io

Leveraging the Narrative plugin can significantly accelerate the development of rich, interactive storytelling elements in your game. By providing a robust framework out of the box, it allows you to focus on crafting compelling narratives without getting bogged down in the technical intricacies of system development. As you continue to explore narrative threads and systems, consider delving deeper into advanced features and customizations to fully realize your game's storytelling potential.

Selling the emotional impact

Once the dialogue has branched into a cutscene, your work isn't done. Player investment comes from *visual and tonal feedback*:

- **Facial animation** (thread: MetaHuman Animator workflows)
- **Camera framing** (tight versus wide angle = power dynamic)
- **Lighting shifts** to reinforce the emotional tone
- **Sound cues and music transitions** based on choice

Even a minor decision can be weighty if it's followed by a cutscene that *looks and feels* unique.

In the next section, we'll cover how to bring these cinematic moments back into gameplay, using techniques for seamless transitions between player-controlled segments and in-world scripted scenes.

Adaptive transitions and camera logic

The most memorable cinematic experiences in games often *don't* begin with a cut to black; they start while you're still in control. The line between gameplay and cutscene is increasingly blurred, and Unreal gives us the tools to make that transition feel smooth, dynamic, and tailored to the player's context.

In this section, we'll explore how to design **adaptive transitions** between player-driven gameplay and Sequencer-driven cinematics, using tools such as **camera blending**, **Trigger Volumes**, and **Fade Tracks**. We'll also explore how to pick the right **camera logic** to keep the moment cohesive with the player's journey up to that point.

Why transitions matter

Cinematic transitions are more than just polish; they're how we *preserve immersion*. An abrupt switch to a new camera angle, a hard fade, or a jarring teleport can immediately remind the player that they're watching a constructed moment.

But with adaptive systems, you can do the following:

- Start a cinematic without ever taking the player out of the world.
- Reflect *how or where* the player entered a space.
- Exit the cinematic seamlessly into gameplay without needing a fade-out.

Setup: Triggering cinematics from gameplay

To begin your adaptive transition, use the following:

- Trigger Volumes or collision checks in the Level.
- **Blueprint logic** that detects entry direction, player state, or context.
- A **sequence selector** to choose the correct Level Sequence for the moment.

> **Tip**
>
> Store player entry direction or last location in the Game Instance for more context-aware transitions.

Camera blend techniques

UE5's Sequencer allows for powerful camera handoff techniques. Instead of cutting harshly, do the following:

- Use blend times on Camera Cuts Tracks.
- Use a Fade Track for soft transitions, especially when shifting tone or location.
- Consider **camera matching** the gameplay camera to ease into the first shot.

Figure 9.7 shows an in-engine screenshot of where you can access a Fade Track within the Sequencer interface (left), and some blending options available between shots by right-clicking on the shot blend (right).

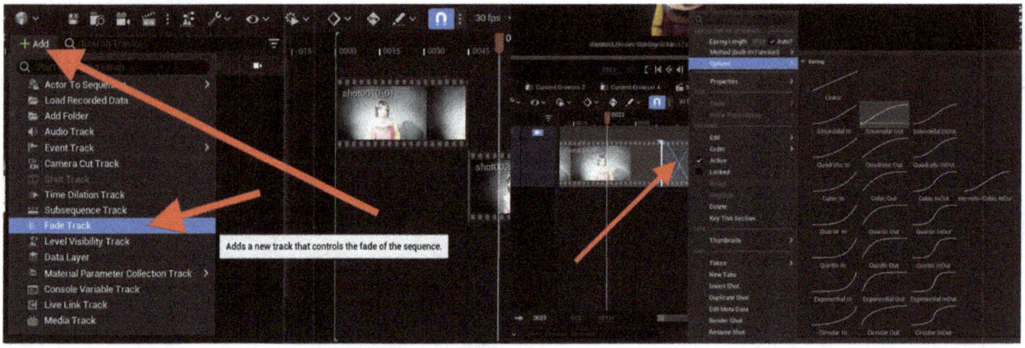

Figure 9.7: Shows an in-engine screenshot of where you can access a Fade Track and Shot Fade

Table 9.2 lists some common camera blend techniques:

Technique	Use Case
Direct cut	Use sparingly. Best for tension or jump scares.
Ease-in blend (1–2 seconds)	Good for emotional scenes or dramatic reveals.
Fade to black/white	Useful for time skips or dream sequences.
Camera match	Align cinematic camera with player camera for invisible transitions.

Table 9.2: Camera blend techniques

Adaptive establishing shots

If your cutscene begins with a wide establishing shot, consider using *contextual logic* to determine which shot to show:

- **Player's entry point** (e.g., entering a town from the north shows a different pan than from the south).
- **Time of day** (e.g., sunset establishes a different emotional tone than daylight).
- **Game progress or world state** (e.g., a peaceful version of the scene versus a war-torn variant).

Figure 9.8 shows another basic flow chart of how a dynamic cutscene could play out based on the following sequence of events:

- Player crosses into a Trigger Volume.
- Sequencer blends camera from gameplay into cinematic.
- Cinematic plays with dynamic elements (e.g., NPCs change depending on previous choice).
- Cutscene ends with a fade or camera blend back to player control.

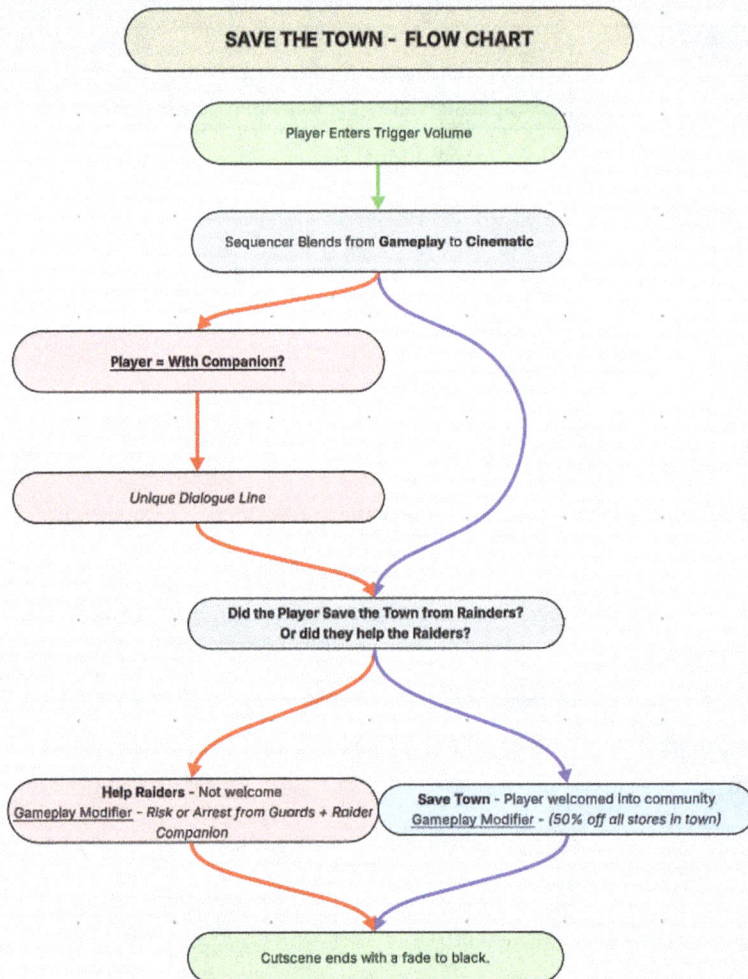

Figure 9.8: A dynamic cutscene flow chart showing one base cutscene with multiple dynamic outcomes

Best practices: "Invisible cuts" that don't break immersion

When possible, do the following:

- Start the cinematic in the player's current environment.
- Match camera framing or player pose at the start.

- Resume gameplay exactly where the cinematic ends.
- Avoid snapping control or teleporting the player.

Use case

The player opens a vault door. The camera slowly pulls back into a wide reveal of the treasure room. After a few seconds, control is handed back, but the camera remains in place, now controlled by the player. No black screen, no control shift; the cutscene and gameplay are one.

In the final section of this chapter, we'll look at some basic best practices for managing and scaling these adaptive systems: how to organize, optimize, and modularize your branching and reactive cinematics to stay production-friendly as your game grows.

Debugging and iterating adaptive cutscenes

As your adaptive cutscene system grows in complexity, with branching paths, dynamic cameras, conditional animations, and gameplay-driven triggers, it becomes *absolutely essential* to *test each condition thoroughly* and to *build your sequences with iteration in mind.*

Even the best-looking dynamic cutscene will fall flat if it plays at the wrong moment, triggers inconsistently, or doesn't reflect the player's past choices. In this section, I'll simply ask you to consider questions about your Sequencers, in preparation for the final chapters of this book. In *Chapters 10–13*, we will also expand on general organization and optimization techniques, so please proceed if you are looking for **key techniques and best practices** for all disciplines we have discussed so far over the past nine chapters.

Keep it manageable: The complexity creep trap

When building adaptive content, it's easy to go overboard. Every new branch multiplies testing needs, design workload, and potential for bugs.

Ask yourself the following:

- Is this branch meaningfully different or just a minor variation?
- Can I achieve this with a single sequence and a conditional animation or camera toggle instead of duplicating the entire scene?
- Will the player even notice this variation, and does it support the story?

With your adaptive cutscenes now responsive, modular, and ready to be optimized, the next step is integrating them seamlessly with your larger game loop, project, and player agency. Let's wrap up the chapter by summarizing the core principles we've discussed and how they tie back to earlier systems, lighting, environment, and real-time storytelling.

Summary

I truly believe the strongest stories in games aren't just *told*; they're *lived and felt* through the player's decisions, actions, and perspective. Adaptive cutscenes empower you to create sequences that feel *personal*, *earned*, and *emotionally resonant*, because they react directly to what the player has done and who they've become.

With UE5's toolset—**Sequencer**, **Blueprint**, **Data Layers**, and more—you're not just making cinematic content; you're *building dynamic narrative systems* that respond in real time.

Your goal isn't just to *show* a story, but to make the player feel like they're *authoring* it alongside you.

Whether it's a subtle glance that changes based on a loyalty variable or a completely different outcome that reshapes a Level's traversal, adaptive storytelling should have the following characteristics:

- Intentional (it's not random)
- Responsive (it reflects what happened)
- Meaningful (it carries emotional or mechanical weight)

> **Important note**
>
> There are, of course, games that are exceptions to the preceding that don't necessarily let you *control the outcome*, but still let the preceding principles shine through with exceptional storytelling and cinematic timing. *God of War (2018)* and *God of War: Ragnarök (2022)* are great examples of this, but are, of course, bolstered by a massive team containing many talented narrative writers.

Throughout this chapter, we explored the following principles:

- **Using Blueprint logic + Sequencer together**: Combine the power of UE5's visual scripting and cinematic tools to drive branching, conditional, and reactive content without excessive duplication.

- **Letting the world reflect the player**: Feed in gameplay data, world state, or narrative flags (e.g., morality, items, or relationships) to change how a cutscene plays out, or whether it plays at all.

- **Prioritizing clarity over complexity**: A simple camera shift, altered animation, or line of dialogue can often feel more meaningful than creating three totally different versions of a scene. Focus on *meaningful moments*, not just mechanical variety.

- **Modularize for scalability**: Use Sub-Sequences, nested structures, and Blueprint-driven systems to keep your scenes manageable as they grow.

Cinematics and cutscenes are no longer just *cutaways*; they can be living, responsive *extensions* of your game's world and systems. With care, clarity, and the right technical foundation, your scenes can *react in the moment*, reinforce the player's story, and deliver the kind of emotional payoffs that define the unforgettable games we all know and love.

Further reading

This list of further readings is from other authors under the Packt Publishing label, and a few of my personal recommendations for getting a deeper understanding of both 3D design in Unreal and general storytelling. These are a bit old at this point, but they're still absolutely solid reads for anyone serious about environmental storytelling within Unreal and beyond.

- *3D Game Design with Unreal Engine 4 and Blender*. Read more here: `https://amzn.asia/d/eyVBBfE`

- *Video Game Storytelling: What Every Developer Needs to Know about Narrative Techniques*. Read more here: `https://amzn.asia/d/j2GVnAA`

- *Procedural Storytelling in Game Design*. Read more here: `https://amzn.asia/d/4AF51yf`

Subscribe to Game Dev Assembly!

We are excited to introduce **Game Dev Assembly**, our brand-new newsletter dedicated to everything game development. Whether you're coding, designing, animating, or managing a studio, we've got insights, trends, and expert advice to help you create, innovate, and thrive. Sign up now and get exciting benefits.

https://packt.link/gamedev-newsletter

Get This Book's PDF Version and Exclusive Extras

UNLOCK NOW

Scan the QR code (or go to packtpub.com/unlock). Search for this book by name, confirm the edition, and then follow the steps on the page.

Note: Keep your invoice handy. Purchases made directly from Packt don't require one.

Part 4

Optimizing Performance and Overcoming Complex Challenges

No project is complete without tackling performance, scalability, and stability. This final part covers the essential practices for profiling, optimizing, and managing assets, as well as strategies for troubleshooting common development hurdles. By mastering these workflows, you'll ensure that your project runs smoothly across platforms and remains production-ready under real-world conditions.

This part of the book includes the following chapters:

- *Chapter 10, Profiling and Performance Techniques*
- *Chapter 11, Advanced Optimization for Real-Time Rendering*
- *Chapter 12, Asset Management Best Practices*
- *Chapter 13, Troubleshooting Common Development Challenges*

10

Profiling and Performance Techniques

Optimizing performance in UE5 is not just about squeezing out higher frame rates; it's about delivering a consistent, high-quality experience that scales smoothly across devices, platforms, and content demands. With modern pipelines pushing visual fidelity further than ever before, *performance is a critical design consideration*, not just a technical afterthought.

Whether you're targeting a cinematic experience on a high-end PC or aiming for stable performance on mobile hardware, understanding *why* your project performs the way it does and how to act on that data is key to maintaining both visual and gameplay integrity. The good news is that Unreal offers an incredibly robust set of profiling and optimization tools to help us surface and solve issues quickly and iteratively.

In this chapter, you will learn:

- **How to profile rendering performance using UE5's built-in tools**: We'll cover tools such as the GPU profiler, stat commands, Unreal Insights, and scene analyzers to help you identify real-time performance bottlenecks.
- **How to optimize key rendering systems for better frame rates**: We'll explore practical strategies to reduce GPU and CPU overhead, simplify Materials, and optimize shadowing, lighting, and post-processing without sacrificing visual quality.
- **How to diagnose asset and Material costs at a granular level**: We'll break down shader complexity, texture streaming, and Nanite usage to help you keep your visuals efficient and scalable.

- **How to optimize large environments using World Partition and HLOD systems**: We'll learn how to streamline open worlds by tuning HLOD settings, controlling streaming cells, and managing data layers effectively.

- **How to implement a feedback loop for testing and iteration**: We'll establish a step-by-step workflow for profiling, fixing, and re-testing performance, turning optimization into a consistent part of your development process.

Whether you're deep in production or just starting to scale your Level design, this chapter will give you the tools and mindset to approach performance with confidence, clarity, and control.

Technical requirements

To follow along with this chapter, ensure you have:

- Unreal Engine 5.4 or later

- A system with real-time ray tracing support (optional but recommended)

- A solid understanding of the Unreal Engine interface

- Have read the previous chapters of this book

- Optional: A project with pre-built assets for testing and practice (or start with Unreal's sample projects)

Performance mindset: Designing with cost in mind

Before we talk about fixing performance issues, it's important to shift the way we *think* about performance. Optimization shouldn't be treated as a clean-up job left to the end of production; by that point, decisions are baked in, content is locked, and performance sacrifices often mean visual compromises. Instead, the best results come when optimization is baked into your design process from day one.

It's important to understand that optimizing for performance doesn't mean sacrificing ambition. I often remind my team that even when we're targeting low-end hardware, we should still aim *high creatively*, because that ambition can be the difference between a memorable game and a forgettable one.

However, it does mean we need to stay mindful of performance costs, understand where bottlenecks typically arise, and make smarter decisions at every level, from asset setup and Level layout to scripting logic and lighting design.

Even now, I still struggle with performance constraints as an artist. But finding ways to make something look *beautiful* while still running smoothly on weaker hardware can be just as satisfying as creating a high-end environment without limits.

"OK, that's all well and good, but what are these constraints?" you may ask. Well, let's have a look at some common ones now.

Recognizing the usual suspects

Performance issues in UE5 often stem from a few common culprits. While we'll go into tools and profiling shortly, it helps to begin with a mental checklist of high-cost systems to watch for:

- **Overdraw and transparency:** Alpha-blended Materials (such as fog, glass, and effects) stack visually and can heavily impact GPU performance, especially on lower-end hardware.

- **Tick rate and Blueprint logic:** Expensive logic running on every frame, especially across multiple Actors, can quickly consume CPU resources. Optimize Actor life cycles and avoid overusing *Tick* when event-driven logic would suffice.

- **Shader complexity and Material Graphs:** Complex Materials with multiple texture look-ups, heavy math operations, or expensive features such as pixel depth offset or refraction can scale poorly.

- **Lumen bounce and reflections:** Lumen offers stunning dynamic lighting, but it comes at a cost. Multiple bounces, emissive Materials, and high surface complexity increase lighting computation.

- **Nanite streaming and distance fields:** While Nanite is efficient for high-poly assets, poor use of virtual textures, MIP biasing, or lack of culling setup can still cause strain, especially in large open-world scenes.

> **Tip**
>
> Mipmaps are pre-calculated, downscaled versions of a texture automatically generated by Unreal Engine. Each level (called a mip level) is a smaller, lower-resolution copy of the original texture. When an object is viewed from a distance, Unreal dynamically switches to a lower mip level. This reduces aliasing and improves performance since the GPU samples smaller textures instead of the full-resolution image.

These systems don't need to be avoided; they just need to be understood. Design with them in mind, and your game will scale more gracefully across hardware and scene complexity.

Building on what we know

Back in *Chapter 4*, we touched on performance-conscious Level layout and asset organization. In *Chapter 11*, we'll dive deep into advanced optimization strategies, LOD generation, culling, instancing, and data-driven streaming. But here, our focus is more foundational: mindset and diagnostics. Before you can fix performance problems, you need to know where the performance is going and *why*.

Now that we've set the stage with a performance-first mindset, let's move from theory to tools. In the next section, we'll explore how to see what's costing you in real time using UE5's profiling systems.

Profiling overview: The right tool for the right job

Performance issues in UE5 rarely have a one-size-fits-all solution. A dropped frame could be caused by overdraw, Blueprint logic, complex shaders, or something as simple as lighting gone rogue. That's why the first step to any performance optimization is knowing which tools to use and when.

UE5 offers a suite of powerful profiling tools, each built to uncover specific aspects of your game's performance. Whether you're chasing frame time drops on a cinematic moment or investigating why a system seems heavier on Xbox than PC, using the *right* tool saves hours of guesswork.

Let's break down the most essential profiling tools available in UE5, with notes on their ideal use cases and what to look for.

stat commands — your real-time radar

For a quick pulse-check on performance, stat commands are your go-to:

- stat unit: Displays real-time frame breakdown, game thread, draw thread, GPU time, and total frame time
- stat fps: Shows frame rate and delta time, which is useful for spotting inconsistencies
- stat SceneRendering/stat RHI/stat Streaming: Display more granular rendering or asset streaming data

> **Unreal 5.6 changes**
>
> - The stat SceneRendering command has been removed
> - The stat RHI command has been renamed to Stat D3D11RHI
>
> The preceding are still relevant for pre-5.6 users/teams and kept for developers on earlier Unreal Engine versions.

> **Tip**
>
> Use these in-editor or in standalone builds for rapid iteration. They're especially
> useful when toggling features such as shadows or VFX to see their immediate impact.

Figure 10.1 shows another way to have performance shown at all times: just go to your editor
settings and under **Performance**, set **Show Frame Rate and Memory**, and it'll appear at the top
of your editor.

Figure 10.1: Where to access alternate performance settings in Unreal

Unreal Insights — long-term trends and deep dives

When you need detailed analysis over time, or you're diagnosing tricky spikes, Unreal Insights
is invaluable:

- It logs both CPU and game thread activity over time.
- It shows event timing, asset loading, thread usage, and more.
- It is great for tracking behavior across Level loads, large cinematics, or gameplay loops.

> **Tip**
>
> Spot a persistent hitch that happens every 30 seconds? Insights can show exactly
> what thread or function caused it.

GPU profiler – frame cost, pass by pass

Hotkey: *Ctrl + Shift + ,* (comma)

If your bottleneck is on the GPU side, such as lighting, post-processing, Nanite, or particles, this is where you look.

- Breaks down GPU cost per render pass.
- Highlights expensive Materials, shadows, translucency, and Lumen bounces.
- Great for visual content debugging, especially on complex scenes.

Tip

Look for high-cost passes such as **Translucency**, **Base Pass**, or **Lumen Reflections**. This can quickly tell you what part of your frame is burning GPU time.

Figure 10.2 shows what you should expect to see when activating the GPU profiler:

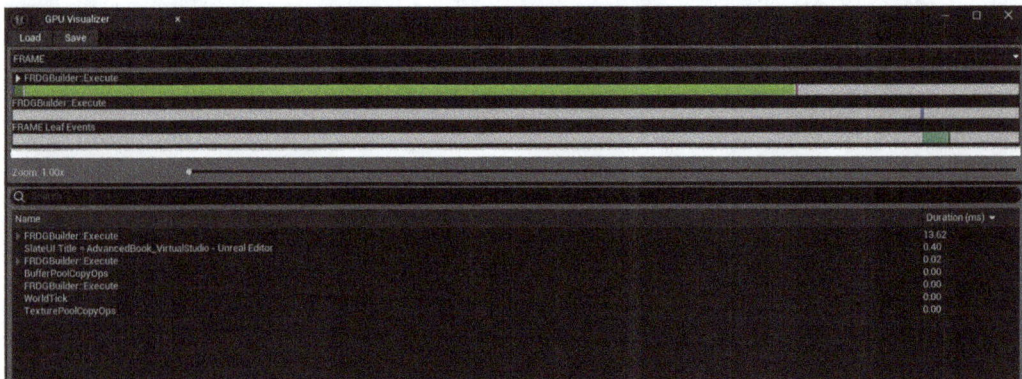

Figure 10.2: Activating the GPU profiler

CPU profiler — investigating logic and tick load

Command: `stat startfile` → then open session in Unreal Insights

The CPU profiler captures performance traces and sends them to Unreal Insights, focusing specifically on tick-heavy systems:

- Analyzes Blueprint logic, AI, tick rate, and custom systems.
- Use this when logic starts slowing the frame, even in visually simple scenes.
- Works great in conjunction with `stat Game` to identify script-based spikes.

Tip

Too many Actors ticking every frame? A few overused delay nodes? The profiler helps you track exactly where time is being spent.

Lumen scene visualizer — light cost debugging

If you're using Lumen for **global illumination** or reflections, this tool helps visualize bounce detail and light complexity:

- Debugs indirect bounce cost and emissive contribution.
- Understands how your surfaces are feeding light back into the scene.
- Reduces unnecessary GI contribution from small or dense emissive areas.

Tip

Use it with `r.Lumen.Reflections.Enable 0` or GI toggles to test trade-offs in bounce cost versus quality.

Figure 10.3 shows where you can access the Lumen scene profiler in the editor:

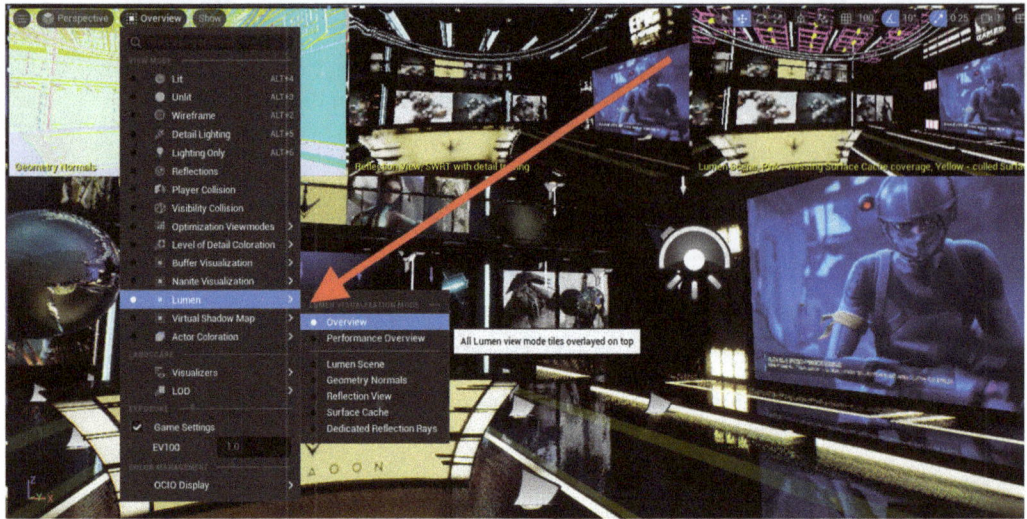

Figure 10.3: Lumen scene profiler in the editor

Now that we know how to access different profile techniques effectively, let's shift focus to how we *interpret* that data, and what actions you can take depending on where the bottleneck lies.

Quick wins: Common bottlenecks and fixes

Once you've profiled your scene and identified the high-cost areas, the next step is knowing where to look first. While every project is unique, certain performance offenders crop up again and again in Unreal Engine workflows, especially in visually ambitious scenes or Blueprint-heavy prototypes.

This section highlights some of the most common bottlenecks in UE5 projects and offers quick, practical fixes to help you stabilize performance early.

Overdraw and transparency — hidden in plain sight

Heavy use of translucent Materials, particles, glass, foliage, or fog can create *overdraw*, where pixels are rendered multiple times per frame. This eats GPU performance fast, especially in Lumen scenes.

Quick fixes

- Replace translucent shaders with *masked or dithered opacity* when full transparency isn't needed.
- Use *foliage LODs* to reduce complexity and eliminate transparency at distance.

- Limit the screen-space coverage of transparent VFX. For example, don't have a fire FX with a thousand transparent textures spawning in front of each other, causing massive translucent overlap.

> **Tip**
>
> Use the **Shader Complexity** or **Quad Overdraw** view in the Viewport to visualize problem areas.

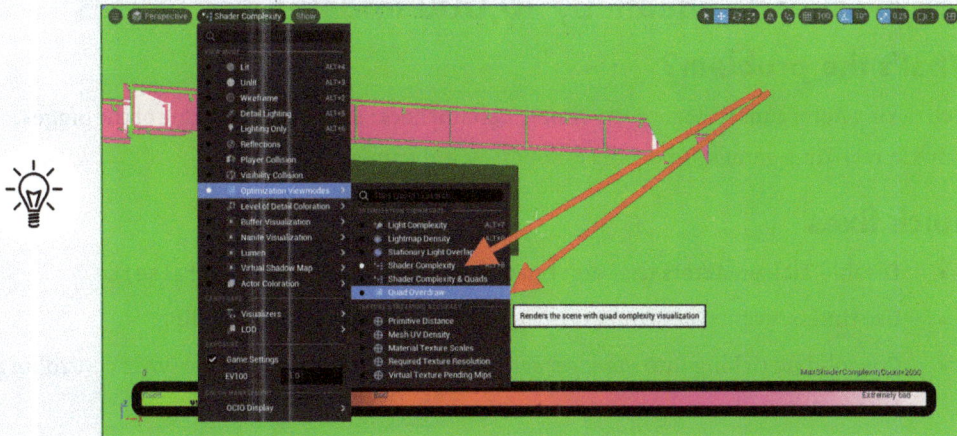

Figure 10.4: Where to access the Shader Complexity and Quad Overdraw views in the editor

Shadow casting – cut the noise

What's the problem?

Every dynamic shadow has a rendering cost. Small props, decals, or interior clutter that cast shadows can create a huge cumulative load, especially when using Lumen or Virtual Shadow Maps.

Quick fixes

- Disable **Cast Shadows** on non-essential objects and lights (e.g., bottles, debris, decals, and candles).
- Use **static or baked lighting** for distant scenery or non-interactive background elements.

- On mobile or performance-limited targets, prioritize shadows only for gameplay-relevant objects.

> **Tip**
>
> Use stat shadow rendering or view the shadow map atlas in the GPU profiler to spot problem Actors.

Tick overhead — death by 10,000 updates

What's the problem?

Each ticking Actor runs its logic every frame. Left unchecked, this becomes one of the biggest CPU drains in real-time games, especially for open-world games.

Quick fixes

- Disable **Tick** on Actors that don't need it (`SetActorTickEnabled(false)`).
- Use timers, events, or Sequencer triggers instead of tick-based polling.
- Consolidate ticking into *manager systems* where possible (e.g., a spawner controlling all enemies).

Blueprint overuse — too much of a good thing

What's the problem?

Blueprints are amazing for rapid development and iteration, but they can become a hidden performance sink if misused, especially on logic-heavy Actors or replicated systems.

Quick fixes

- Move critical or loop-heavy systems to **C++** if they impact frame time.
- Use **Blueprint Nativization** for builds, especially on shipping platforms. This is a great topic for a thread—check out the following Epic documentation: `https://dev.epicgames.com/documentation/en-us/unreal-engine/nativizing-blueprints?application_version=4.27`.
- Optimize Blueprint logic: Avoid deep loops, redundant casting, and tick usage.

These optimizations don't need to wait until the end of production. Treat them as part of your regular development process, especially if you're targeting multiple platforms.

Now that we've tackled some of the biggest (and most fixable) issues, let's look at how to interpret your profiling data to make smart decisions about where to optimize next.

Unreal Insights: Capturing and reading performance data

Once you've applied some quick fixes, deeper optimization requires understanding *why* and *where* your performance is dipping. This is where **Unreal Insights** comes in, a powerful, real-time profiler that records granular performance data across all major systems.

Unlike on-screen `stat` commands, Unreal Insights gives you a *full timeline of events*, letting you trace performance spikes, monitor logic execution, and see exactly how your game is behaving under the hood.

Setting up and recording a session

Here's how you can set up and record a session:

1. **Launching Unreal Insights**: Unreal Insights is built into UE5, and you can start Unreal Insights directly from the Unreal Editor or by running `UnrealInsights.exe`, located in your engine's binaries folder, like so: `"Drive:\UE_5.4\Engine\Binaries\Win64\UnrealInsights.exe"`.

2. **Recording a trace session**: In the Unreal Editor, go to **Trace** at the bottom of the editor, then do the following:

   a. Navigate to the tab to edit your settings:

      - **Channels** lets you choose what Insights will track (e.g., lighting, animations, etc.).

      - **Trace Storage** takes you to where your recordings are stored externally (great for sharing with teammates if needed).

      - **Recent Traces** shows your most recent trace recordings for easy access and the easiest way to *open* them for viewing.

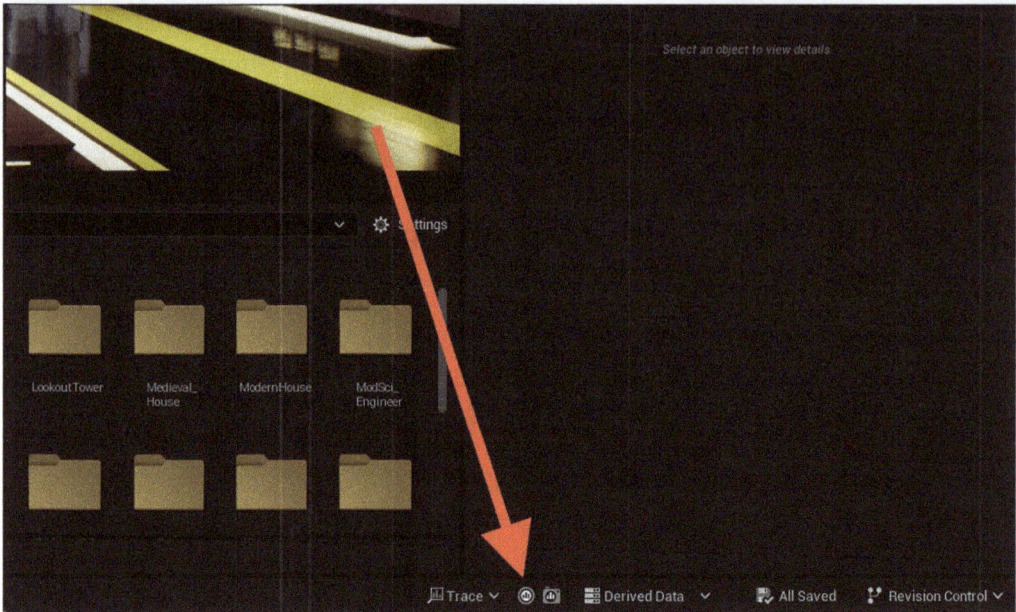

Figure 10.5: Where to access Unreal Insights in the editor

b. Click on **Start Tracing** to begin recording performance data.

c. Perform the actions in your game that you wish to profile.

d. Click on **Tracing** to end the session.

e. The recorded session will appear in the **Recent Traces** list. Click to open Unreal Insights.

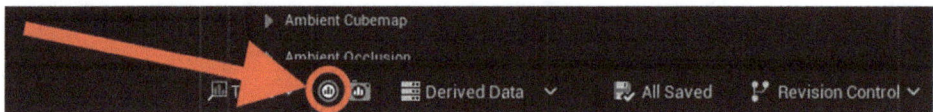

Figure 10.6: Where to start recording an Unreal Insights session

> **Tip**
>
> Tick **Stat Named** events to make things clearer as you initially learn insights. It costs a bit more to run but can be worth it as a learning experience.

Interpreting the Timeline: Threads and spikes

Once inside the viewer, the Timeline is divided into major thread lanes:

- **Game thread**: Logic, events, AI, input, and blueprints
- **Render thread**: Scene submission and draw calls
- **GPU**: Actual rendering work, lighting, post, and particles

Each thread shows a timeline of frames and the tasks executed within them.

Here's how you can look for spikes:

1. Hover over tall spikes in the Timeline and identify the function or task causing it.
2. You can zoom in and filter by thread or event type.

> **Tip**
>
> The game thread is usually your first stop for logic bottlenecks. The render thread and GPU spikes usually indicate Material, lighting, or scene complexity issues.

Finding Expensive Functions

Use the **Event Timers** tab to do the following:

- View the *most expensive functions* by cumulative time.
- Sort by thread, time per frame, or call count.
- Identify unexpected outliers, which are functions you didn't expect to cost as much as they do.

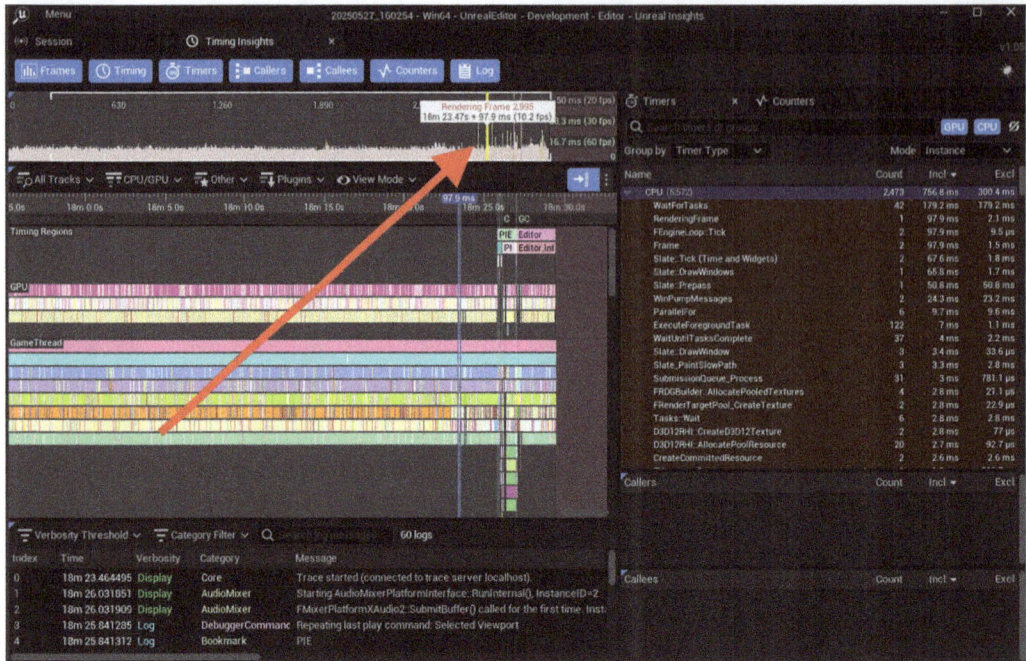

Figure 10.7: A screenshot of Unreal Insights and an arrow pointing to a performance spike

Use case

A simple Blueprint animation trigger might show a surprisingly large CPU cost if it's being called every frame instead of on demand.

Insights is a beast of a system and a **thread** (a callback to *Chapter 6*!) you should follow on your own if you want to be truly proficient at optimization (it is a job in itself), but now you at least know how to start identifying performance issues in your project in the most efficient way possible.

Now that you know how to capture and analyze performance at the frame level, the next step is prioritizing your fixes and applying the right strategies. Let's explore that in the next section.

Real-time GPU debugging: Understanding rendering costs

When your game feels slow or stutters, and you're confident it's not a logic or CPU issue, it's time to dive into **GPU profiling**. Unreal's **GPU profiler** allows you to break down rendering costs in real time, frame by frame, pass by pass.

This tool is essential for visual-heavy scenes where lighting, Materials, or post-processing could be dragging performance down, and is the primary tool I use as a cinematic and lighting artist.

Using the GPU profiler

To open the GPU profiler in the editor, do the following:

- Press *Ctrl + Shift +* , (comma) while in the engine, or while the game is running.
- Alternatively, use the following console command: "profilegpu".

This displays a *per-frame GPU cost breakdown*, showing how much time each rendering pass takes.

Reading the pass names

Here are common passes you'll see in the profiler, and what they mean:

Pass	Description	Common Bottlenecks
BasePass	Main rendering of opaque geometry (Materials and lighting)	Expensive shaders, layered Materials
ShadowDepths	Shadow maps and cascaded shadows	Overlapping lights, large shadow casters
Translucency	Transparent objects and particles	Overdraw, large transparent Materials
PostProcessing	Bloom, tone-mapping, and color grading	Complex post stacks or custom effects
LumenSceneLighting	global illumination and reflections	High bounce counts, dynamic lighting overload
NaniteRaster	Rendering of Nanite meshes	Excessive triangle counts, poor fallback settings
DiffuseIndirectAndAO	Screen space and Lumen reflections	Multiple reflection captures, rough surfaces

Table 10.1: Common passes in the profiler

Figure 10.8 shows the previously mentioned render passes in the GPU profiler:

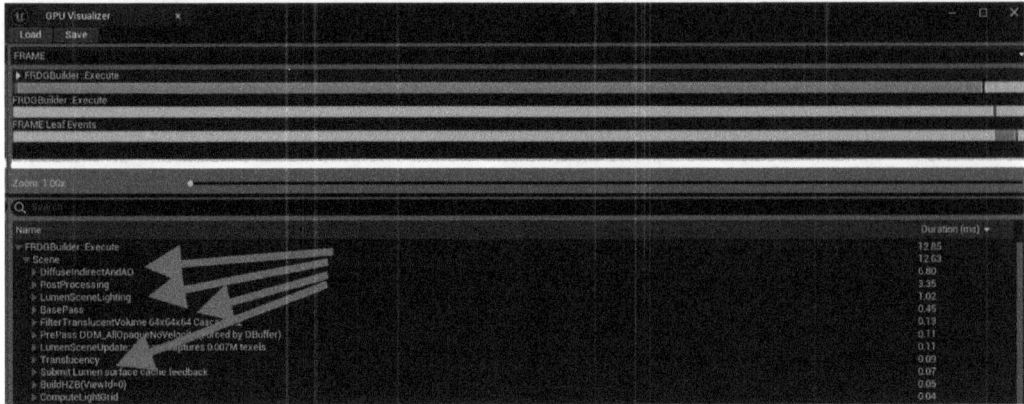

Figure 10.8: Render passes in the GPU profiler

Interpreting the numbers

Once you've identified the different render passes in the profiler, the next step is understanding what the numbers actually mean. Interpreting these values correctly will help you spot bottlenecks and decide where to focus your optimization efforts:

- Look for **high millisecond values** (anything above 2–3 ms per pass is worth investigating)
- Sort the entries by **time consumed** to find your top offenders
- Use **GPU Visualizer (profilegpu)** and **Shader Complexity viewmode** together to correlate data

Optimization tactics

Once you know which pass is causing the slowdown, apply targeted fixes:

- **BasePass:**
    - Simplify layered Materials and complex shaders.
    - Use Material instances instead of dynamic parameters where possible.
    - Remove excessive per-pixel effects (e.g., high-cost normals or parallax occlusion).
- **Translucency:**
    - Use **Dithered Opacity** or masked Materials instead of full transparency.
    - Avoid large overlapping translucent meshes (especially in particles and fog).
    - Limit the number of transparent layers stacked in view.

- **Lumen:**

  - Reduce **Bounce Intensity** in the Post Process Volume.

  - Limit dynamic lights casting shadows.

  - Use static lighting or mesh cards for distant emissive detail.

  - Disable **Global Illumination** or **Reflections** where not needed.

- **Decals:**

  - Turn off **Receive Decals** on assets that don't need them.

  - Reduce **Decal Draw Distance** and the lifespan of particles.

- **Lights:**

  - Avoid overlapping shadow-casting Movable Lights.

  - Use Stationary or Static lights where you can.

  - Cap **Light Complexity** using the **View** mode (*Alt + 7*).

Figure 10.9 shows how light complexity increases as you have more overlapping shadow-casting lights:

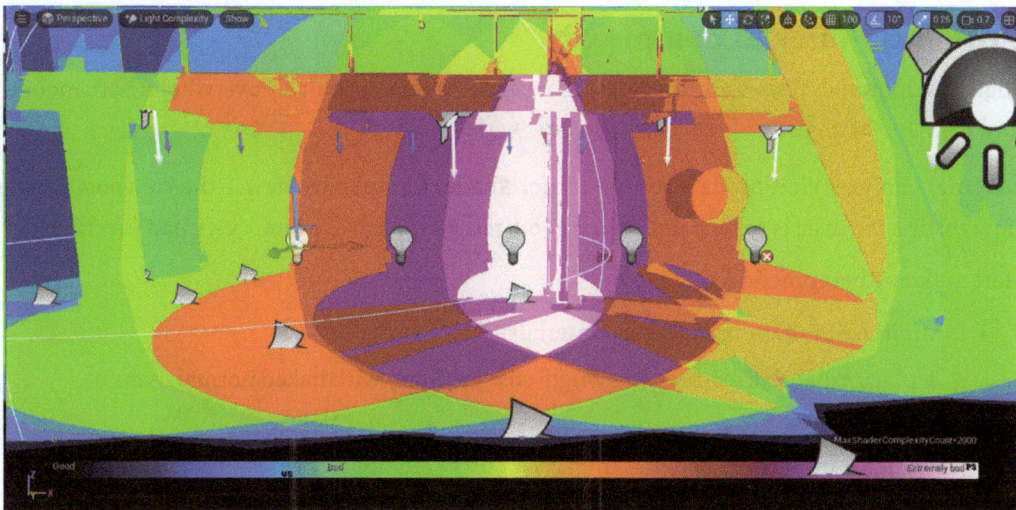

Figure 10.9: Increased light complexity with more overlapping shadow-casting lights

Tip

Lumen and Nanite are incredibly efficient when used as intended, but they are not magic. Overusing dynamic shadow casters, high-emissive Materials, or improperly configured Nanite fallback meshes can lead to steep costs.

Now that you know how to identify GPU bottlenecks in greater detail, the next step is actual optimization strategies and processes. Let's move on to asset and Level optimization.

Asset-level optimization: Materials, LODs, and streaming

Beautiful assets are great, but even the most stunning visuals can tank performance if they aren't optimized. In UE5, most performance spikes tied to assets stem from **Material complexity**, **mesh density**, and **texture streaming pressure**.

This section covers how to profile and optimize asset-heavy scenes using built-in tools and smart asset practices.

Profiling Material complexity

High-cost Materials (especially translucent or layered ones) can quickly overwhelm both mobile and high-end systems.

Material Analyzer View Mode is your *go-to* tool. **Shader Complexity** view in the Viewport shows how costly each pixel is to render: Green = good, red = expensive, white = very bad (overdraw).

Here are some best practices to follow:

- Minimize if/else branches in Materials.
- Replace expensive features (e.g., high-cost parallax) with baked normal maps or detail textures.
- Reduce transparency and masking; prefer **dithered opacity** when possible.

Using LODs and Nanite intelligently

Nanite handles mesh complexity brilliantly, but it's not a silver bullet.

You can follow these best practices:

- Use **custom fallback meshes** for animated objects.
- Review the Nanite fallback settings to avoid over-drawing small objects.
- For non-Nanite assets, do the following:
    - Set up LOD chains with aggressive screen-size thresholds.
    - Use impostors or billboards for far-distant background assets.

> **Tip**
>
> For mobile or non-Nanite platforms, LOD setup is still king. Prioritize LOD creation early in your asset pipeline.

Optimizing texture streaming

Textures eat a lot of memory and can cause hitches if streaming is poorly managed.

Here are some useful commands:

- `r.TextureStreaming 1`: Ensures UE5 streams in only needed textures.
- `r.Streaming.PoolSize`: Controls how much texture memory Unreal Engine can use.
- `r.Streaming.FullyLoadUsedTextures 1`: Loads all visible textures immediately for debugging.

Here are some best practices to follow:

- Keep texture sizes to **power-of-two**, and use **lower MIP bias** for performance.
- Use **Virtual Texture** for landscapes and large surfaces.
- Watch out for high-res textures on small objects; set the correct LOD bias and streaming distance.

With assets tuned for runtime efficiency, let's finish by zooming out, reviewing holistic project profiling and a few production-ready optimization workflows.

Optimization workflow: Step-by-step loop

Performance optimization isn't a one-off task; it's a continuous loop of analysis, improvement, and validation. Whether you're shipping on console, PC, or mobile, this repeatable workflow will help you stay in control of your game's performance throughout development.

Step 1: Profile baseline performance

Begin by establishing a clear performance baseline:

- Use stat unit, stat fps, and stat Streaming for real-time diagnostics.
- Use Unreal Insights to record deeper performance sessions for CPU/GPU/thread timing data.
- Test both worst-case and average gameplay conditions (e.g., dense scenes, VFX-heavy moments, or large crowds).

> **Tip**
>
> Record multiple data points; frame rate alone isn't enough. Capture frame time consistency, hitching, and thread pressure.

Step 2: Identify bottlenecks

Once you have your data, pinpoint which systems are underperforming:

- *GPU-bound?* Check for expensive rendering passes (Lumen, translucency, and shadows).
- *CPU-bound?* Check logic-heavy blueprints, ticking Actors, or animation overhead.
- *Scene-bound?* Look at overdraw, HLODs, streaming stutter, or memory pressure.

> **Tip**
>
> Focus on the top 1–2 bottlenecks first; tackling everything at once dilutes your effort.

Step 3: Optimize targeted systems

Now that you've found the culprits, apply focused optimization strategies:

- Reduce shader complexity, LOD costs, or shadow cascades.

- Disable unnecessary ticking or move logic off the main thread.
- Simplify complex Materials or dynamic lights.

Don't aim for perfection in one pass; refinements can build up over time.

Step 4: Re-profile and iterate

Re-test your scene after changes:

- Did the optimizations improve performance measurably?
- Did any new issues appear (e.g., visual bugs or regression in other areas)?
- Validate both peak and average performance improvements.

This step ensures you're not "fixing" one system while quietly breaking another.

Step 5: Automate where possible (thread)

Build automation into your performance workflow:

- Use automation tools to track FPS and memory across builds.
- Build custom performance checkpoints into your test maps.
- Log results over time to catch performance regressions early.

Optimization is a cycle, not a sprint, and in the next chapter, we'll build on these fundamentals with advanced optimization strategies, digging deeper into memory management, streaming systems, and high-end rendering trade-offs. For now, let's finish up by summarizing what we have discussed in this chapter and prepare to move forward to some more advanced concepts.

Summary

Performance isn't just a checkbox at the end of development; it's a mindset that should be baked into every stage of production. The goal is not simply to hit 60 FPS but to deliver a stable, consistent experience that feels good to play, looks great, and runs well across all target platforms. UE5 offers wonderful profiling and optimization tools that empower you to make informed decisions, not compromises.

By adopting a performance-first approach, you avoid late-stage panic and make space for artistry within technical constraints. A scalable scene is a sustainable scene, one that won't collapse under complexity as your project grows.

Throughout this chapter, we explored the following principles:

- **Profile early, profile often**: Use UE5's built-in tools to monitor performance consistently.

- **Optimize what matters**: Don't guess. Let real data guide your decisions.

- **Stay modular and clean**: Scalable environments are easier to debug, iterate, and ship.

- **Test across real hardware**: Simulate your players' experience before they do.

- **Build a feedback loop**: Small, focused improvements made regularly go further than last-minute overhauls.

When combining these tools with strategies from other chapters in this book, you will begin to have a complete development pipeline and production strategies within your own projects, which will allow you to create games that are both beautiful and performant.

Further reading

This list of further readings is from other authors under the Packt Publishing label, and a few of my personal recommendations for getting a deeper understanding of game performance and profiling in Unreal. They are definitely programming-heavy, since that naturally lends itself to optimization, but I'll try to cover the artist side in greater depth in the next chapter to make up for the lack of books covering the topic.

- *Unreal Engine 5 Game Development with C++ Scripting: Become a professional game developer and create fully functional, high-quality games.* Read more here: `https://amzn.asia/d/0KDx5Nc`

- *Unreal Engine Pro: Advanced Development Secrets.* Read more here: `https://amzn.asia/d/91eNRO0`

- *Unreal Engine 5 Game Development with C++ Scripting: A Practical Guide for Developers of all Levels, Optimize & Troubleshoot High-quality Games from Start to Finish.* Read more here: `https://amzn.asia/d/gNa1y4q`

Subscribe to Game Dev Assembly!

We are excited to introduce **Game Dev Assembly**, our brand-new newsletter dedicated to everything game development. Whether you're coding, designing, animating, or managing a studio, we've got insights, trends, and expert advice to help you create, innovate, and thrive. Sign up now and get exciting benefits.

https://packt.link/gamedev-newsletter

Join our community on Discord

Join our community's Discord space for discussions with the authors and other readers:

https://packt.link/unrealengine

11

Advanced Optimization for Real-Time Rendering

In high-end real-time development, optimization isn't about stripping your project down to the bare minimum; it's about making deliberate, efficient decisions that support both performance and visual quality. In fact, many of the best-looking projects in Unreal Engine 5 are also some of the most optimized. Why? Because optimization encourages clarity, intention, and control over what the player sees and experiences.

This chapter builds directly on the profiling workflows explored in *Chapter 10*. Now that you know how to find performance issues, we'll focus on render-specific strategies to solve them. These are practical, high-impact techniques you can apply right now to get better results on any platform, from cinematic PC builds to performance-constrained mobile devices.

In this chapter, you will learn:

- How to diagnose expensive rendering features such as translucency, shadows, and post-processing
- Techniques for optimizing materials and lighting setups for scalability
- Improve streaming and LOD strategies in a way that supports level design
- Balancing real-time visual fidelity with project-specific frame budget goals

Let's begin with some of the most common rendering cost drivers and how to reduce them without sacrificing what makes your project visually special.

Technical requirements

To follow along with this chapter, ensure that you have:

- Unreal Engine 5.4 or later

- Basic understanding of the UE interface and general pipeline best practices in Unreal Engine

- Read the previous chapter (*Chapter 10*) of this book

- Optional: A project with pre-built assets for testing and practice (or start with Unreal's sample projects)

Rendering cost breakdown: what's really expensive?

Before you can optimize your visuals, you need to understand where your GPU time is actually going. In UE5, rendering performance is shaped by several core systems that can quickly become expensive when pushed too far. These areas should be your first stop when diagnosing slow frames or poor scalability.

Common high-cost rendering systems include the following:

- **Lumen Reflections and Global Illumination (GI)**: Lumen provides beautiful dynamic lighting, but bounce lighting, screen traces, and software ray tracing can become costly, especially in complex indoor scenes or with too many bounce surfaces. Watch out for excessive bounce light, high roughness surfaces reflecting Lumen GI, and non-static geometry affecting reflection stability.

- **Virtual Shadow Maps (VSMs)**: VSMs offer fine shadow detail and support Nanite, but can become a drain on GPU time if many shadow-casting lights or large scenes with dynamic objects are in play. Use shadow distance settings, light channeling, and selective shadow casting to reduce overhead.

- **Transparency and overdraw**: Translucent materials, such as glass, smoke, and UI, can cause significant overdraw. These materials bypass depth testing and require extra passes, especially when layered. Use masked or dithered materials when possible, and keep overlapping transparent effects minimal.

- **Material complexity**: Highly layered materials with multiple texture samplers, expensive math operations (e.g., world position offsets, parallax, etc.), or per-pixel lighting models will impact rendering performance. Complex master materials should be simplified for use on background or less important assets.

Tools for diagnosis include the following:

- **GPU Profiler** (*Ctrl + Shift + ,*): Get a real-time snapshot of your scene's render passes, including **Base Pass**, **Translucency**, **Shadow Depths**, and **Lumen Costs**.

- **Shader Complexity View** (**Lit | Shader Complexity**): Visualize the pixel cost of your materials directly in the viewport. Green is cheap, red is expensive, and white is where you need to start fixing things fast.

Figure 11.1 shows an in-engine example of a heatmap screenshot from the **Shader Complexity** view, where to find it, and areas of high material cost, excessive transparency, or Lumen-heavy surfaces.

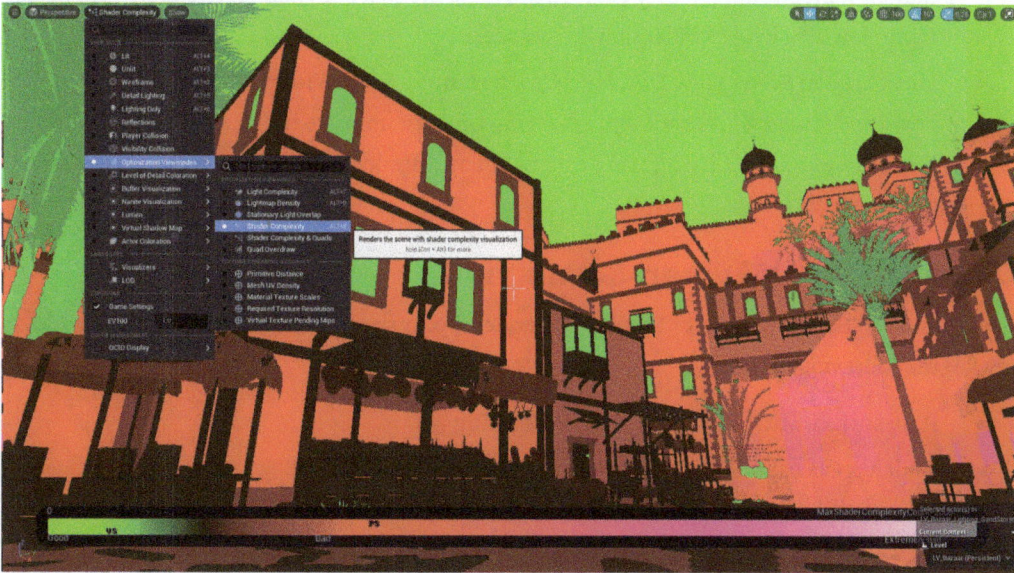

Figure 11.1: A heatmap screenshot from the Shader Complexity view

Now that we understand where rendering costs really come from, let's focus on one of the biggest performance hitters in UE5—**Lumen**—and explore how to get the most from it without sacrificing quality.

Lumen optimization: getting the most from GI

Lumen is one of UE's standout features, offering dynamic GI and reflections without baking, but it can also be one of the most performance-intensive systems in your scene. Optimizing it effectively lets you maintain visual richness while staying within your rendering budget.

Practical tips for reducing Lumen overhead include the following:

- **Use Static or Stationary lights when appropriate**: Dynamic lights are expensive, especially when there are many. If a light doesn't need to move or flicker dynamically, consider converting it to **Static** or **Stationary** to reduce cost.

- **Adjust Lumen GI quality**: Use the **Lumen Scene Lighting Quality** slider in your **Post Process Volume** to lower overall lighting detail. Reducing this can significantly boost performance, especially on lower-end hardware.

- **Lower Lumen Reflections quality**: In the same **Post Process Volume** settings, reduce the **Lumen Reflections | Quality** value to decrease the cost of dynamic reflections. This helps minimize GPU load in reflection-heavy scenes.

- **Limit Lumen Scene View Distance**: Use the **Lumen Scene View Distance** slider to control how far detailed GI is rendered. Lowering this can improve frame rates by reducing the amount of high-fidelity lighting calculated at distance, with visual trade-offs in far-off geometry, and so on.

Diagnostic tool: Lumen Scene view

Use the **Lumen Scene** view (**Lit | Lumen | Overview**) to inspect how Lumen sees your world. It reveals the following:

- How surface attributes affect bounce lighting
- Which areas use surface cache data
- When and where screen traces are applied

This view is essential for understanding what's contributing to bounce cost and reflection behavior, and for catching hidden performance traps such as emissive spam or over-bright surfaces.

Figure 11.2 shows an in-engine example of the **Lumen Scene** view and where to find the setting.

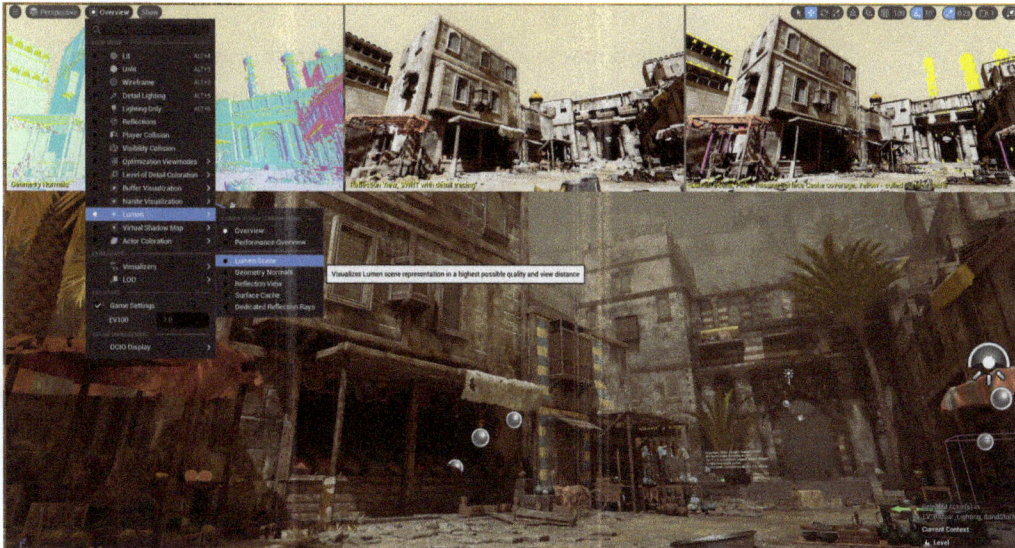

Figure 11.2: An overview of the Lumen Scene view

> **Tip**
>
> Lumen behaves differently across quality tiers. Always test your scene at multiple
> scalability levels to ensure consistent performance across devices and player settings.

Nanite optimization: geometry that performs

Nanite revolutionizes real-time rendering by allowing massive triangle counts with minimal draw call cost. But using Nanite effectively requires more than just enabling it; smart usage can mean the difference between peak performance and hidden slowdowns.

Use Nanite wisely, not blindly, by following these tips:

- **Avoid Nanite for translucent or deforming meshes:** Nanite does not support translucent materials, skinned meshes (limited), or vertex animations. Applying Nanite to such assets can lead to rendering issues or unintended behavior. It's advisable to exclude foliage, character meshes, FX elements, and glass objects from Nanite usage.

> **Note**
>
> Epic Games continues to make significant progress in addressing many of these limitations. For example, Nanite support for foliage is reportedly in development, and the engine evolves rapidly with each new release. As a result, some of the information in this book may become outdated, depending on when you're reading it. Be sure to consult Epic's official documentation for the most current details on these cutting-edge features.

- **Bake detail when the silhouette allows**: For surfaces where intricate details don't significantly affect the silhouette, consider baking those details into normal maps. While Nanite excels at preserving geometric fidelity, not all meshes require high triangle counts. This approach can optimize performance without compromising visual quality.

- **Implement effective culling strategies**: Nanite meshes remain rendered if they're within the camera's view, regardless of their size or occlusion status. To enhance performance, use the following:

  - **Cull Distance Volumes**: Utilize **Cull Distance Volumes** to define distances at which Actors are no longer rendered.

  - **Hierarchical Level of Detail (HLOD)**: Employ HLOD systems to merge and simplify distant meshes.

  - **Packed Level Instances**: Use **Packed Level Instances** to convert static meshes into instanced static meshes, enabling distance culling.

Diagnostic tools

- **Nanite Stats**: Use `r.Nanite.ShowStats 1` in the console to inspect instance counts, memory usage, and triangle budget per mesh. This helps pinpoint unexpected performance drains from specific assets.

- **Nanite Visualization Overlays**: In the **Viewport | Nanite Visualization** menu, options such as **Triangles**, **Instances**, and **Overdraw** can help you visually inspect geometry density and scene composition at a glance.

Figure 11.3 shows an in-engine example of the **Nanite Overview** and where to find it from my currently in-development indie game, *Primordials Legends: Hollow Hero*.

Figure 11.3: The Nanite Overview window and where to find it (image source: Primordials Legends: Hollow Hero, by Toybox Games Studios)

Nanite's triangle streaming is powerful, but in very dense scenes, it can become a bottleneck, especially on lower-spec machines. Test your environments early and often, especially during fast traversal or when many Nanite assets are visible simultaneously.

Shadowing techniques: performance without compromise

Shadows play a major role in visual realism, and as a lighting artist, I find them essential to achieving the mood and tone I am looking for with so many of my environments and scenes, but they're also one of the most expensive and dangerous rendering features in Unreal Engine, especially for those who do not know how to handle them. However, with careful shadow setup, you can retain fidelity while keeping performance under control.

Let's compare Virtual Shadow Maps with Cascaded Shadow Maps:

- **Virtual Shadow Maps (VSMs)**: UE5's default system for Nanite-compatible scenes. Offers sharper, more stable shadows at various distances, but can be costly on lower-end hardware. Great for high-end visuals, but be sure to monitor memory and per-light shadow cost.

- **Cascaded Shadow Maps (CSMs)**: Traditional system, still performant on non-Nanite or mobile projects.Cheaper but less detailed. Great for use in broad, large-scale outdoor scenes with many static objects.

You can optimize what casts shadows, as follows:

- **Limit dynamic shadow casters**: Disable dynamic shadows on small or flat decorative assets. Set **Cast Shadow** to **false** in the **Details** panel or via Blueprint for runtime control.

- **Use light channels for selective shadowing**: Assign lights and meshes to separate lighting channels to limit which objects affect which lights. This is great for hero objects needing special treatment.

- **Distance fade for shadow drop-off**: Set shadow fade distances to reduce shadow rendering for distant objects. This maintains fidelity up close while saving rendering cost over distance. Also, limit whole lights' **Draw Distance**, reloading them when they are not needed.

- **Bake when you can—baked shadows on Static elements**: For props, architecture, and background set dressing, use **Stationary** or **Static** lights with baked shadows and Lightmass GI. This reduces real-time load dramatically; however, it doesn't scale well, and isn't realistic from a development perspective for large maps, as baking times can become untenable.

Even perfectly optimized lighting can't save a scene if the materials are too heavy. Let's look at how simplifying material setups can dramatically improve frame times, whether your project is stylized or photoreal.

Material complexity: keep it simple, stylized or not

Whether your project is photoreal or stylized, complex materials can quickly tank performance. Optimizing material logic is one of the easiest ways to reduce GPU cost without sacrificing style or detail. Let's look at how:

- **Material tips for better performance**:

  - **Limit texture samplers and instructions**: Each texture lookup adds cost. Stick to fewer samplers when possible. Consolidate masks into channels and reuse textures across materials.

- **Prefer simpler blend modes: Opaque** materials are fastest. **Masked** is costlier, and **Translucent** is the most expensive; avoid it unless necessary.

> **Tip**
>
> Use dithered opacity for fake transparency on compatible assets.

- **Precompute expensive effects**: Fancy math means expensive shaders. Bake effects such as curvature, dirt, or edge wear into textures or decals instead of generating them dynamically.

- **Profiling material performance:**

  - **Shader Complexity view** (*Alt + 8*): This is a visual heatmap of how complex each pixel is to render:

    - Green = Good.
    - Red = Expensive. Aim for green or light yellow wherever possible.
    - White = Expensive!

  - **Stat GPU**: This gives per-material and per-draw call cost during gameplay.

> **Tip**
>
> Material layers and functions are great for modularity, but don't over-nest or overbuild them. Keep logic efficient and reusable.

Figure 11.4 shows what you should expect to see when using **Stat GPU**:

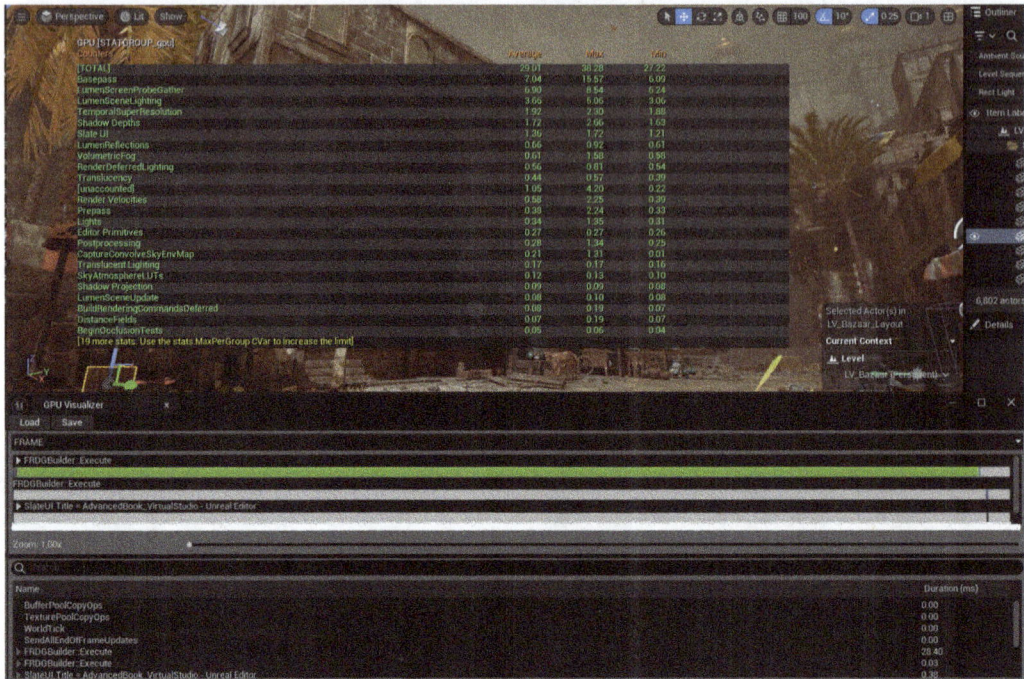

Figure 11.4: Stat GPU

Once your world is efficiently structured, the next challenge is managing what data loads, and when. Let's explore texture and asset streaming to keep your game's memory footprint lean and responsive.

HLODs and instancing: world optimization

Large, detailed worlds can strain performance, especially if every asset is rendered independently. HLOD and mesh instancing are essential tools for optimizing draw calls, memory usage, and streaming speed in UE5.

Here is a list of key techniques for world rendering efficiency:

- **Leverage HLODs**: UE5 can automatically merge distant actors into simplified proxy meshes. These HLODs reduce draw calls and material complexity at range.

- **Group Static Actors using instanced static meshes (ISMs)**: If you're repeating the same static mesh (e.g., rocks, crates, trees), convert them into ISMs or hierarchical ISMs. This significantly reduces draw call overhead by batching identical geometry.

- **Reduce Actor count in dense scenes**: Every actor has a tick cost, even static ones. Combine static meshes in densely populated areas (e.g., set dressing or debris) into single mesh assets to lighten the scene load.

- **World Partition integration**: HLODs work directly with World Partition streaming cells. Test streaming transitions and visibility logic in complex scenes using the **World Partition Debug** view.

Figure 11.5 shows an in-engine example of my recommended **World Partition** and **HLOD** settings within the **World Settings** tab:

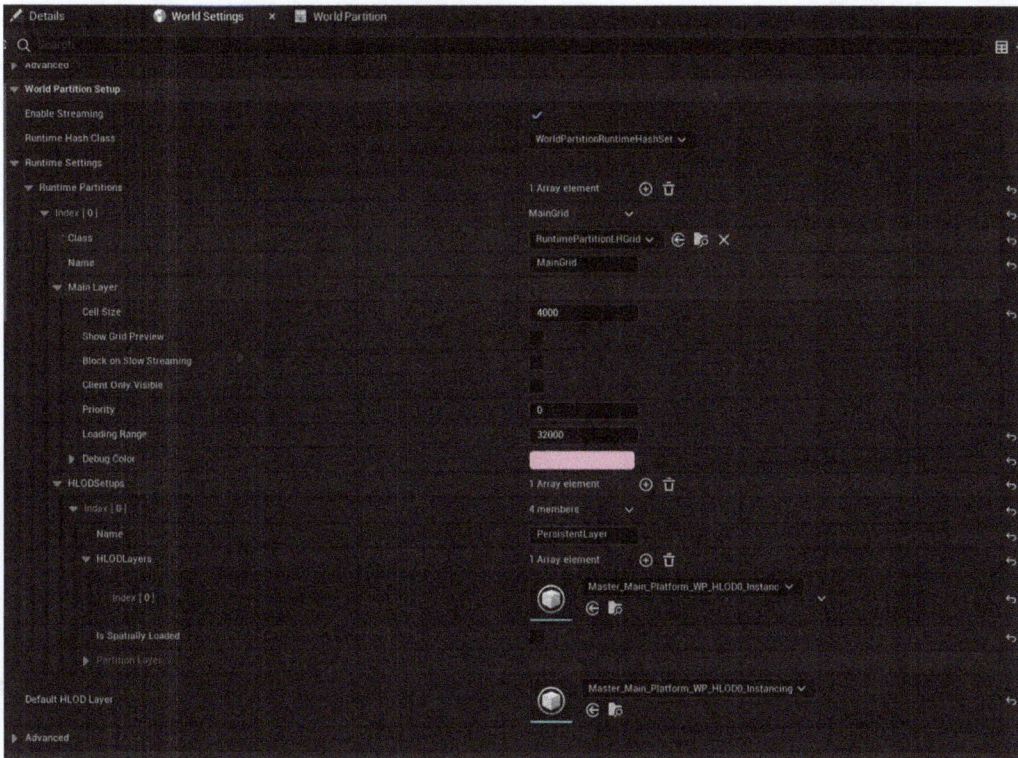

Figure 11.5: Best settings for World Partition and HLOD in World Settings

Once your world is efficiently structured, the next challenge is managing what data loads and when. Let's explore texture and asset streaming to keep your game's memory footprint lean and responsive.

Streaming and memory footprint

Efficient asset streaming and memory management are critical for real-time rendering, especially on memory-constrained platforms such as mobile or consoles. Poor streaming setups can lead to pop-in, long load times, or even crashes.

Here are some texture streaming best practices:

- **Use texture pool budgets**: Control texture memory with `r.Streaming.PoolSize` based on your target platform (e.g., 1,000–1,500 MB for mid-range PC, and 500–800 MB for mobile).
- **Adjust mip bias**: Lower mip bias values (`r.MipMapLODBias`) to reduce texture sharpness in favor of memory savings. Ideal for background objects or distant scenery.
- **Avoid oversized textures**: Limit 4K or 8K textures to hero assets only. Most objects can use 2K or even 1K with minimal quality loss.
- **Use real-time streaming commands**: Use runtime commands during play or test sessions to evaluate streaming performance:
    - `r.Streaming.FullyLoadUsedTextures 1`: Force-loads all textures currently used.
    - `r.Streaming.CheckBuildStatus`: Validates whether assets are prepped for streaming.
    - `stat Streaming`: Monitors streaming stats such as pool usage, required mip levels, and more.
- **Optimize asset and mesh LODs**:
    - Use more aggressive LODs for assets that are frequently seen from a distance.
    - Minimize material complexity per LOD.
    - Bake down complex geometry where Nanite isn't suitable or supported.

With the foundations of optimization covered, we can now dive into more advanced techniques that fine-tune system-level performance and bring all these principles together.

Advanced tips and systemic optimization strategies

Advanced optimization means looking beyond individual elements, focusing instead on how systems interact at scale. Many rendering slowdowns aren't caused by one thing, but by several overlapping processes.

Reduce render thread load

A surprising amount of performance loss can come from an overloaded render thread. Before looking at GPU-heavy systems, it's worth learning how to reduce this hidden bottleneck:

- **Minimize post-process overlap**: Avoid stacking heavy post-process effects (e.g., chromatic aberration + heavy DOF + screen-space reflections). Each layer adds cumulative cost.

- **Clean up visual Blueprint logic**: Any visual change driven by Blueprints—such as toggling VFX, changing materials, or updating the UI—can generate render thread spikes. Cache results or delay updates when possible.

- **Lower effect resolution**: Use lower-resolution buffers for the following:

  - **Motion Blur** (`r.MotionBlurQuality`)
  - **Depth of Field** (`r.DepthOfFieldQuality`)
  - **Ambient Occlusion** (`r.AmbientOcclusionLevels`)

These have a significant cost at high settings and often provide minimal visual gain in fast-paced gameplay.

Use scalability groups wisely

Scalability settings let you define visual quality per device class. Key groups include the following:

Group	Key settings	Performance impact
`sg.ShadowQuality`	Shadow resolution, distance	High
`sg.EffectsQuality`	Particle FX, decals	Medium
`sg.PostProcessQuality`	DOF, SSAO, bloom	High
`sg.ViewDistanceQuality`	LOD bias, streaming range	Medium

Table 11.1: Key scalability groups

Use these groups to tune for performance without touching asset content directly.

Automate performance testing

Use or find someone who can use tools such as Commandlets or the **Automation Framework** to do the following:

- Run headless builds for perf capture
- Test across device configurations
- Detect regressions early in your pipeline

This is especially powerful for large teams or live-service games where performance needs to be tracked continuously.

Summary

Optimizing for real-time rendering isn't just about squeezing out more frames per second; it's about making deliberate, informed visual decisions that scale with your project. Performance and quality aren't opposing forces; they can coexist through thoughtful design.

UE 5 gives you powerful tools such as Lumen, Nanite, and VSMs, but they come at a cost. The key is understanding when, where, and how to use them effectively.

Throughout this chapter, we explored the following principles and workflows behind optimizing for real-time in UE5:

- **Lumen and Nanite are powerful, but not free**: Use them strategically, profile often, and test across hardware.
- **Simplify materials and shadows**: Reducing shader complexity, transparency, and dynamic shadow casters leads to major wins.
- **Embed optimization into your workflow**: Make profiling, streaming budgets, and scalability testing part of your daily development loop, not a final step.

Performance-aware creativity leads to content that looks great, runs well, and reaches more players. And that's what great real-time development is all about. The things discussed here usually require some form of code support from a dedicated team, but for indies, sometimes, you just need to get your hands dirty, and this is where we start expanding our horizons, not just as artists, but as efficient game makers.

> **Important note**
>
> Like "modeling" or "design" in the previous chapters, "optimization" is a massive and diverse discipline that can easily fill the pages of several books, and something I still struggle with over a decade into my career. I hope that what you have read in this chapter provides you with some solid tips and tricks on how to approach optimization in Unreal Engine itself, but I also recommend self-research and the following *Further reading* resources to really expand on this complex and nuanced discipline.

Further reading

The following resources are excellent companions to the optimization principles we've covered in this chapter. While some focus directly on Unreal Engine 5, others provide broader insights into performance profiling, rendering pipelines, and real-time graphics optimization. These are solid reads for anyone serious about getting the best possible performance from their projects, whether targeting cinematic fidelity or pushing for 90+ FPS in gameplay.

These books are especially useful if you're building performance-critical experiences for VR, mobile, or console with the tightest possible frame budgets:

- *Real-Time Rendering (4th Edition)*: A gold standard for graphics programmers and technical artists alike. While not Unreal-specific, it explains the underlying concepts that affect rendering performance in any real-time engine. Read more here: `https://amzn.asia/d/7ACAaAo`.

- *3D Math Primer for Graphics and Game Development*: A foundational book that covers the math behind spatial transforms, culling, level-of-detail, and other optimizations often implemented under the hood. Read more here: `https://amzn.asia/d/iEtexFn`.

- *Unreal Engine 5 Shaders and Rendering Cookbook*: Offers hands-on recipes for building efficient materials, reducing shader complexity, and understanding how UE5's rendering systems work. Read more here: `https://amzn.asia/d/6XE0AFJ`.

Subscribe to Game Dev Assembly!

We are excited to introduce **Game Dev Assembly**, our brand-new newsletter dedicated to everything game development. Whether you're coding, designing, animating, or managing a studio, we've got insights, trends, and expert advice to help you create, innovate, and thrive. Sign up now and get exciting benefits.

`https://packt.link/gamedev-newsletter`

Get This Book's PDF Version and Exclusive Extras

UNLOCK NOW

Scan the QR code (or go to `packtpub.com/unlock`). Search for this book by name, confirm the edition, and then follow the steps on the page.

Note: Keep your invoice handy. Purchases made directly from Packt don't require one.

12

Asset Management Best Practices

Efficient asset management is the backbone of any successful game project, UE5 or otherwise. Whether you're building a high-fidelity cinematic experience or targeting optimized mobile performance, how you structure, organize, and maintain your assets directly impacts the stability, scalability, and speed of your development pipeline.

Without a clear system, even the most visually stunning projects can become difficult to manage, leading to bloated builds, broken references, and hours of unnecessary cleanup. With a *strong asset management foundation*, however, teams can iterate faster, collaborate seamlessly, and scale projects with confidence.

In this chapter, we'll explore the essential principles, workflows, and tools for managing assets effectively in Unreal Engine 5. From folder structure and naming conventions to source control and redirector cleanup, this chapter aims to provide you with a practical toolkit for keeping your projects clean, consistent, and future-proof.

In this chapter, you will learn:

- Why asset management matters in UE5
- Folder structures and naming conventions that scale
- Best practices for importing and organizing assets
- Managing asset dependencies and redirectors
- Practical asset cleanup and optimization tips

By the end of this chapter, you'll have a clear, structured approach to organizing and maintaining your UE project's asset library, one that supports both solo workflows and advanced full-scale team production. You'll gain practical knowledge that helps eliminate chaos in your **Content Browser**, reduce project bloat, and ensure your files remain accessible and performant, from pre-production to final shipping.

Whether you're importing hundreds of assets from DCC software, setting up materials for reuse, or collaborating across a team with version control, these best practices will help you save time, reduce errors, and scale your projects with confidence.

Let's begin by understanding *why* asset management is so critical in Unreal, and what can happen when it's ignored.

Technical requirements

To follow along with this chapter, ensure you have:

- Unreal Engine 5.4 or later
- Basic familiarity with the Content Browser and import workflows
- Read the previous chapters of this book
- Optional: Access to source control (e.g., Git, Perforce) for version control examples
- Optional: A project with pre-built assets for testing and practice (or start with Unreal's sample projects)

Why asset management matters

In Unreal, it's easy to get swept up in the excitement of importing stunning assets, building intricate scenes, and pushing visual fidelity to new heights—I know I do! But beneath every great-looking game or cinematic lies an invisible structure: a well-maintained, intelligently organized asset library. Without it, even the most beautiful projects can collapse under the weight of inefficiency.

Good asset management isn't just about keeping things tidy; it's a crucial part of your project's *health*. It directly affects everything from performance and iteration speed to collaboration and scalability. When overlooked, poor asset management becomes one of the biggest sources of bottlenecks, bugs, and burnout in a production pipeline.

Here's why it matters:

- **Faster load times and editor performance**: Unreal loads and indexes assets as you work. A bloated, disorganized project can lead to longer startup times, sluggish editor performance, and unnecessary memory usage. Keeping your asset library lean and logically structured means faster loading, smoother editing, and fewer slowdowns, especially critical when working on large levels or projects.

> **Example**
>
> I've worked on projects where a poorly managed `Content` folder ballooned the project size to over 100 GB, half of which was unused textures and duplicate materials. Once cleaned up, not only did the engine load significantly faster, but crashes during packaging vanished almost entirely.

- **Stable references = fewer bugs**: Unreal uses a system of soft and hard references to link assets together. When you *rename*, *move*, or *delete* assets without proper cleanup, you risk breaking references in Blueprints, Levels, Sequencer timelines, and more. These *invisible* errors often surface much later, costing time and sanity during crunch.

> **Pro tip**
>
> If you've ever encountered a level that fails to load because of a missing asset or a blueprint that suddenly throws null errors, you've likely encountered the consequences of unmanaged redirectors or broken references.

- **Scalability for teams and long-term projects**: Small projects can *get away with chaos*—even I've gone down this route for projects such as high-intensity game jams, with tight development timelines, and so on. But as soon as your team grows or your project hits a certain scale, disorganized assets become a roadblock for everyone. Clear folder hierarchies, naming conventions, and consistent structure make onboarding easier, reduce miscommunication, and ensure everyone can find what they need.

> **Pro tip**
>
> Asset naming conventions aren't just for programmers. Artists, designers, and VFX teams all benefit from predictable patterns. When you search for `SM_Chair_Oak`, you shouldn't also find a dozen `chair_1`, `test_obj`, or `import_042` files.

- **Optimized builds and reduced bloat**: Without regular cleanup, projects accumulate unused textures, old geometry, placeholder assets, and temp files. These inflate build sizes, increase cooking and packaging times, and eat up disk space, especially painful when working with version control or sending builds to QA or publishing platforms.

  Regular audits and automated tools can help identify what's actually being used, what's duplicative, and what can safely be removed, ensuring your project remains lightweight and performant.

- **Improved collaboration and source control integration**: If you're using Perforce, Git, or any source control system, consistent asset structure is vital. Renaming or moving assets arbitrarily can break other people's working copies or cause massive conflicts. A structured, intentional approach to asset management reduces these risks and enables smoother team collaboration.

In short, asset management is what keeps your project *sane*.

I'll be honest, it may not be the flashiest part of Unreal Engine, and I sure don't get the same *buzz* from doing it as I do from lighting a beautiful scene, but it's the foundation that makes everything else possible: faster iteration, fewer bugs, cleaner levels, and happier teams. Whether you're a solo dev or working with a studio, the habits you build around asset hygiene will pay off tenfold over the course of development.

Now that we've explored the *why*, let's look at the *how*, starting with building a folder structure that scales.

Structuring your Content Browser: folder conventions

A strong folder structure is your first defense against chaos in Unreal 5. Whether you're working solo or in a team, organizing your Content Browser early and sticking to a clear system will save you hours (if not days) of future headaches.

Unreal doesn't force a particular structure, which is both a blessing and a curse. Left unchecked, assets can pile up in a flat, unreadable sprawl. But with just a bit of planning, you can create a layout that supports scalability, collaboration, and long-term maintenance.

Recommended folder layout

Figure 12.1 shows a battle-tested top-level structure that works as a strong starting foundation for both small and large projects:

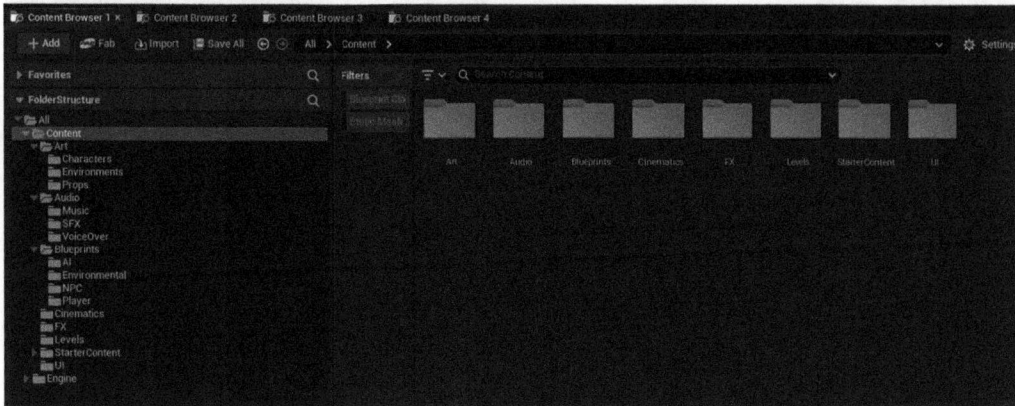

Figure 12.1: Screenshot of a foundational folder structure in Unreal

This structure separates asset *types* rather than *scenes*, which helps avoid duplication and keeps related content centralized. You can always add subfolders, such as `Art/Environments/Forest` or `Blueprints/AI`, as your project grows.

> **Pro tip**
>
> Avoid naming folders after specific scenes or levels (e.g., `/Level01Assets`). It encourages repetition and makes global changes harder to manage.

Smart subfoldering

Don't bury assets five levels deep; it slows down navigation and makes migration painful. Aim for clarity over complexity.

Figure 12.2 shows an Unreal documentation flowchart that represents what some solid subfolder-Ing can look like.

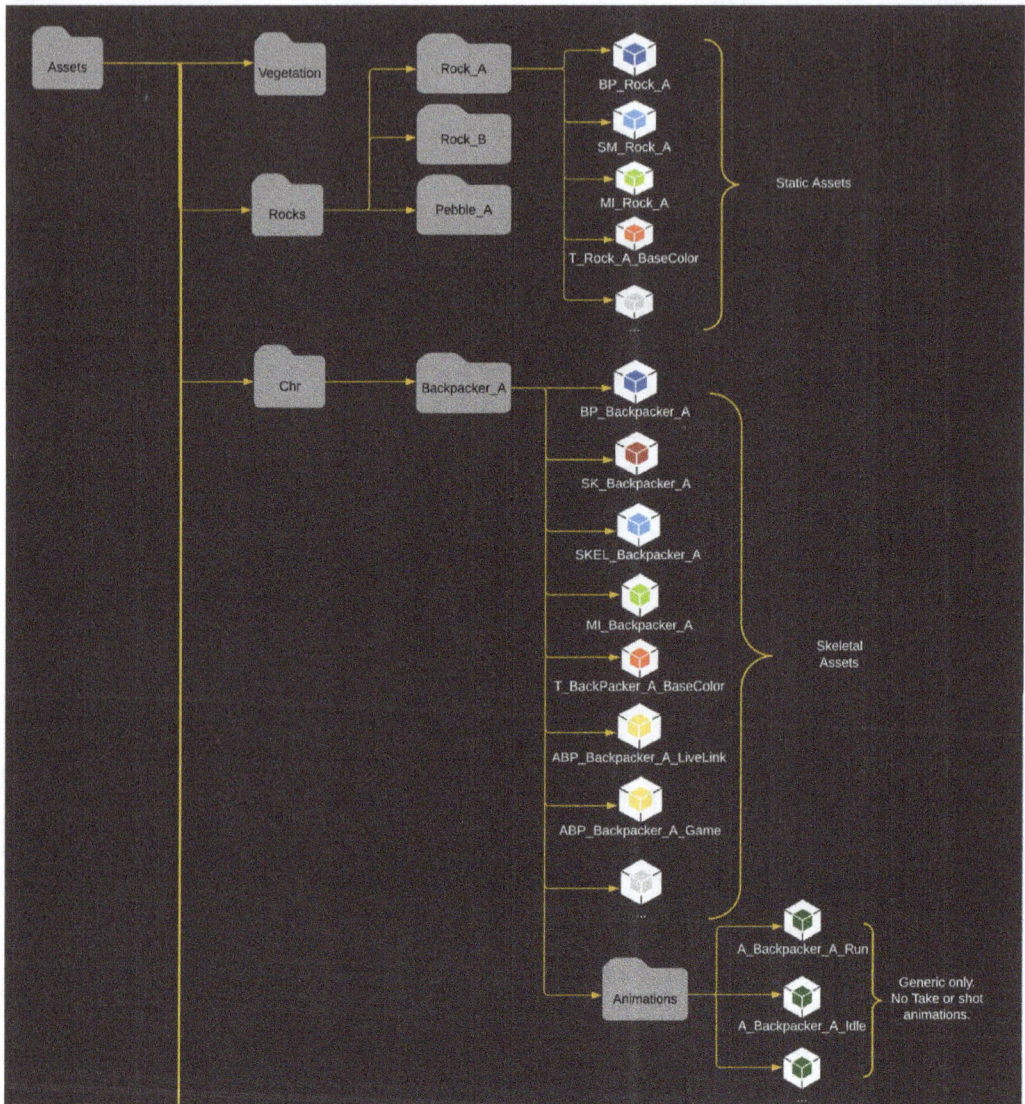

Figure 12.2: An Unreal documentation subfolder flowchart

Figure 12.3 follows on from the previous figure, showing the same structure in Unreal.

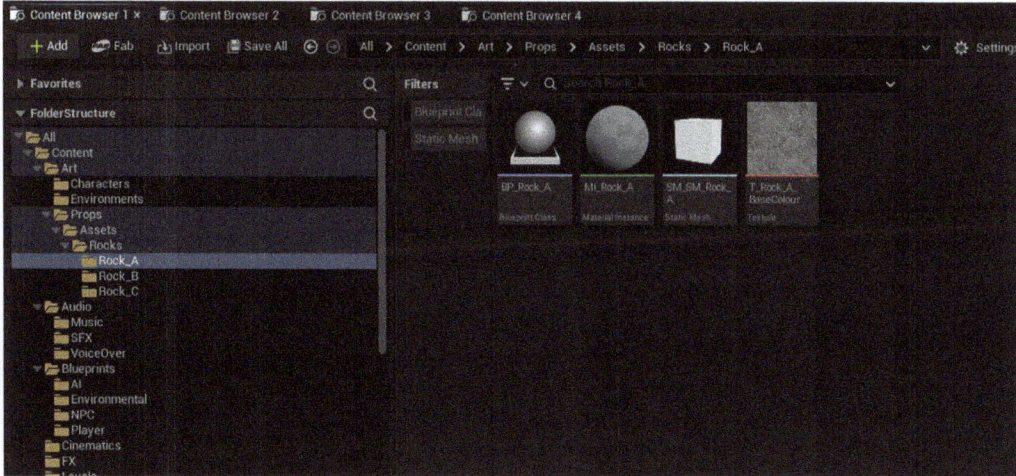

Figure 12.3: Flowchart in Figure 12.2 represented in Unreal Engine

> **Pro tip**
>
> Use short, consistent folder names. `Materials` instead of `MaterialLibrary_v2`; `FX` instead of `SpecialEffects_Market`.

A clean folder structure helps everyone move faster, locate assets quickly, and understand the project at a glance. In the next section, we'll reinforce this clarity by defining consistent

naming conventions, because good names matter just as much as good folders.

Naming conventions: the unsung hero

If folder structure keeps your project clean, naming conventions keep it *usable*. A consistent naming system makes assets easier to search, manage, and reference, especially when working in Blueprints, Sequencer, or with source control.

Without naming standards, you'll quickly end up with a mess of files such as `mesh_1`, `NewMat`, or `Final_Final_V2`, and no one will know what anything is. Multiply that by a team, and the problem compounds.

Quick rule

Every asset should be immediately identifiable by its name alone; no need to open or preview it to understand what it is.

Here is a list of some recommended common prefixes and suffixes:

Asset Type	Prefix	Suffix
Level/Map	LV_	
SubLevel (Audio)	SLV_	_Audio
SubLevel (Lighting)	SLV_	_Lighting
SubLevel (Geometry)	SLV_	_Geo
Blueprint	BP_	
Material	M_	
Material Instance	MI_	
Static Mesh	SM_	
Skeletal Mesh	SK_	
Texture	T_	_[X] (describes texture type, e.g., _D for diffuse)
Particle System	PS_	
Widget Blueprint	WBP_	
Level Sequence	LS_	_Master (For Master Shots) | _SH[XX] (describes shot number, etc.)

Table 12.1: Prefixes and suffixes for naming folders/subfolders

Example

SM_Chair_Wood_Oak is far more useful than WoodChair_Mesh or Chair_123.

Here are some additional best practices for naming conventions:

- **Be specific and readable:** MAT_Glass_Stained is better than MAT_01.
- **Avoid spaces or special characters:** Stick to underscores and alphanumerics.

- **Use suffixes where needed**: For variations or LODs (e.g., SM_Tree_Large_LOD1).
- **Use lowercase or Title_Case**: Just be consistent!

Naming conventions may seem small, but they scale exponentially. One clear system helps everyone, from artists to programmers, stay on the same page and avoid duplication, confusion, or bugs caused by misidentified assets.

With folders and names in order, let's move on to importing assets cleanly and keeping them that way.

Importing assets: clean pipelines from the start

How you import assets into UE5 sets the tone for everything that follows. Sloppy imports lead to naming mismatches, broken materials, scale issues, and wasted time redoing work. A clean import process ensures consistency, reduces manual cleanup, and speeds up iteration, especially when assets are handed off between teams.

> **Golden rule**
>
> Prepare your assets properly *before* bringing them into UE5. Fix it once in your DCC tool, don't patch it five times in-engine.

FBX and static mesh import checklist

- **Name your files correctly** before import. Avoid generic names such as model1.fbx.
- **Reset transforms** and apply scale in your DCC tool (e.g., Blender: *Ctrl+A* → **Apply All**).
- **Use .01 to 1.0 scale ratio** for Blender or Maya (Unreal uses centimeters).
- **Turn off Import Materials** if you're using custom shaders or instancing.
- **Enable Combine Meshes** only if the object should be a single asset (e.g., modular wall versus multiple props).

> **Pro tip**
>
> For modular kits, import pieces as individual FBXs with consistent pivot points aligned to the grid. This makes them easier to snap together in-engine.

Materials and textures

- **Use master materials + instances**; don't create new shaders for every asset.
- **Import textures at the correct resolution**; don't upscale later.
- **Compress textures before import where possible**, but feel free to use Unreal's powerful compression settings as well!
- **Match naming to the asset they're for** (e.g., T_Chair_Oak_Albedo).

Skeletal assets and animations

- **Ensure skeleton hierarchies are consistent** across animations.
- **Avoid importing skeletons multiple times**; reuse a single base skeleton where possible.
- **Verify animation frame rate and root motion** settings before import.

A clean import pipeline avoids tech debt down the line. Whether you're sourcing from Megascans, the Marketplace, or your own 3D suite, start with structure and discipline; it's much easier than cleaning up chaos later.

Up next, we'll look at keeping your assets healthy by understanding dependencies and cleaning up redirectors.

Managing asset dependencies and redirectors

Every asset in Unreal Engine is connected; meshes rely on materials, Blueprints reference animations, and levels load textures. As your project grows, these **dependencies** can quickly become tangled. And when assets get renamed, moved, or deleted? That's where **redirectors** come in, and why it's so important to manage them properly.

What are redirectors?

When you move or rename an asset in UE5, it doesn't delete the original reference. Instead, it leaves behind a **redirector**, a placeholder that points to the new location. Redirectors help keep references intact during development, but over time, they pile up, and they do the following:

- Slow down asset loading and cooking
- Break packaging if not cleaned up
- Cause false file conflicts in source control

Warning!

Moving assets without fixing redirectors is one of the most common causes of "can't find asset" or "failed to cook" errors.

How to clean them up

Unreal makes it easy:

1.   In the Content Browser, right-click the top-level folder you want to clean.
2.   Choose **Update Redirectors References.**
3.   Save all assets when prompted.

Tip

Do this regularly, especially after large refactors or asset reorganizations. *But* make sure redirectors are pushed to source control before cleaning them, as this too can cause breaks in referencing for other team members.

Managing dependencies with the Reference Viewer

The Reference Viewer (*Right-click asset* | **Reference Viewer**) shows a visual map of what an asset depends on, and what depends on it. Use this to do the following:

* Track down unused or redundant assets.
* Find out why an asset can't be deleted.
* Avoid circular dependencies that can cause compile or cook errors.

Staying on top of redirectors and dependencies keeps your project light, reliable, and ready for shipping. Now let's wrap things up with some final cleanup and optimization workflows to keep everything running smoothly.

Practical cleanup and optimization tips

Even with the best structure and workflows, projects can get messy over time, especially under deadline pressure. That's why periodic asset cleanup is essential. Regularly reviewing and optimizing your Content Browser can improve performance, reduce the project size, and make future iterations faster and safer.

Here are a few targeted strategies to help you stay on top of asset hygiene.

Use the Asset Audit tool

UE5 includes a built-in **Asset Audit** tool (*Right-click asset*/**Folder → Asset Audit**) that gives a quick overview of the following:

- Asset memory usage
- Asset load times
- Texture resolution and compression

This is a great way to catch oversized textures, unused materials, or high-poly models slipping into your build.

Figure 12.4 shows an in-engine example of the preceding concept of **Control the "Player Eye"**, showing a scene designed and lit to clearly show the statue as the key element.

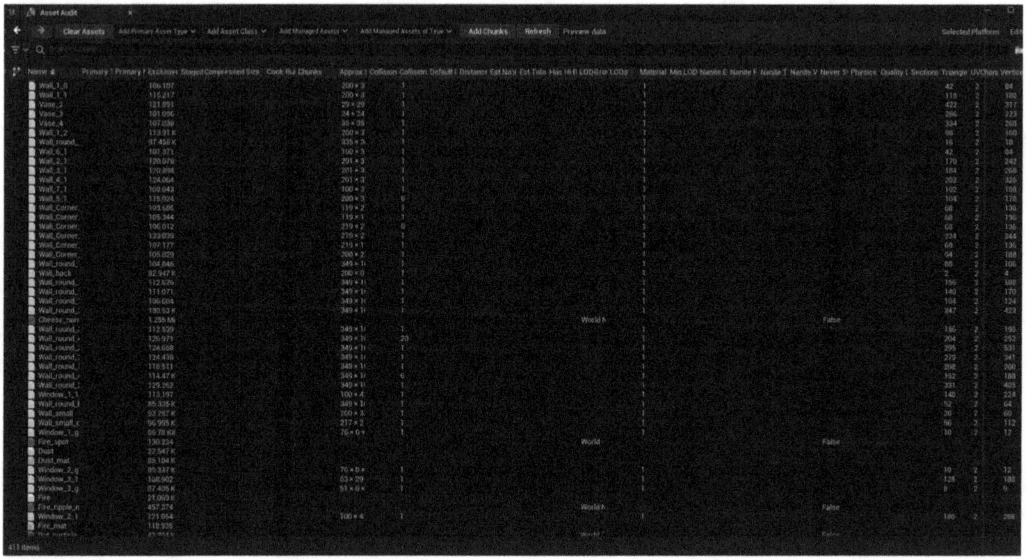

Figure 12.4: A screenshot of Unreal's Audit window

Identify and remove unused assets

Use the Size Map or Reference Viewer to identify unreferenced assets. If an asset has no dependencies and isn't used in levels or Blueprints, it's probably safe to delete.

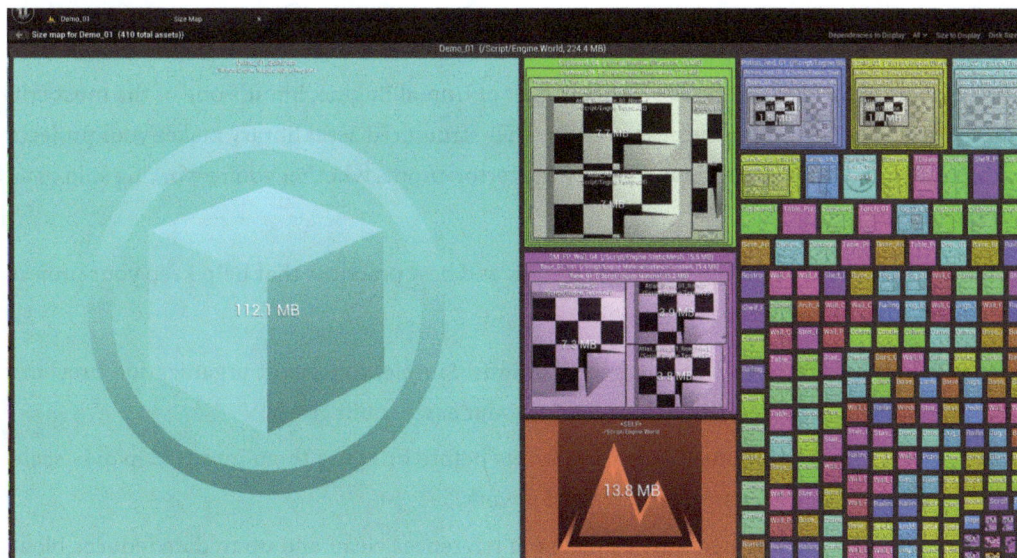

Figure 12.5: An example of Unreal's SizeMap windowReduce material complexity

Complex materials slow down rendering and increase shader compile times. When possible, do the following:

- Bake out material complexity into textures (normal, AO, roughness)
- Use *material instances* instead of full duplicates
- Combine static meshes that share materials to reduce draw calls

Clean up redirectors

As covered earlier, make redirector cleanup part of your milestone wrap-up process. Don't wait until the end of the project; fix them as you go.

Keeping your project lean and efficient doesn't just help with performance; it also saves hours of debugging, speeds up shipping, and helps maintain your artistic vision without technical compromise.

Let's wrap up with a quick summary of everything we've covered in this chapter.

Summary

Asset management may not be the flashiest part of Unreal Engine, but it's one of the most critical, especially for long-term success. A clean, well-structured asset library makes your projects easier to navigate, more performant, and far less error-prone, whether you're working solo or as part of a team.

In this chapter, we covered the core foundations and best practices that help keep your project organized, scalable, and healthy:

- **Folder structure and naming conventions**: Simple, consistent organization prevents confusion and duplication, especially as your asset count grows.
- **Clean import pipelines**: Preparing assets before bringing them into UE5 avoids scale issues, broken references, and wasted rework.
- **Redirectors and dependencies**: Keeping references clean and up to date reduces bloat and prevents hidden bugs from creeping into your builds.
- **Cleanup and optimization workflows**: Regular asset audits, unused asset checks, and material streamlining help you maintain a lean, performant project.

By applying these principles from the start, and reinforcing them as your project grows, you'll build a content pipeline that supports faster iteration, fewer bugs, and better collaboration across disciplines.

Whether you're shipping a cinematic trailer, an open-world RPG, or a mobile game, strong asset management will help ensure your project stays clean, stable, and ready for whatever comes next.

Let's carry that momentum forward into the next and final chapter, where we'll dive into *troubleshooting common development challenges* to get the best of my final Unreal tips and tricks to go with your stunning worlds and your beautifully managed content.

Let's get started, we're on the home stretch!

Further reading

This list of further reading includes some standout books from the Packt Publishing label and other trusted sources. While not all of them are Unreal-specific, they offer excellent insights into asset pipelines, digital production workflows, and scalable game development practices that complement what we've explored in this chapter. If you're looking to deepen your understanding of asset management and production structure, especially in 3D and real-time projects, these are solid places to start.

- *Unreal Engine 5 Game Development with C++ Scripting*: Covers the full pipeline of UE5 development, including organizing assets, managing references, and structuring content around gameplay systems. Read more here: `https://amzn.asia/d/5WtChh1`
- *Game Development Projects with Unreal Engine*: A great step-by-step guide with strong emphasis on setting up reusable systems, importing assets cleanly, and maintaining project scalability. Read more here: `https://amzn.asia/d/74g7j05`
- *Agile Game Development with Scrum*: While not about assets per se, this book offers key insights into organizing game production efficiently. Read more here: `https://amzn.asia/d/2Lzihmt`

Subscribe to Game Dev Assembly!

We are excited to introduce **Game Dev Assembly**, our brand-new newsletter dedicated to everything game development. Whether you're coding, designing, animating, or managing a studio, we've got insights, trends, and expert advice to help you create, innovate, and thrive. Sign up now and get exciting benefits.

`https://packt.link/gamedev-newsletter`

Join our community on Discord

Join our community's Discord space for discussions with the authors and other readers:

`https://packt.link/unrealengine`

13

Troubleshooting Common Development Challenges

No matter how experienced you are or how well-structured your project is, roadblocks in development are inevitable. UE5 is an incredibly powerful toolset, but with that power comes complexity. Crashes, bugs, performance issues, broken references, and *"it worked yesterday but not today"* problems are all part of the journey.

The reality is this: *every Unreal project will break at some point*. That's not a failure of planning; it's a normal part of building ambitious real-time content. What separates experienced developers from frustrated ones is the ability to *troubleshoot with intent*. Knowing *how* to solve problems is just as important as knowing *how* to build systems.

Over time, you'll start to recognize the signs of common issues, lighting bugs caused by incorrect UVs, broken materials that don't support Nanite, and gameplay events not firing due to Blueprint scope errors. The trick is learning how to approach these challenges *methodically*, using UE5's built-in tools and a few battle-tested workflows.

Whether you're working solo or across a multidisciplinary team, being able to isolate and fix problems efficiently will save you time, reduce risk, and give you more creative control over your project.

In this chapter, you will learn:

- How to approach problems methodically and isolate issues
- The most common causes of crashes and freezes
- Troubleshooting material and lighting bugs

- Fixing broken references, redirectors, and invisible assets
- Debugging Blueprint logic and gameplay behavior
- Diagnosing performance hitches and runtime stuttering
- Core troubleshooting tools every UE5 developer should know about

By the end of this chapter, you'll have a practical troubleshooting toolkit you can rely on across any UE5 project, and one that helps you navigate the technical challenges of everything we have discussed in this book with confidence and clarity. We are on the home stretch, so let's start by reframing how to approach problems when they appear.

Technical requirements

To follow along with this chapter, ensure you have:

- Unreal Engine 5.4 or later
- A solid understanding of the UE interface
- Read the previous chapters of this book
- Optional: A project with pre-built assets for testing and practice (or start with Unreal's sample projects)

Developing a troubleshooting mindset

Before we dive into common issues and fixes, let's talk about the mindset you need to trouble-shoot effectively. In my experience, one of the most underrated skills in Unreal development isn't technical; it's *how you think through problems*. The best game devs I know aren't just great creators; they are great problem solvers.

Unreal 5 is a complex environment. It's built on a mix of C++, Blueprints, shaders, streaming systems, asset references, live rendering, and editor tooling. When something breaks, it's tempting to panic, hit random settings, or hope a restart fixes it. But the most efficient developers don't panic; they *observe, isolate, and test*.

Here's a practical mindset to follow when something goes wrong:

Step 1: Reproduce the problem consistently

Before anything else, make sure the issue can be triggered reliably. Can you reproduce the bug in a clean scene? Does it only happen after a certain input or at a specific time?

If you can't reproduce it, you can't fix it. Find the trigger first.

Step 2: Narrow the scope

Ask yourself the following:

- Is this issue level-specific, asset-specific, or global?
- Did this start happening after a recent change or import?
- Is the problem tied to rendering, logic, audio, or packaging?

Strip the scene down to basics. Temporarily disable features, remove actors, or migrate the scene to a blank map. Isolate variables one by one.

Step 3: Rule out common culprits

Some issues are just...*unreal*. Being Unreal. Start by checking the following:

- **Corrupt assets** (especially from external sources or version mismatches)
- **Missing dependencies or redirectors**
- **Unsupported material settings** (Nanite, Lumen, translucency)
- **Plugins or Marketplace content** that override engine behavior
- **Project settings** that may have been altered accidentally

> **Pro tip**
>
> A huge number of bugs are caused by assets being moved, renamed, or deleted without redirectors being cleaned up.

Step 4: Use the tools available

UE5 gives you a powerful toolkit to investigate issues:

- Use **Output Log** and **Message Log** to catch missing references or compile errors
- Use **Blueprint Debugger** to step through logic at runtime
- Enable **Buffer Visualization** view modes to analyze lighting/rendering problems
- Run **Unreal Insights** for performance bottlenecks
- Use **stat commands** (e.g., stat unit, stat fps) to get instant feedback

We've covered these in previous chapters, and we'll cover each of these again in more detail later in this chapter.

Step 5: Test in isolation

When in doubt, create a **test level** or a stripped-down version of your scene. Start with only the asset or system that's causing issues. If it works in isolation, the problem is likely caused by an interaction between systems, not the asset itself.

This approach is especially helpful for debugging complex Blueprints, lighting bugs, or runtime logic failures.

Adopting this structured mindset helps you stay calm under pressure, reduce downtime, and solve problems more confidently. Now that we've set the foundation, let's explore some of the most common crashes and freezes developers encounter, and how to fix them.

Common editor crashes and freeze fixes

Unreal Engine 5 is incredibly powerful, but it's also sensitive. When something goes wrong at the engine level, the result is often a crash, a freeze, or a project that won't even load. These moments can be stressful, especially if you're on a deadline, but many crashes follow recognizable patterns and can be solved quickly if you know where to look.

Below are some of the most common causes of editor instability, along with practical fixes and prevention tips.

Corrupt assets

Assets that are partially imported, renamed externally, or migrated improperly are a major source of crashes.

Symptoms

- UE crashes during project startup
- Level crashes when opened
- Crash references an asset path or UUID

Fixes

- Open the project in a blank level (`DefaultEmptyMap`)
- Use **Output Log** to identify the last asset loaded before the crash
- Move or delete the suspected asset manually from the file system and reimport it properly

> **Pro tip**
>
> If you have a project you can't open due to the level on startup being corrupted, you can change the startup level within `DefaultEngine.Ini` as a way to force your way back into the engine to try and start fixing problems.

Overloaded materials or shaders

High-instruction materials can cause slow compiles or complete freezes, especially when previewing them on large Nanite meshes.

Fixes

- Reduce material complexity (especially with translucency or heavy world position logic).
- Use **Material Stats** to evaluate shader instruction counts.
- Disable preview meshes when editing high-complexity materials.

Plugin conflicts or engine version issues

Third-party plugins (or even Marketplace content) can break after engine updates or improperly migrated projects.

Fixes

- Disable plugins one by one in the `.uproject` file or via the **Plugin** window.
- Rebuild your project files after major version upgrades (*right-click* → **Generate Visual Studio Project Files**).
- Always back up before enabling unfamiliar plugins.

Broken level issues

Streaming levels and partitioned worlds can sometimes be corrupted, especially after undo-heavy sessions or source control merge errors.

Fixes

- Load into a different level and open the problematic one manually.
- Remove faulty actors from the level via the World Outliner (if accessible).

General recovery tips

- **Try autosaves:** Check **Saved | Autosaves** for recent versions of maps or Blueprints.
- **Clear Intermediate/Saved/DerivedDataCache:** Especially after crashes during compile.
- **Use log files: Saved | Logs | YourProject.log** contains detailed crash info (search for Critical Error).

Crashes will happen, but they're rarely the end of the world. Once you're familiar with the common causes, they become just another part of the creative workflow. Next, we'll dig into a more targeted topic: rendering and lighting bugs that impact your visuals.

Material and lighting bugs

Visual bugs can be some of the most confusing to diagnose, especially when everything looks fine in the editor but falls apart in play or in a packaged build. Whether it's flickering shadows, black materials, broken Nanite surfaces, or incorrect lighting responses, these issues often boil down to a few key culprits.

Let's walk through some of the most common material and lighting bugs in UE5 and how to fix them.

Black or broken materials

This is one of the most frequent issues, especially after importing Marketplace assets or migrating content between projects.

Causes

- Missing or disconnected texture inputs
- Unsupported shading models (e.g., translucency on Nanite meshes)
- Shader compile errors

Fixes

- Open the material and check the **Material Stats** tab for errors or warnings.
- Ensure all texture sample nodes are properly connected.
- Avoid using **refraction, translucent blend modes,** or **volumetric shading** with Nanite.

Lighting looks wrong or inconsistent

Lighting issues can stem from a range of things: UVs, normals, engine settings, or even Lumen's unique characteristics.

Symptoms

- Overly bright/dark surfaces
- Light leaking or glowing edges
- Shadow artifacts or flickering

Fixes

- Check mesh **Lightmap UVs (Channel 1)** in the **Static Mesh Editor**.
- Rebuild lighting if using static/stationary lights (even in Lumen).
- Make sure **Normal maps** aren't flipped or inverted (especially if authored in non-standard formats).
- Use **Buffer Visualization → Lighting Only** to isolate contribution issues.

Lumen-specific lighting glitches

UE5's dynamic GI system, Lumen, is powerful, but still has a few quirks developers need to watch out for.

Issues

- Soft shadows not appearing correctly
- Bounced lighting looking "washed out" or noisy
- GI appearing to lag behind dynamic changes

Fixes

- Avoid using unsupported platforms. Unfortunately, Lumen is expensive, and even on a PC, it can sometimes be too much; sometimes the fix is simply to not use it.
- Set the **Lumen Quality** and **Reflection Quality** settings in your Post Process Volume.
- Confirm that meshes are not affecting **Global Illumination** in their **Details** panel if not intended.

Materials flickering or Z-fighting

Flickering, especially at a distance, is often caused by overlapping geometry or mismatched LOD transitions.

Fixes

- Ensure only one surface occupies the same space (no duplicate meshes).
- Tweak LOD transition distances and material **Dither** settings.
- Avoid stacking planes with alpha or masked blend modes unless absolutely needed.

Viewport versus packaged build visual differences

Sometimes things look perfect in the editor but fall apart when cooked.

Fixes

- Avoid referencing assets only via the editor (e.g., through Level Editor Utility Widgets).
- Use **Primary Asset Labels** or **Asset Manager** to guarantee inclusion in packaged builds.

Lighting and material bugs can be frustrating, but with a clear understanding of how Unreal handles shaders, GI, and mesh rendering, they're also some of the easiest to isolate and fix.

Up next: let's look at another common headache, missing, invisible, or mysteriously broken assets.

Missing or "invisible" assets

It's a classic UE problem: something that was there yesterday has vanished today. Whether it's a mesh not appearing in-game, a material that shows up blank, or an actor that loads fine in-editor but disappears at runtime, missing or "invisible" assets are a common challenge, especially in larger projects with layered streaming or version control.

Here's how to diagnose and fix them quickly.

Redirectors not cleaned up

If assets have been moved or renamed without fixing redirectors, references can silently break.

Fixes

- In the Content Browser, right-click your top-level project folder and select **Update Redirector References**.
- Rebuild or recompile affected Blueprints, materials, or levels afterward.

> **Tip**
>
> Always clean up redirectors after reorganizing assets, especially before packaging or migration, but be sure to push redirectors if using source control so other team members' projects also know about the redirectors, and that they have been cleaned, and so on.

World partition or level streaming issues

Streaming levels or partitioned world cells can cause assets to unload unexpectedly or fail to appear at runtime.

Symptoms

- Actors visible in-editor but not in-game
- Objects load when the camera moves closer, then disappear again
- Assets missing in packaged builds only

Fixes

- Open the **World Partition Outliner** and verify that streaming cells are active.
- Check whether your actor is on a **Data Layer** that's disabled or filtered out.
- Make sure **Is Spatially Loaded** is checked for the assets you want to stream, and that they are on the correct runtime grid in the **Details** panel.
- Make sure **Is Spatially Loaded** is unchecked if the asset must be present from the start.

Incorrect actor scaling or LOD settings

If a mesh appears invisible, it may simply be scaled to zero, culled by distance, or swapped out by an empty LOD.

Fixes

- Check **Actor Scale** in the **Details** panel (especially after duplicating or importing).
- Open the Static Mesh Editor and inspect the LOD settings.

Missing texture or material references

If a material or texture is missing, a mesh may render with the default gray checker or go completely invisible, depending on the settings.

Fixes

- Reassign the correct material manually.
- Check **Output Log** for *missing asset* warnings on loading.
- Ensure the material domain is set correctly (**Surface**, **Post Process**, etc.).

Assets not included in packaged builds

UE5 sometimes excludes assets that aren't referenced directly or are only used via editor scripts or utility widgets.

Fixes

- Use **Primary Asset Labels** to explicitly mark assets for inclusion in builds.
- Avoid relying on **Get Asset by Name** unless backed by an Asset Registry entry.
- Confirm your maps and streaming levels are listed under **Packaging Settings | List of Maps to Include**.

Vanishing assets can feel overwhelming, but they're usually just a matter of narrowing the problem and using the right tools. Next up: let's look at those tools in detail, and how they help you track down even the sneakiest issues.

Tools and techniques for debugging in UE5

Unreal gives you a surprisingly robust suite of built-in tools to help you track down logic errors, performance issues, visual bugs, and packaging problems. Learning how to use these tools effectively can save you hours of guesswork and turn random issues into solvable tasks.

Following is a focused breakdown of the essential debugging tools every UE5 developer should know.

Output Log and Message Log

These are your first stop for any unexpected behavior. I know it seems obvious, but that's for good reason—you'll use them always!

- **Output Log (Window | Developer Tools | Output Log)**: Shows compile errors, runtime warnings, asset load issues, and plugin problems.
- **Message Log:** Highlights Blueprint compile errors and material warnings in real time.

> **Pro tip**
>
> Watch the log while packaging or loading levels; it often points directly to the culprit.

Blueprint Debugger

This is vital for gameplay logic and variable flow testing.

- Set **Breakpoints** on nodes to pause gameplay and step through logic.
- Supports stepping through **Tick**, **timelines**, and custom events.

> **Tip**
>
> Use **Simulate** instead of **Play** if you want to debug without possessing a character.

Stat commands (in-editor or console)

Quick, in-engine performance snapshots:

- `stat unit`: Shows frame time breakdown (game, draw, GPU).
- `stat fps`: Displays current frame rate.
- `stat memory`: Monitors texture pool and asset streaming.
- `stat anim`: Category-specific metrics.

These are lightweight and don't require Unreal Insights, though realistically, this is where you'll end up. Speaking of...

Unreal Insights

This is UE5's full-featured performance profiler:

- Records gameplay and rendering performance over time.
- Tracks spikes, hitching, asset loads, and thread timings.
- Ideal for diagnosing CPU/GPU bottlenecks or runtime memory pressure.

Buffer visualization view modes

These are essential for diagnosing lighting and shading issues:

- `viewmode lightingonly`: Direct lighting only.
- `viewmode roughness`: Visualize roughness values.
- `viewmode naniteoverview`: See Nanite mesh status.
- `viewmode virtualtexturing`: Useful for debugging VT-based materials.

These modes help isolate problems with GI, shadows, or surface properties.

Used together, these tools turn *What is happening?* into *Here's exactly where it broke.* Whether you're building a cinematic, a system-driven game, or a high-performance level, these are your go-to instruments for stability and polish.

A lot of these, as you can tell, are art-tech, art-driven solutions. I recommend further research or help from a dedicated programmer for more complex solutions; however, these should be perfect for any artist, game designer, filmmaker, or even junior programmer.

In our final section, we'll wrap things up with some general habits and troubleshooting tips to keep in mind across *any* kind of Unreal project.

Practical tips and habits

Troubleshooting isn't just a reaction; it's a habit. The best way to deal with bugs, crashes, and technical issues in Unreal Engine 5 is to develop daily practices that *prevent* problems before they snowball. The following are some real-world-tested habits that I use to save time, reduce stress, and keep my projects stable from start to finish.

Save incrementally and often

Use versioned saves such as `Level_Forest_v03` or `BP_BossFight_v07`. It's faster than source control rollbacks and lets you quickly compare between working and broken states. This can get out of control, though, and requires self-discipline; do not fall into the bad habits we learned to avoid in *Chapter 12*!

> **Tip**
>
> Use the **Save All** shortcut (*Ctrl + Shift + S*) regularly, especially before compiling or cooking.

Test in cooked builds early

Don't wait until the end of production to test a packaged build. Many bugs (especially logic errors, asset omissions, and shader issues) only show up when cooked.

- Create a *test map* with critical systems and test **development packaging** regularly.

Back up before major changes

Before engine upgrades, large refactors, or plugin installs, make a backup or zip of your project. You'll thank yourself if something breaks.

> **Pro tip**
>
> Use source control tags or branches before doing heavy restructuring or overhauls.

Use Print String (strategically)

Print String may be basic, but it's still one of the fastest ways to debug logic. Drop a print at key points in your Blueprint to confirm execution or check variable values.

Just remember to clean them up before final delivery!

Create a dedicated debug level

A minimal "debug map" lets you isolate problems without needing to load a full environment. Use it to test assets, lighting setups, or system prototypes in isolation.

Log and document fixes

If you're working on a team, or even for future you, keep a shared document of known issues and their fixes. It can save hours when a problem returns six months later.

Use community resources

If you're stuck, you're not alone. The Unreal forums, AnswerHub, Discord servers, and dev communities are full of developers who've likely solved the same issue.

> **Tip**
>
> Always include engine version, platform, reproduction steps, and error logs when asking for help.

Good habits won't eliminate every bug, but they *will* make you better equipped to find, fix, and learn from every issue you encounter. Now let's wrap up this chapter and reinforce the core ideas.

Summary

Troubleshooting in Unreal Engine is part of the creative process, not a detour from it. As projects grow in complexity, so too do the ways things can break. A popular quote among seasoned game developers is *"Video Games, really don't want to be built...They'll fight the whole time."* But with a clear mindset, the right tools, and a little patience, even the most intimidating issues can be broken down, diagnosed, and resolved.

In this chapter, we walked through some of the most common technical challenges in UE5 and how to approach them:

- Developing a *methodical troubleshooting mindset*
- Solving *crashes, freezes, and project startup issues*
- Fixing *material and lighting errors*, from Nanite conflicts to Lumen quirks
- Resolving *missing or invisible* assets due to redirectors, LODs, or streaming
- Leveraging tools such as *Unreal Insights, Blueprint Debugger, stat commands*, and more
- Building healthy daily habits for *preventing and documenting bugs*

By developing strong troubleshooting instincts, you'll not only save yourself hours of frustration, but you'll also become a more adaptable, reliable developer. Problems are inevitable in game development, but they're also opportunities to grow your skills and deepen your understanding of Unreal's inner workings.

No matter the project size, platform, or scope, stability, clarity, and problem-solving will always be part of the job. With the knowledge from this chapter, you'll be ready to face those challenges head-on.

Aaaaannnnnd CUT! That's a Wrap!

With this final chapter complete, you've now explored a full visual pipeline of advanced Unreal Engine 5 development, from lighting and cinematic storytelling to performance, optimization, and stability. You've delved into the technical depths, wrestled with creative challenges, and gained insight into workflows that can help bring even the most ambitious ideas to life.

Thank you for joining me on this journey. Together, we've navigated the intricate systems that power Unreal Engine 5, building a deep understanding of not only *how* things work but *why* they matter, and how to expand our knowledge beyond the teachings here. Let's take a moment to reflect on how far you've come...

We started by learning how to harness Unreal Engine's lighting, atmospheric effects, and modeling tools to shape visually stunning and emotionally rich environments. Along the way, we explored how mood, tone, and storytelling can be embedded directly into the world itself, while streamlining creative workflows inside the engine.

From there, we moved on to designing interactive and adaptive spaces that respond dynamically to player actions and physics-driven systems. We also discovered how to use cinematics and environmental storytelling to blend gameplay and narrative seamlessly, creating experiences that feel both immersive and cinematic.

Finally, we focused on the technical backbone of development—profiling, optimization, and asset management. These practices ensure that ambitious visual and gameplay ideas remain performant and scalable.

We closed by equipping ourselves with strategies for troubleshooting and overcoming common challenges, helping us move forward with confidence on any project.

This book has been about more than just features or tools; it's been about empowering you to think like a problem-solver, an artist, and a developer who can navigate Unreal Engine 5's complexity with confidence.

Whether you're a solo developer, a student, or part of a studio team, I hope this book has given you not just practical tools but the confidence to tackle complex projects, the ability to learn concepts beyond the scope of this book, and the inspiration to push your craft further.

Remember, every great project starts with a spark of curiosity, and every challenge you overcome adds to your strength as a creator. Unreal Engine 5 is an incredible canvas. And now, wherever your next project takes you, whether it's a small personal prototype, a cinematic experience, a game destined for millions of players, or a tool to inspire others, **you now have the knowledge and discipline to bring it to life**.

So, here's to what comes next: build boldly, iterate wisely, and never stop exploring, learning, and growing.

Cheers!

Tyson Butler-Boschma

Subscribe to Game Dev Assembly!

We are excited to introduce **Game Dev Assembly**, our brand-new newsletter dedicated to everything game development. Whether you're coding, designing, animating, or managing a studio, we've got insights, trends, and expert advice to help you create, innovate, and thrive. Sign up now and get exciting benefits.

https://packt.link/gamedev-newsletter

Get This Book's PDF Version and Exclusive Extras

UNLOCK NOW

Scan the QR code (or go to packtpub.com/unlock). Search for this book by name, confirm the edition, and then follow the steps on the page.

Note: Keep your invoice handy. Purchases made directly from Packt don't require one.

14

Unlock Your Exclusive Benefits

Your copy of this book includes the following exclusive benefits:

- ☁ Next-gen Packt Reader
- 📄 DRM-free PDF/ePub downloads

Follow the guide below to unlock them. The process takes only a few minutes and needs to be completed once.

Unlock this Book's Free Benefits in 3 Easy Steps

Step 1

Keep your purchase invoice ready for *Step 3*. If you have a physical copy, scan it using your phone and save it as a PDF, JPG, or PNG.

For more help on finding your invoice, visit `https://www.packtpub.com/unlock-benefits/help`.

> **Note:** If you bought this book directly from Packt, no invoice is required. After *Step 2*, you can access your exclusive content right away.

Step 2

Scan the QR code or go to `packtpub.com/unlock`.

On the page that opens (similar to *Figure 14.1* on desktop), search for this book by name and select the correct edition.

Figure 14.1: Packt unlock landing page on desktop

Step 3

After selecting your book, sign in to your Packt account or create one for free. Then upload your invoice (PDF, PNG, or JPG, up to 10 MB). Follow the on-screen instructions to finish the process.

Need help?

If you get stuck and need help, visit `https://www.packtpub.com/unlock-benefits/help` for a detailed FAQ on how to find your invoices and more. This QR code will take you to the help page.

Note: If you are still facing issues, reach out to `customercare@packt.com`.

‹packt›

packtpub.com

Subscribe to our online digital library for full access to over 7,000 books and videos, as well as industry leading tools to help you plan your personal development and advance your career. For more information, please visit our website.

Why subscribe?

- Spend less time learning and more time coding with practical eBooks and Videos from over 4,000 industry professionals
- Improve your learning with Skill Plans built especially for you
- Get a free eBook or video every month
- Fully searchable for easy access to vital information
- Copy and paste, print, and bookmark content

At www.packtpub.com, you can also read a collection of free technical articles, sign up for a range of free newsletters, and receive exclusive discounts and offers on Packt books and eBooks.

Other Books You May Enjoy

If you enjoyed this book, you may be interested in these other books by Packt:

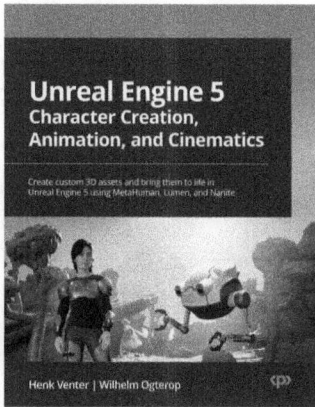

Unreal Engine 5 Character Creation, Animation, and Cinematics

None Venter, None Ogterop

ISBN: 978-1-80181-244-3

- Create, customize, and use a MetaHuman in a cinematic scene in UE5
- Model and texture custom 3D assets for your movie using Blender and Quixel Mixer
- Use Nanite with Quixel Megascans assets to build 3D movie sets
- Rig and animate characters and 3D assets inside UE5 using Control Rig tools
- Combine your 3D assets in Sequencer, include the final effects, and render out a high-quality movie scene
- Light your 3D movie set using Lumen lighting in UE5

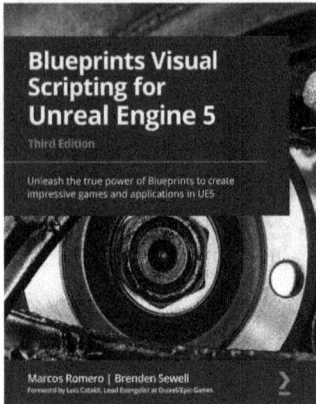

Blueprints Visual Scripting for Unreal Engine 5

Marcos Romero, Brenden Sewell

ISBN: 978-1-80181-158-3

- Understand programming concepts in Blueprints

- Create prototypes and iterate new game mechanics rapidly

- Build user interface elements and interactive menus

- Use advanced Blueprint nodes to manage the complexity of a game

- Explore all the features of the Blueprint editor, such as the Components tab, Viewport, and Event Graph

- Get to grips with OOP concepts and explore the Gameplay Framework

- Work with virtual reality development in UE Blueprint

- Implement procedural generation and create a product configurator

Packt is searching for authors like you

If you're interested in becoming an author for Packt, please visit authors.packt.com and apply today. We have worked with thousands of developers and tech professionals, just like you, to help them share their insight with the global tech community. You can make a general application, apply for a specific hot topic that we are recruiting an author for, or submit your own idea.

Share your thoughts

Now you've finished *Unreal Engine 5 Best Practices*, we'd love to hear your thoughts! Scan the QR code below to go straight to the Amazon review page for this book and share your feedback or leave a review on the site that you purchased it from.

https://packt.link/r/1836205651

Your review is important to us and the tech community and will help us make sure we're delivering excellent quality content.

Index

A